A huge thank you to the following for th ng Pure Potential to provide university a thousands of state school s

PRIFYSGOL ABERYSTWYTH UNIVERSITY

accenture High performance. Delivered.

agr

aspiringsolicitors access | opportunity | assistance

Baker McKenzie.

Bank of America Merrill Lynch

THE DIANA AWARD

Essex Collaborative OUTREACH Network

EY Building a better working world

FULBRIGHT COMMISSION

GetMyFirstJob Where it all starts.

GOWLING WLG

VE RI TAS HARVARD

HERBERT SMITH FREEHILLS

THE HONOURABLE SOCIETY OF THE INNER TEMPLE

ICAEW

Imperial College London

University of Kent

KPMG

LinkedIn

MANCHESTER 1824 The University of Manchester

MillionPlus The Association for Modern Universities

MoneySavingExpert.com

NAO National Audit Office

Pathwaystolaw

RREF Reading Real Estate Foundation

RUSSELL GROUP

STEPHENSON HARWOOD

THE SUTTON TRUST

UBS

UCAS

UCL

Unilever

University Alliance Making the difference

VSO

UNIVERSITY OF WESTMINSTER

What CAREER LIVE

What UNIVERSITY LIVE

Yale University

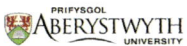

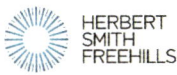

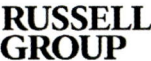

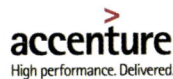

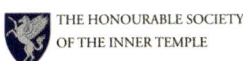

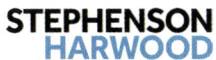

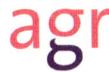

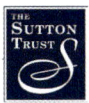

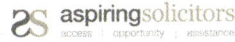

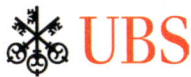

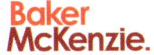

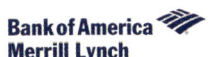

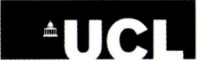

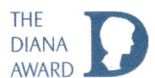

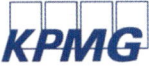

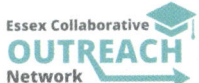

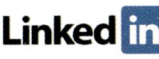

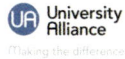

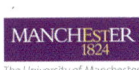

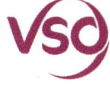

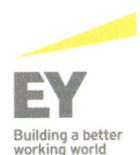

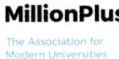

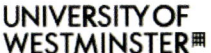

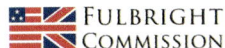

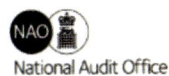

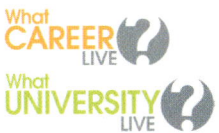

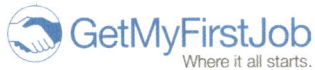

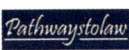

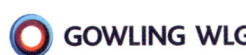

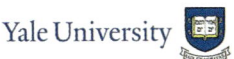

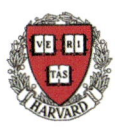

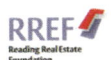

EXPLORE YOUR OPTIONS

It can be hard to figure out where to start when thinking about the future. Follow the decision tree below to give you an idea of what next steps you could take. We always recommend exploring all your options before making a final decision, so approach this with an open mind.

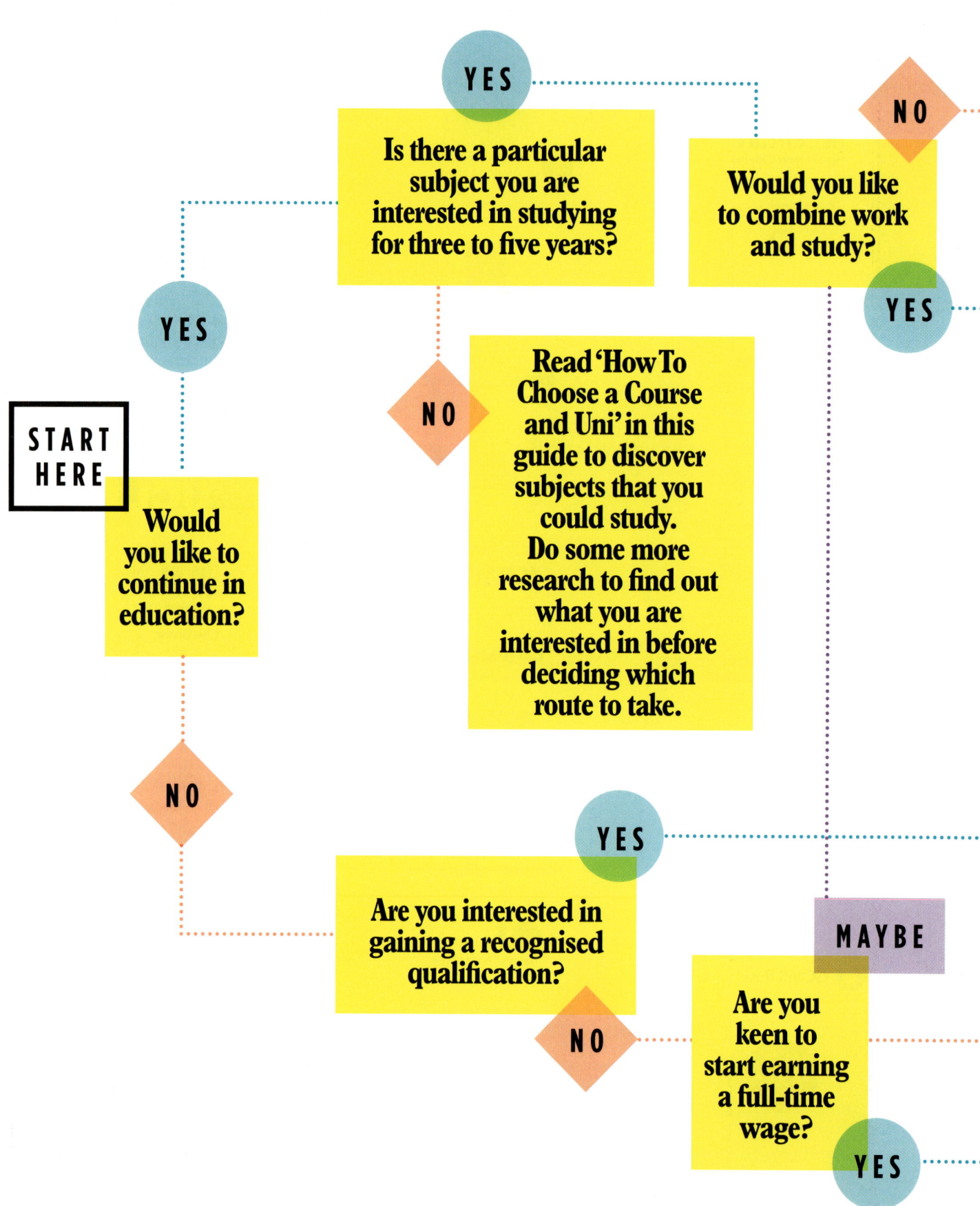

Do you want to experience university life?

- YES → **EDUCATION**
- NO → **Would you prefer to be based in a workplace or an educational institution?**
  - EDUCATION
  - WORKPLACE

Do you learn best by reading or doing?
- READING
- DOING → NO

DEGREE

Studying towards a degree at university has many benefits. It means you can engross yourself in a subject that really interests you. Alongside the academic side of university, you will also make lots of new friends, have the opportunity to take up new hobbies and experience living away from home. Finding part-time work alongside your studies or during the holidays will enable you to gain skills and earn some extra money. Read through the university section of APPLY for information on how to research universities, choosing a subject and the whole UCAS application process.

SPONSORED DEGREE

A sponsored degree is a way that you can work towards a degree AND be employed at the same time, meaning generally you have your fees paid and earn money along the way, as well as developing contacts and skills that a degree alone won't offer you. Your time will usually be split between attending university and working for the company that is sponsoring your degree. Read more about sponsored degrees in the careers section.

APPRENTICESHIP

Apprenticeships offer a great way to learn on the job and work towards a recognised qualification. Apprenticeships are offered in 170 industries covering over 1,500 job roles. You can read more about the range of apprenticeships in the careers section. Even if you answered that you didn't want to combine work and study, an apprenticeship isn't like going to college or university. As an apprentice, you will be doing a real job in a real workplace – and getting paid for it. Learning in an apprenticeship will be different to learning at school, so if you didn't enjoy school, it doesn't mean education isn't for you! Having a nationally recognised qualification will stand you in good stead for your future career.

WORK

For some people, going into work straight away has many benefits. Spend some time while at sixth form or college gaining some work experience, networks and employability skills. There are lots of great opportunities out there for school leavers so make sure you read the school leaver section. Remember that you can return to education at any age and there are many options for studying part time alongside work if you change your mind about education in the future.

INTRODUCTION	How Can Pure Potential Help You?	2
	Explore Your Options	4

THE UNI SECTION

APPLYING TO UNI	The Benefits of Higher Education	8
	How to Choose a Course and Uni	10, 12
	University League Tables	14
	The Best Online Resources	16
	Uni Open Days	18
	University Mission Groups	20
	Applying to Oxford or Cambridge	22
	Applying through UCAS	24
	The UCAS Application Timeline	26
	How to Handle A-Level Results Day	28 - 31
	The Pure Potential Personal Statement Masterclass	32 - 41
	Example Personal Statement	42
	Enrichment	43
	Boost Your Personal Statement	44
	University Interviews	46 - 49
	You Can Afford to Go to Uni – Student Finance 2017–18	50 - 55
	Student Finance 2017-18 – Wales, Scotland & NI	56
UNI LIFE	Freshers' Week	58
	Making the Most of Your Time at Uni	60
	Changing Your Course or Dropping Out	61
STUDYING ABROAD AND GAP YEARS	Studying Abroad	62
	Studying in the USA	64
	Studying in Australia and New Zealand	65
	Studying in Europe	66
	My Experience – Studying Abroad	67
	Gap Years	70
	My Experience – Gap Years	71
UNIVERSITY PARTNERS	University of Kent	11
	University College London	13
	University of Manchester	15
	Imperial College London	17
	Aberystwyth University	19
	University of Westminster	21
	Yale University	68
	Harvard University	69

THE CAREERS SECTION

JOB APPLICATIONS	What Are You Going to Do with Your Life?	74
	Work Experience	78
	The Pure Potential CV Writing Masterclass	80
	CV Template	82
	LinkedIn	83
	The Covering Letter	84
	Application Forms	86
	Competency-Based Questions	87
	Motivation- or Strength-Based Questions	88
	Assessment Days	89
	Job Interviews	90
	Questions to Expect	91
	Sponsored Degrees	92
APPRENTICESHIPS by Get My First Job	Kick Start Your Career with an Apprenticeship	94
	Earn While You Learn	95
	Weighing Up Your Options	96
	Top 5 Benefits of Apprenticeships	98
	Go Higher with Your Education	99
	Focus on Finance Apprenticeships	100
	Focus on Law Apprenticeships	103
CAREER PROFILES	Healthcare	106
	– Medical Applicants	107
	– Getting into Medical School	108
	– Alternative Routes into Medicine	110
	Hospitality & Catering	112
	Media, TV & Radio	114
	Finance	116
	– Chartered Accountancy	124
	Entrepreneurs	126
	The Third Sector	128
	Technology	130
	Property	132
	Engineering	134
	Retail	136
	Law	140 - 150
PARTNERS	The Diana Award	27
	Voluntary Service Overseas	72
	What Career Live?	76
	KPMG	117
	National Audit Office	118
	Bank of America Merrill Lynch	120
	EY	121
	ICAEW	122
	Pathways to Property	133
	Unilever	138
	Aspiring Solicitors	145
	Baker McKenzie	146
	Stephenson Harwood	147
	Herbert Smith Freehills	150

THE UNI SECTION

The benefits of higher education are endless – what you will learn both inside and outside the lecture room will stay with you well beyond graduation day.

With around £9,000 a year tuition fees, many students will be wondering whether it's worthwhile going to university. Not everyone's dream will involve higher education, and nor should it. Many top athletes, musicians, tech pros and business gurus choose not to go to university, but go on to achieve great things.

There is nothing wrong with opting out of the university route, but you should carefully consider all your options before you make a decision (you can read about the alternatives to university later on).

In many areas of life, however, a university degree is still an essential route. If you want to become a doctor, dentist or vet, develop new treatments, delve into history and the arts or understand the sciences and our environment, then going to university is a must. Adapting to life at university can be one of the most rewarding challenges you will ever face. Whatever subject you decide to study, going to university will equip you with skills that you can apply to your academic work, your career and in your personal life. The chance to nurture an academic passion over several years guided by an expert in that field, while simultaneously enjoying independence, extracurricular activities and new friends is not to be easily dismissed.

If you're still not sure if university is right for you, talk to your teachers, speak with your family and friends, ask some students a few years above you to tell you about their experiences and consider what it is you want to do for a career. Remember, this is a decision based on your aspirations and career dreams – put yourself and your feelings first. Think about the school subjects you enjoy and which classes you look forward to. In the end, however, the decision will be down to you. If you decide it's what you want, you'll need to fully understand the application process, select your course and pick your universities. Turn over to find out how.

WHY GO TO UNIVERSITY?

IMMERSE YOURSELF IN YOUR CHOSEN SUBJECT

Ever since you began your education, you probably had very little choice in the subjects you studied and the topics you covered, but university offers you the chance to explore a subject you are really interested in. Whether you choose a subject that you enjoy, a subject that you're good at or both, university offers you the chance to study a subject of your choice for three years or more with guidance and tuition from experts in their fields, and in a place with excellent resources.

ENHANCE YOUR CAREER PROSPECTS

Getting a degree from a top university will enhance your career prospects in a number of ways. Employers like the commitment shown through studying one subject for three years. It also shows that you are able to work independently and are able to flourish in new, challenging environments (much like when you start a new job). Not only do you look highly attractive to employers because of your degree and the skills you develop along the way, but you will also increase your earning potential.

EXPAND YOUR SOCIAL LIFE

Universities offer a whole host of new experiences, which is often reflected in the lively nightlife of most university towns. That said, it's not all cheap beer and nights out; university is a great place to meet like-minded people from all walks of life. It will offer you the chance to immerse yourself in a new culture and environment, and make friends with people who you may stay in touch with long after graduation.

EXTRACURRICULAR ACTIVITIES

Don't forget, university is not just about studying! It is unlikely that you will ever have the opportunity to take part in such a wide range of activities as you will come across at university. You can join all sorts of clubs, societies and teams, from the usual things like sports, culture, theatre, debating and faith-based societies to things like belly dancing, tea drinking and Hollyoaks fan clubs. And the best thing of all is that if there isn't a society for what you love, then it's easy to start one yourself! Whatever your interests, you can pursue them in a social capacity and the increase in confidence and awareness you develop by spending time with different people through social and extracurricular activities will often contribute to your education as much as your degree.

GAIN INDEPENDENCE

Whatever subject you decide to study, going to university will equip you with skills that you can apply to your academic work, your career and in your personal life. Independence is one of the key skills that you will develop while a student. Living and studying on your own will be totally different from your pre-university life. To be able to study when you like, buy your own groceries, learn self-discipline and indulge yourself is something you may not have done before. You'll learn so much so fast – some of it the hard way – but you'll have a great time laughing about it with your new friends. The university experience is to be grasped with both hands, to be appreciated as so much more than the venue of your studies

"Studying maths at City University was definitely a worthwhile way to spend three years. It was a lot of hard work, trust me, but while working hard, I have been able to bank three years worth of valuable skills and knowledge that has been vital in securing a job."

"I picked a course that really reflected what I enjoyed & loved. Having the passion definitely made the late nights spent working on coursework and revising for exams that little bit easier."

"I was really unsure of what I wanted to study at university, so I decided to take a gap year, which was one of the best decisions I made! It helped me to gain some perspective on university and gave me some direction on what I wanted to study."

HOW TO CHOOSE A COURSE AND UNI

CHOOSE A SUBJECT YOU ENJOY

Generally speaking, you shouldn't pick a course you're good at over one you really love, because innate ability just isn't a match for passion in the long run. Ideally, you will excel at the course you enjoy, but if you happen to have a gift for a subject but find it boring and uninspiring, then reconsider because you will have to motivate yourself to study in your own time at university and if that fundamental interest isn't there, you just won't do it!

WHAT IF I HAVE NEVER STUDIED THE SUBJECT BEFORE?

The great advantage of choosing a course based on something you studied at school is that you have an idea of what it involves, and you have a strong foundation of knowledge and skills to build on. That said, be aware that there's a big difference between the way a subject is taught in school and at university, and even the topics covered.

If you're interested in a subject that you either haven't studied at school, or wasn't available, then the onus is on you to discover everything you need to know to make sure it's right for you. There are over 37,000 courses on offer via UCAS, the highest in Europe, so there are plenty to choose from! Do some reading around your subject; the recommended reading lists on the university websites are a good place to start. As always, read the prospectus very carefully for information on how the course is taught and assessed.

Many universities offer a service where you can email students currently taking the course to ask them questions about their experiences. If you do decide to take a course you haven't studied before, don't worry if other students applying for the course have already taken the subject at school; the admissions tutor and syllabus will take account of these discrepancies, and you won't be behind for long.

UCAS TARIFF POINTS

Once you've chosen your course, you need to see if the grades you're expecting match up to the grade requirements. Every course on offer at any university will have an entry requirement that is set by the university. These can be found on both the university and UCAS websites. Different universities will set different entry requirements for the same subject. Think carefully about the requirements and be realistic when choosing your universities. If you are predicted 340 UCAS tariff points, and a university is asking for a minimum of 360, there is a chance your application will be unsuccessful. Wise students spread their choices across universities with a range of requirements to cover all eventualities come results day.

CAREER PROSPECTS

Are you absolutely certain what you want from your future career? If you are, then great, but many students find that their aspirations change between their teens and twenties. Though no one can be absolutely certain of how their ambitions may shift, you should try to get some practical experience in the field you want to work in to check if it's for you. This will also help beef up your UCAS form.

If you are as sure as you can be, then perhaps you should consider a vocational course. A vocational course is one that is specifically designed to qualify you for a defined career – for example, medicine, dentistry or nursing. If you are considering this kind of course, you should be aware of the pros and cons before you sign on the dotted line (or, in the case of the UCAS form, press the submit button).

If you do have a career in mind, you must also love the idea of studying the subject theoretically. It doesn't matter how committed you are to becoming a lawyer, you will find yourself falling behind your peers if you do not love the academic disciplines of law because the academic study of the subject is very different to its practical application. You should also check if it really is necessary to study that subject to pursue a career in that field – for example, lawyers are NOT required to study law at undergraduate level, and you don't have to study finance or economics to work in the financial sector.

The law conversion course (GDL) and the medical fast track programme are two examples of postgraduate courses that allow you to catch up on all the stuff that everyone else did during their degree. Many employers value the breadth of knowledge that people who did different degrees at university can bring to their professions.

If, like most students, you are not sure yet, or have absolutely no idea, then just choose a course that you find interesting and keep your options open.

EXCELLENT STUDENT EXPERIENCE

Kent offers academic excellence, inspirational teaching and a superb student experience.

- £2,000 scholarship to all students achieving AAA (A level) / DDD (BTEC) / IB35*
- 4th highest score for overall student satisfaction
- Our Canterbury campus has fantastic facilities including a nightclub, cinema and sports centre all set in 300 acres of parkland.
- Our Medway campus has high-tech facilities, a great riverside location and is only 30 miles from London.

To find out more come along to an Open Day
www.kent.ac.uk/opendays

01227 827272
www.kent.ac.uk/ug

* see website for specified equivalents and conditions

HOW TO CHOOSE A COURSE AND UNI
CONTINUED

Remember that no single person or organisation, not even UCAS, can be an expert on all courses or universities. It is up to you to do your own research for the most up-to-date facts.

You'll want to consider what is most important to you. A good reputation? New facilities? Near to home or as far away as possible? A tight-knit community, or large campus? In a city, or a leafy campus? Spacious accommodation, or shared rooms? What's the local nightlife like? Is it safe? Do you have to share bathrooms or are they en suite? Does the uni have high employment statistics and a great careers service? Is the accommodation catered, or will you have to cook for yourself? How far away is your local supermarket or bank? How much will it cost you to travel between home and university? Does the library have good facilities like online journals and e-books? Is there a broad range of societies? Can you get involved in theatre or sport?

Prospectuses, university league tables, and UCAS are all useful resources in helping to answer these questions, but nothing beats an open day, which allows you to get a feel for a place.

Although practical considerations can make a big difference to your university years, you're going away to study and, ultimately, the content of the course should be your guiding principle, no matter how much fun Freshers' Week sounds, or how many nightclubs the town has! Create your own league table based on the factors that are most important to you.

Don't be influenced by where friends are headed – people can have very different priorities when choosing universities and one of the most wonderful things about university life is the new friends that you will make.

QUESTIONS TO ASK YOURSELF

ARE YOU QUALIFIED?

Don't waste one of your five precious choices on a course you're not qualified to do! In addition to grade requirements, some courses require specific A-Levels, extra qualifications or experience – make sure you've checked. If you're not sure of something, call the university admissions office to check.

HAVE YOU LOOKED INTO IT FULLY?

Course choice is consistently the top reason why students drop out of uni in the first year, so make sure that you have researched extensively and are confident you know what you are in for. Every course will approach the subject from a different angle. For instance, if you take French at Oxford, you will find yourself reading a great deal of French literature. Take the French course at Newcastle and there'll be a lot less literature, but a lot more language and sociology.

HAVE YOU SELECTED SIMILAR COURSES?

Make sure the five courses you select are similar to each other – you only get to submit one personal statement, so you'll have a hard job convincing an admissions tutor you're interested in economics but also zoology. The only exception here is for medical applications; you can have a course such as biomedical sciences as a back-up. Read more on healthcare in the careers section.

WHAT ARE THE DIFFERENT ROUTES AVAILABLE?

It can be easy to get swept up in the standard UCAS process that it seems everyone else is doing, but there are alternative options out there that could be right for you, such as part-time study, apprenticeships, distance learning or working while gaining a degree. For more on sponsored degrees or school leaver programmes, see the careers section.

HAVE YOU BEEN TO THE CAMPUS?

Visit as many open days as you can – you will never get 'the feel' of a place just through reading a glossy prospectus. Speak to lots of current students while you're there – they will be able to give you that all-important insider knowledge. You should also look into summer schools and insight days – many universities offer students the chance to stay on campus, attending talks by lecturers and exploring the course.

UNIVERSITY LEAGUE TABLES
(AND HOW TO USE THEM)

University league tables can be a useful tool to use when choosing your future place of study. You can find plenty of them online, but with different tables ranking universities in different orders, it's important to find out what factors are involved, and consider how much attention you should be paying to them.

USEFUL FACTS TO KNOW

DEGREES OF SEPARATION

According to the Higher Education Liaison Officers Association, you shouldn't read too much into universities that are five or ten places apart on the league table. A university in 20th place is usually separated from one in 30th place by only a few percentage points.

CHANGING PLACES

Universities that are right at the top of the league tables are obviously doing well according to all of the relevant criteria. However, the top of the league tables is consistently dominated by Oxford and Cambridge, LSE and Imperial College, London. It might be worth looking more carefully at those universities that have dropped or risen dramatically compared with their positions in the last few years and finding out why.

SUBJECT RANKING

It is also useful to look at how the subject ranks, not just the institution as a whole. Some universities have particularly strong faculties that are internationally famous, even if the institution itself may be lower on the league tables. Look out for these types of courses and make sure you do your research, particularly in specialist areas. The results can be very surprising. For example, Glasgow is currently number 30 on the Complete University Guide's table, but their law faculty is rated number 7 in the country.

A GOOD FIT FOR YOU

Choosing the right course for you is ultimately the most important thing. Looking at league tables does not replace the need for you to thoroughly research available modules, course structure and assessment methods. Other factors like the distance from your home to university, entry requirements and long-term career options are also very important. Attending university open days can be a really good way of finding out whether a university suits you.

FUTURE EMPLOYERS

Employers will also use university league tables when assessing which candidates to select from. Try to apply to at least one or two universities that consistently appear in the top 50 – they are likely to be the ones held in higher regard by future employers.

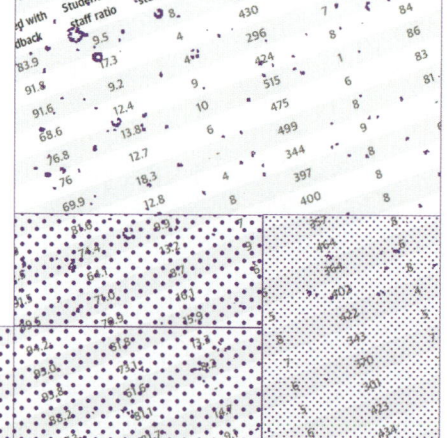

BE AWARE

STUDENT SATISFACTION

The student satisfaction score can show you what current students think about their university experience. Bear in mind that this percentage might not just be based on the university's academics but on the student experience as a whole, and that scores don't vary that much between different universities.

STUDENT TO STAFF RATIO

This gives you an idea of how much money a university invests in its staffing. This does not necessarily tell you how many hours of teaching you personally will get, or who will be teaching you.

GRADUATE PROSPECTS

These scores can tell you what graduates go on to do after university. Statistics are collected six months after graduation, so can sometimes give you a skewed idea of what the graduate prospects actually are.

ENTRY GRADES

Normally, the league table will show what the average UCAS tariff score was for each student starting at the specific institution. Most students' UCAS tariff scores are usually higher than the course requirements, and so it can make it look like some universities are out of reach. Make sure you always look at the university's individual course requirements, rather than relying on the tariff scores produced by the league tables.

USEFUL RESOURCES

thecompleteuniversityguide.co.uk
timeshighereducation.co.uk
theguardian.com/education

UNDERGRADUATE OPEN DAYS

THE UNIVERSITY OF MANCHESTER

FRIDAY 23 JUNE 2017
10am-4pm

SATURDAY 24 JUNE 2017
10am-4pm

SATURDAY 30 SEPTEMBER 2017
10am-4pm

SATURDAY 14 OCTOBER 2017
10am-4pm

 www.manchester.ac.uk/opendays

THE BEST ONLINE RESOURCES

Choosing your university can be a daunting prospect, but the wonderful World Wide Web is a great place to start. Spending a little time doing online research can enable you to eliminate certain courses and universities and start to hone in on the ones that are going to be the right fit for you.

USE ONLINE TOOLS

An obvious place to start is the UCAS website, which will give you information about which university runs which courses. But there are also a host of other sites that are specifically geared to help you dig a little deeper. Whatuni.com lets you filter your results to look for a specific module you're interested in or prioritise universities that are a certain distance from your home postcode. Similarly, Which? University enables you to filter by your predicted grades and create your own 'shortlist' as you look through different courses. You can even sign up to Which? University alerts for tips and advice about decision making and reminders of upcoming deadlines.

CHECK OUT ONLINE RANKINGS

The internet is a great place to look at all of the major university league tables and compare their rankings. Check out websites such as the Complete University Guide.

FIND OUT WHAT CURRENT STUDENTS THINK

Community sites like The Student Room allow you to get involved in discussions with current students, ask any questions you may have, and read about other peoples' personal experiences of applying to university.

It's also worth checking out the student satisfaction rankings that help make up university league tables and reading some student reviews of universities (Whatuni.com has loads on their website).

FIND OUT MORE ABOUT LOCATION

It's important not to forget to give due consideration to location when choosing your uni. Once you've narrowed your choices down a little, a quick Google Maps search will be able to give you an indication of how long it will take you to get back home and doing some basic online research should enable you to start to build a picture of the area – how safe it is, how urban or rural, how new or historic, how far the uni facilities are from the nearest town or city.

OPEN DAYS (BOTH VIRTUAL AND REALITY)

We understand that it might not be logistically possible to get along to the open day of every single one of the universities that you're interested in – this is where virtual tours can help. UCAS now has a nifty page on their website with links to virtual open days at most of the big universities. Watching these can give you a 'feel' for the university and help you to narrow down which ones you might want to actually visit in person.

Once you've decided which universities you want to pay a visit to, it is a good idea to do some planning. Universities will have details of upcoming open days on their websites and you will normally be able to book onto these online. Make sure you check out the rest of the website so that you head to the open day armed with any questions you may wish to ask.

TWITTER

Almost all universities now have a range of affiliated Twitter accounts, for their departments, their careers service, their student union, etc. which you can follow to keep up-to-date with news and events. Doing so can provide a useful insight into the day-to-day activities of a university and help you work out which universities are doing stuff that's of most interest to you. You can also follow lecturers from the university to stay informed with progress in their fields – this can be particularly useful for keeping in touch with your subject of choice and making sure you're ready for any potential academic interviews.

USEFUL RESOURCES

ucas.com
linkedin.com/edu
whatuni.com
university.which.uk
thestudentroom.co.uk

Imperial College London

Exclusively

science + engineering + medicine

Top 10 best university in the world
The Times Higher Education World University Rankings 2016–2017

No.1 in UK for career prospects
The Guardian University Guide 2017

WWW.IMPERIAL.AC.UK/STUDY/UG

UNI OPEN DAYS

Choosing which university to go to out of so many options can seem impossible, but open days are on hand to help. They are a brilliant way to find out more about a university, see it for yourself and decide what you think.

In order to get the most out of your visit and ensure you get the information you need to make the right decision, you will need to do some preparation beforehand. Make sure you've at least researched the university and found out if they offer the course you're after and grade requirements you can meet – don't waste time visiting and falling in love with a university that you're not going to be able to get into. Better still, check out the course structure and make sure you find it appealing.

PLAN AHEAD

Most universities will include a timetable of what lectures, talks and events will be going on during the day on their website. Make sure you take a look at this and plan your day to maximise what you can find out about and ensure you don't miss any of the key things you've travelled there for.

GO ARMED WITH LOTS OF QUESTIONS

And make sure you ask them! There's no point driving miles and miles to visit a university just to sit quietly through a sample lecture, grab a prospectus and head home. Make sure you talk to the staff who will be leading your course, interrogate some current students about how they're finding the experience and visit the people working at the careers service, the sports facilities and the student support services to find out more about what's on offer from each. Open days are a great opportunity to ask any of those burning questions that haven't been answered in the prospectus. Use the opportunity to check out the range of accommodation options. Universities use open days to try and sell themselves and, as such, it's likely you'll be shown the nicest lecture halls and taken to see the best accommodation on campus. Try, where possible, to get a good look at the whole of the campus and all of the different accommodation types on offer.

VENTURE INTO THE NEAREST TOWN OR CITY

You'll probably be spending a fair bit of time there if you go to that university, so it's important that you like it and feel comfortable in it.

GOOD QUESTIONS TO ASK AT AN OPEN DAY:

What will you be doing as part of your course on a weekly basis?

How many hours of contact will you have?

What's the balance between practice and theory?

Are there opportunities to study abroad as part of the course you're interested in?

Could you study a joint or combined course?

Are all the buildings on campus or are they spread over a town?

Will your course seminars and lectures take place in a certain area or will you be heading to different buildings?

What clubs and societies does the university have?

What kind of social life is there?

Is there nightlife on campus?

USEFUL RESOURCES

www.opendays.com
www.ucas.com
www.whatuni.com

ABERYSTWYTH UNIVERSITY

Learn and Live in an Exceptional Environment

www.aber.ac.uk

Visit a top 4 UK university

2017 Open Days

12th July | 16th September | 14th October | 11th November

Book your place now at aber.ac.uk/openday | 01970 622065 | openday@aber.ac.uk

2017 Online Open Days | 6th April | 6th December | Book your place now at aber.ac.uk/virtual

TOP 4 IN THE UK AND 1st IN WALES — NSS 2016 FOR STUDENT SATISFACTION

@AberUni_UG | @AberUni | #AberOpenDay
www.facebook.com/AberystwythUniversityNewStudents
www.youtube.com/aberystwythuni

UNIVERSITY MISSION GROUPS

WHAT IS A UNIVERSITY MISSION GROUP?

A mission group is a group of universities united around a common purpose or (as you can guess from the name) mission, with shared strengths, origins or priorities.

WHO ARE THEY?

The three main groups are as follows.

The Russell Group is the mission group that people are most likely to have heard of. It is an association of 24 historic research-intensive universities of the UK. The group is so called because it originally met at a hotel in Russell Square, London.

MillionPlus is the association for modern universities in the UK, and the voice of 21st century higher education. The association champions and promotes the role played by modern universities in the UK and throughout the world, highlighting the focus of these universities on teaching, research and enterprise.

University Alliance is a mission group representing 19 universities in England and Wales. Its member institutions have strong links with employers and businesses, are passionate about high-quality teaching (particularly in technical and professional education) and deliver research with impact and a large proportion of professionally-accredited degrees.

HOW CAN THEY HELP?

Mission groups can be useful in categorising similar universities. Knowing the differences between the various mission groups and which group, if any, the universities you're looking at belong to can help you to understand the priorities and aims of the universities you're considering.

Mission groups can also give an indication of what external perceptions there are of a university. This can be helpful when thinking about what aspects of different universities will most impress future employers.

It should be noted that the universities within a mission group are all different and will all have their own individual histories, identities and set of values. You will need to research each university carefully to make sure that it is going to be the right one for you – mission groups are just another of the many factors that can help you in your considerations.

WHAT'S THE DIFFERENCE BETWEEN THEM?

There are a few key differences between the main mission groups. The universities that make up the Russell Group tend to lead all of the major university league tables and are generally considered the most academically prestigious. On the other hand, University Alliance and MillionPlus tend to contain 'newer' universities that, in keeping with their reputation as younger institutions, provide a range of more modern courses that you might not find at the older, more traditional institutions of the Russell Group. Entry requirements tend to be lower and more flexible outside of the Russell Group, with the newer universities that make up MillionPlus and University Alliance providing additional opportunities for mature and part-time students who aspire to build upon their education or use education to facilitate a career change. Teaching often takes place in groups, focused on problem solving and tackling real-world challenges.

While the Russell Group tends to have the most respected academic standing, University Alliance emphasises its strong links with industry and the professions and its focus on innovation, entrepreneurship and employability. In comparison, MillionPlus promotes the essential role played by modern universities in areas such as international business, enterprise, professions, commerce, industry, and the public & charitable sectors.

IN THEIR OWN WORDS:

Dr Wendy Piatt, Chief Executive of the Russell Group, says:

"The educational offer of Russell Group universities is characterised by three key components: a good learning environment; rich and interesting learning experiences; and the long-term benefits students gain from studying at a Russell Group university."

Maddalaine Ansell, Chief Executive of University Alliance, says:

"Alliance universities work hand in hand with employers to develop courses that give our students the skills they need to thrive in their chosen career. We provide opportunities to work on real-world problems in practical settings – a great foundation for success in the workplace and in life. Many of our students will graduate with both a degree and a professional accreditation, as well as an entrepreneurial attitude.

We are passionate about ensuring all our students achieve their potential and invest in innovative and high-quality teaching and research with impact."

Pam Tatlow, Chief Executive of MillionPlus, says:

"Modern universities offer a rich variety of high-quality courses that are taught by lecturers and researchers who are experts in their field. From industry visits and internships, student union societies and scholarships, to cultural visits, volunteering and masterclasses, modern universities offer not just the chance to get a degree but an opportunity for students of all ages to develop their talents and future careers."

MORE THAN JUST A DEGREE

With a global student network and career-focused courses, we offer a wealth of opportunities.

To find out more about our next Open Day and to book your place, visit: **westminster.ac.uk/opendays**

#LondonIsOurCampus

UNIVERSITY OF WESTMINSTER

APPLYING TO OXFORD OR CAMBRIDGE

The universities of Oxford and Cambridge, sometimes collectively referred to as Oxbridge, are internationally famous for their research, their excellent teaching and the quality of their graduates.

- Are you consistently at the top of your class?

- Are you on course for strong A or A* grades at A-Level?

- Did you get excellent GCSE grades?

- Do you enjoy reading about your chosen subject in your own time?

- Does the stuff you learn at school or college inspire you to do your own research?

- Do you find that your schoolwork throws up questions that you would like to devote more time to trying to answer?

- Do you enjoy discussing your views with classmates, parents and teachers?

As well as having extraordinary resources, both materially and in terms of the expertise of their staff, they practise something called the tutorial (at Oxford) or supervision (at Cambridge) system. This means that, in addition to the normal course of lectures, students will spend two hours per week individually or in very small groups, discussing their work with a world-class academic in their field. This not only allows students to develop their written work, but also encourages the development of confidence and verbal fluency. Furthermore, both universities are made up of a number of smaller colleges, which means that settling in is much easier than in other universities. For that reason, each college will be able to provide a very high level of academic and pastoral care to each student. It may also be of great interest to learn that the terms are much shorter than other universities (8 weeks compared to 10–12 weeks) but are considerably more intense!

Oxbridge graduates enjoy unparalleled career prospects, and having one of these universities on your CV will impress employers, and stand you in good stead for the rest of your career. Many of the top employers visit Oxbridge finalists to try and recruit them early on, as they recognise the value of the skills students have developed during their studies.

The application process is more rigorous than many other universities, but don't let this put you off – they are looking for bright, ambitious students with lots of potential, whatever their social or economic background. Don't be distracted by the myths surrounding Oxbridge either. Oxford and Cambridge are teaching institutions just like anywhere else and all they are looking for is the sharpest young minds available to study their subjects.

WHO DO THEY WANT?

Nearly everybody goes to Oxbridge worrying that they won't be as clever as all their new classmates, and each new student discovers that the image of a university filled with geniuses is entirely a media illusion. Equally, Oxford and Cambridge are not full of posh people punting down rivers. The majority of students (57–63%) come from state schools and both universities are taking active measures to encourage applications from non-traditional backgrounds. Look into the Oxford and Cambridge Access Schemes on their websites.

SHOULD I APPLY TO OXFORD OR CAMBRIDGE?

You cannot apply to both, so you need to pick one. In reality, there is very little difference between the two institutions and both have the same academic reputation. You can also apply to up to four other universities.

THE APPLICATION PROCESS

The deadline for applications to both Oxford and Cambridge is 15th October, so ideally you should be working on your personal statement throughout the summer holiday after Year 12, so that you are ready to apply come October.

HOW DO I CHOOSE A COLLEGE?

Both universities are made up of around 30–40 colleges, and you can apply directly to the college of your choice.

Each college holds its own open day, often in conjunction with the main university open day. It might be a good idea to attend a few of these to get more of a feel of what life at the college could be like. Alternatively, the colleges are usually open to the public every day except in the examination period, so if you are unable to attend the prescribed open day, it is possible to visit on a day that suits you.

If you are finding it difficult to choose a college, you can do what is called an open application. The university will then allocate you a college at random. Your application will not be negatively affected by choosing this route.

FACTORS TO CONSIDER WHEN CHOOSING A COLLEGE

SUBJECT
Whether your chosen degree course is offered at the college.

SIZE
Colleges usually range between about 60 and 200 students per year group.

LOCATION
The cities of Oxford and Cambridge are both relatively small, especially since most colleges are located in the city centre. Living five minutes away from your lectures, the university sports pitches, the town centre or Sainsbury's is convenient. A lot of students choose to cycle while at university, so journeys are usually very short.

APPEARANCE
Would you prefer to attend an old college or a more modern one?

ACCOMMODATION
Is it offered for all three years?

GENDER
If you are female, there are some all-girls colleges that you might consider applying to.

FACILITIES
Some colleges will have their own sports pitches, theatres, cinemas, music practice rooms and chapels, for example.

STRENGTHS
Is the college renowned for music, sport, drama, etc.?

SCHOLARSHIPS & BURSARIES
Are you considering applying for a choral, sport or instrumental scholarship? Check to see whether the college of your choice offers these awards. Many colleges also offer bursaries and hardship funds.

ACADEMIC STAFF
Does the Director of Studies or do other Fellows at the college match your own academic interests?

WHAT HAPPENS AFTER I SUBMIT MY APPLICATION?

If you applied to Cambridge...

You will be asked to fill in an online form (the Supplementary Application Questionnaire, SAQ). You will have to supply your AS-Level module results and answer a few other questions about your experience so far and possible career paths. You are not expected to know what you want to do after graduation at this point.

If your application is successful, you will be invited for interview, which normally takes place at the beginning of December. The interview process is different for each subject, so you must check the college website for guidelines on what to expect. Normally, you will have about three interviews lasting roughly 20 minutes each. There is no typical Cambridge interview, but you will definitely be asked further questions on what you wrote in your personal statement, and what you have studied so far in your A-Level course. You should be well prepared for obvious questions such as 'why Cambridge?' and 'why your chosen subject?'. You might also be given a short test beforehand or during the interview. It is easy to be put off by horror stories surrounding the Oxbridge interview process. The interviews are difficult, but they are also your chance to speak to a leading expert in your subject. The interviewers will push you as hard as they can, and if you cannot answer a question that does not necessarily mean that you have failed the interview stage. They are much more interested in your potential than your current knowledge.

If you applied to Oxford...

The Oxford application process is very similar. The only difference is that, for Oxford, there is no extra application form to fill in, so the university does not see your AS-Level module results. Instead, most subjects require their applicants to sit a short test before they choose which candidates will progress to the interview stage. These tests are normally taken at your school. Again, it is important to check the department and college websites for details specific to your subject. The same interview advice applies for applications to Oxford. It is the norm for students applying to Oxford to spend a few days and stay overnight in the college. Accommodation and food are provided free of charge by the college, and social events are organised for the evenings.

You will be notified of either university's decision in December or January. The exact timings vary depending on which faculty you applied to.

USEFUL RESOURCES

ox.ac.uk
cam.ac.uk
thestudentroom.co.uk

APPLYING THROUGH UCAS

If you decide that university is right for you, and you have chosen your course and the universities you'd like to study at, you will have to fill in an application. All applications are handled through a centralised agency, the University and Colleges Admissions Service (UCAS). UCAS is the meeting place for applicants and has 380+ member institutions. Almost everyone will apply through UCAS and not directly to the university concerned.

You can apply individually or through your school (most students apply via their school to get that additional support). If you're applying as an individual, you will need to answer a few simple questions to confirm your eligibility before you can start your application. If applying through your school or college, they will issue you with a unique 'buzzword' that enables UCAS to link you to your school.

You can fill out the form in stages and make changes as you go along – just make sure you don't pay the fee until you are completely ready.

SECTIONS OF THE UCAS FORM

PERSONAL DETAILS
This section will ask for your name, address, date of birth, nationality, residential status (e.g. EU citizen) and if you have any special needs.

PASSWORD
You will be asked to create your own password and answer four security questions. Please make a note of your username, password and your personal ID, and keep the information in a safe place.

ADDITIONAL INFORMATION
Here, you will be asked to state your ethnic origin and the occupation of your parents. This information is used by UCAS and other organisations for research on the demographic make-up of university applicants and not for selection purposes. You will also have the opportunity to include any activities you have participated in to prepare for higher education. Summer schools would be ideal for this, as would campus visits, summer academies, taster courses and booster courses. This does not include open days, so if you haven't done anything leave it blank.

STUDENT FINANCE
Students in the UK will have to fill in this section. This isn't your actual student finance application, but filling in this part of the form will speed up the application process for when you apply for student finance.

UP TO FIVE CHOICES (INSTITUTIONS AND COURSES)
The majority of students can make applications through UCAS to up to five courses. You can select just one course, but this is unusual and risky. There are some exceptions. For example, applicants for medicine, dentistry, veterinary science or veterinary medicine can apply for no more than four of these courses and if you decide you want to go to Oxford or Cambridge, you have to choose between the two, though you can still put down other universities. Look at the UCAS website to find out if any exceptions could apply to you.

This section of the form requires you to list each of the universities and courses applied for. The universities appear in alphabetical order, not by order of preference. When the individual universities look at your application, they will NOT be able to see which other universities you have applied to. Each institution and course has a code, which can be found on the UCAS website, and you will have to state if you will be living at home or in student accommodation.

EDUCATION
Fill in your exam results so far and the exams you plan to take. You will have to enter all qualifications, even if you are retaking your exams, awaiting your exam results or if you got unsuccessful grades.

EMPLOYMENT
You will be asked to give details of any employment to date. This includes weekend and holiday jobs.

PERSONAL STATEMENT
We'll look at this rather daunting aspect of the form in detail later in this section.

REFERENCE
After completing all of the above, you have to send the whole document online to your referee (a teacher) so he or she can confirm the accuracy of the details you've given. The

referee is there to comment on your academic achievement and potential, suitability and motivation. They also help the admission tutors assess your personal qualities, career aspirations and exam predictions. Make sure you ask your teacher about your reference as early as possible – they're likely to be writing a lot!

DEFERRED ENTRY

If you are deferring your entry to university, please note that the same deadlines apply for submitting your UCAS application. You will still need to make your choices, but remember to check with the university whether you are able to defer your entry. In fact, some universities may not offer the course the following year, so make sure you check. Note that maths applicants are not encouraged to take this option and, in some cases, refused… Speak to your chosen institutions to find out the score.

PAYMENT

UCAS has a fee for processing each application and this amount is dependent on how many universities you are applying to. They charge £23 to apply to more than one university, and £12 to apply for one course at one university. Your school will send you more information about how to go about paying this fee, so hold tight until then. If you feel that you are unable to pay this fee, speak with your teachers and they will be able to give you advice. It is worth noting that there is a 14-day cooling-off period within which you are entitled to a refund if you decide against applying to university.

Once you have filled everything in to your satisfaction, you will then pay for the application, which will enable your teacher to add the reference. Once this has been completed, your school/college will then submit it electronically. UCAS will then process it for you and pass your application on to the universities you applied to.

ANOMALIES

ADDITIONAL QUALIFICATIONS

Sometimes you will need to provide further evidence of your suitability for the course. For example:

– Art & Design or Performing Arts applicants may need to attend an audition or submit a portfolio (there may be a fee for this).

– You may have to send in an essay or written piece of work.

– You might be called for interview. An increasing number of universities are calling students to interview in addition to the UCAS form. This shouldn't put you off but you need to be prepared, so do your research.

– Some will require an admissions test.

Places on top university courses have become increasingly competitive in recent years, and more applicants than ever achieve top grades and receive excellent references from their schools. In response to this, admissions tests are now used in certain subjects with the aim of providing an alternative method of assessing a their aptitude, in addition to your exam results and personal statement. These tests are important but are only an alternative method of assessment and should be seen as another way to demonstrate your strengths rather than something to be concerned about!

This list is not exhaustive – UCAS Apply will warn you if additional information such as the above is required, but find out as early as you can so you can prepare.

BTEC STUDENTS

Before applying, always check entry requirements carefully, in particular for universities such as Oxford, Cambridge, UCL, Imperial College London and LSE who may not offer places to students studying BTECs – have a look on the university's website or visit ucas.com for university-specific information.

INDEPENDENT LEARNERS

If you are homeschooled, you will be classified as an independent learner and the process is slightly different. When registering, you'll need to select the independent option and then complete the UCAS form in the same way, but adding the details of your chosen referee in the reference section. Once you've finished, it allows you to generate an email that will be sent to your referee. Make sure you have contacted them first to ask if this is OK! They will need to confirm their identification and then give their reference and your predicted grades. It will only be once they complete this that you will be able to pay your fee and submit the application.

WHAT HAPPENS NEXT?

Once UCAS has your application, you will have to play the nail-biting waiting game. It can take a while for the responses to trickle through because UCAS has to process hundreds of thousands of applications. Also, don't expect them all to come at once – it can be as quick as a week or two, or as long as months.

OFFERS AND REJECTIONS

You will be able to view the status of your application via UCAS Track on their website, and UCAS will email you whenever there is news. When you do finally hear back, you will get one of the following:

Offer Conditional
A conditional offer means that you must get certain grades on results day in order to be accepted.

Offer Unconditional
In rare cases, an unconditional offer is given, and it means that, whatever you get, your place is guaranteed!

Unsuccessful
If you have not been awarded a place, you will be sent a notification that your application has been unsuccessful.

FIRM & INSURANCE

You will be asked to pick two offers when you hear from all the universities, and you will choose one 'Firm' and another 'Insurance'. Usually, the best thing to do is put your first choice university with the higher grade requirements as your Firm offer, and have a back-up uni that you would still like to attend with lower grade requirements as your Insurance. If you don't get any offers at all, you can go through what is known as UCAS Extra – read about this on the UCAS or Pure Potential website.

If you've got your responses and chosen your Firm and Insurance, then all that remains is to study hard, and smash those exams.

USEFUL RESOURCES

ucas.com
purepotential.org

THE UCAS APPLICATION TIMELINE

SUMMER 2017
CHOOSE YOUR COURSE AND UP TO FIVE UNIVERSITIES.
WRITE THE FIRST DRAFT OF YOUR PERSONAL STATEMENT.
REGISTER WITH UCAS AND BEGIN YOUR ONLINE APPLICATION.

1ST SEPTEMBER 2017
APPLICATIONS OPEN.
YOUR SCHOOL OR COLLEGE WILL WRITE YOUR REFERENCE.

15TH OCTOBER 2017
ADMISSIONS DEADLINE FOR OXFORD, CAMBRIDGE, MEDICINE, DENTISTRY AND VETERINARY MEDICINE.

OCTOBER–NOVEMBER 2017
MOST ADMISSIONS TESTS, UKCAT MAY TAKE PLACE IN MAY.

OCTOBER 2017–MAY 2018
INTERVIEWS.
START TO HEAR BACK FROM THE UNIVERSITIES: CONDITIONAL, UNCONDITIONAL OR UNSUCCESSFUL OFFERS.

15TH JANUARY 2018
ADMISSIONS DEADLINE FOR THE MAJORITY OF COURSES.

LATE FEBRUARY–EARLY JULY 2018
EXTRA – CHANCE TO ADD ANOTHER CHOICE IF YOU'VE USED ALL FIVE CHOICES AND ARE NOT HOLDING ANY OFFERS.

MARCH 2018
DEADLINE FOR SOME ART & DESIGN COURSES.

MARCH 2018
APPLY FOR STUDENT FINANCE.

MAY–JUNE 2018
EXAMS.

EARLY JULY–SEPTEMBER 2018
CLEARING – USED IF APPLIED AFTER 30TH JUNE, DIDN'T RECEIVE ANY OFFERS (OR NONE YOU WANTED TO ACCEPT) OR DIDN'T MEET THE CONDITIONS OF YOUR OFFERS.

AUGUST 2018
A-LEVEL RESULTS DAY. CLEARING OR ADJUSTMENT.

SEPTEMBER 2018
UNIVERSITY OR GAP YEAR BEGINS.

D
NOMINATE
A YOUNG PERSON FOR THE DIANA AWARD

The Diana Award is bestowed in Diana, Princess of Wales' name to young role models who are going above and beyond in their daily lives to create and sustain positive change in their communities and around the world.

For more information visit
diana-award.org.uk/nominate

"Everyone needs to be valued. Everyone has the potential to give something back"

#DianasLegacy

© Mario Testino

HOW TO HANDLE A-LEVEL RESULTS DAY

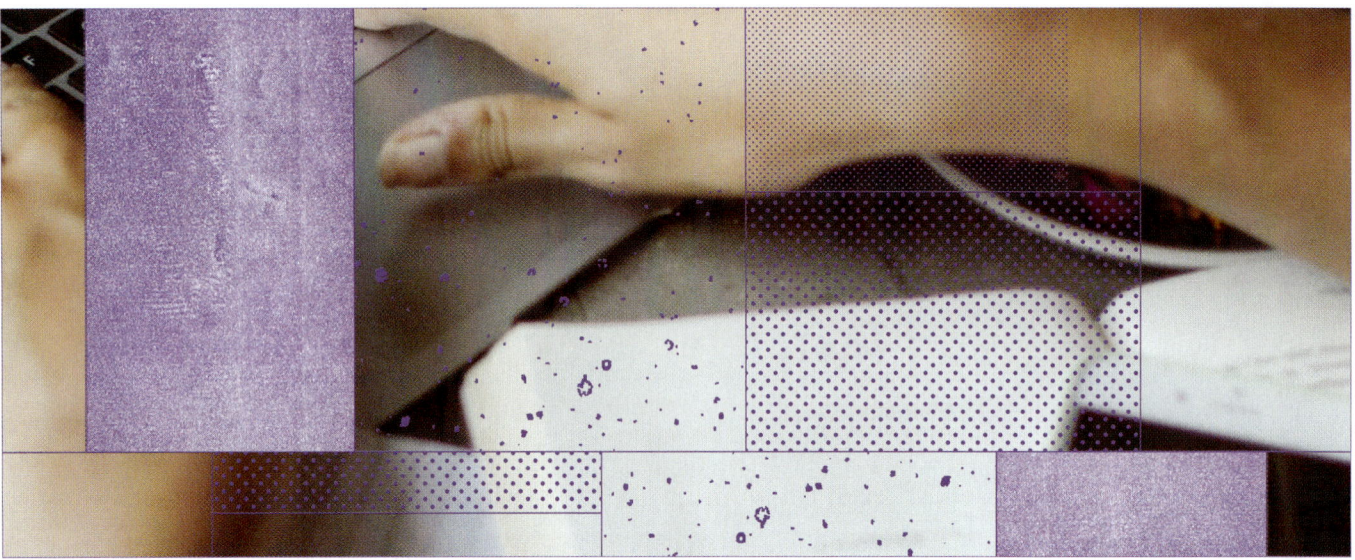

It's been a black mark in your calendar all summer and you break out in a cold sweat just by thinking about it. Every sixth form student in the nation will go to bed the night before with a little fear in their hearts, no matter how confident they felt when they walked out of the exam hall, or what they were predicted.

There are several options for Year 13 students on A-Level results day and, depending on the grades you get, one of them will apply to you. We strongly recommend reading all of the options before the big day so that you are fully prepared for any outcome.

Your future is not something to make hasty decisions over, so take your time to consider your next step. If you don't meet your expected grades, and you don't think you could improve if you retake, then perhaps you should consider if academia really is for you (if you get higher grades than expected, then see Option Five, Adjustment). There are plenty of highly regarded alternatives to university, so if you think that going straight into employment could be the route for you, have a look at the careers section. There are plenty of programmes that combine studying for qualifications with practical, vocational experience – investigate all the options available and don't have the blinkered and outdated view that the only route to success is through higher education.

BE HERE

Make sure you have nothing scheduled on the big day so you can go to school first thing to find out your grades. If you do have to be away, ensure you have reliable, fast internet and telephone access! You will need to sign into UCAS Track to see the outcome of your application. UCAS Track will not display your actual grades, but you should be able to get these via your school, so ask your teacher beforehand.

BE PREPARED

However confident you are of meeting your grade requirements, it's always a good idea to research your alternatives in advance. Just as you researched your first choice universities and courses, or school leaver programme or apprenticeship thoroughly, it is important to do the same again using websites and prospectuses (or even open days if you still have time) so you know what your options are. Having a broad, objective view of what you would consider doing if you missed or exceeded your expected grades will allow you to make an informed and rational decision on the day, should you need to.

It's also important to speak to staff at your school and find out what support they offer on the day, what time they open, who will be there, and if there will be anyone you can talk to.

Your six options are:

1. ACCEPTING
2. CLEARING
3. RE-MARKING
4. RETAKING
5. ADJUSTMENT
6. DEFERRING

OPTION ONE: ACCEPTING

If you got the results you were expecting, then well done. If you are still sure that you want to go to university, embark on the school leaver programme or job you've applied for or head off on your gap year, then that's fantastic! Or, if you haven't made any plans yet but you're pleased with your results, then you can get on with thinking about what you'd like to do next, safe in the knowledge that you got the grades you wanted.

PLEASE NOTE:
If you change your mind about what you want to do, then make sure you let the relevant people know. You never know when your paths may cross again in the future, so it is important to thank them for the opportunity, and briefly explain your reasons for withdrawing. They will understand.

OPTION TWO: CLEARING

If you get poorer-than-expected exam results but these are just a blip in an otherwise good academic performance to date and you still want to go to uni, then Clearing could be for you. Don't worry, not getting the grades you hoped for really isn't the end of the world, even though it might feel that way at first. Last year, over 45,000 students secured a place at university through Clearing, so don't be disheartened. The rule of thumb here is not to jump the gun and go with the first half-decent offer you get!

YOU ARE ELIGIBLE FOR CLEARING IF…

· You have not received any offers.

· You have declined all your offers or not responded by the due date.

· Your offers have not been confirmed because you have not met the conditions (e.g. you have not achieved the required grades).

· You applied for one course that has been declined/unsuccessful and you have paid the full £23 fee (if you only applied to one university through 'single choice', then you will need to pay the full fee of £23 to enter Clearing).

· UCAS receives your application after the 30th June deadline (UCAS will not send it to any universities and colleges if your application is late).

MIDNIGHT – VACANCIES PUBLISHED

All vacancies will be published on the UCAS website just after midnight of A-Level results day. Most students don't get much sleep that night anyway so it's worth staying up to have a thorough scroll through this list and pick out any courses or universities that might be of interest.

Many leading universities offer well-respected courses through Clearing, so don't be under the impression that it's only the dregs left!

PLEASE NOTE:
It is possible that if you only just missed your grades by a few marks, your chosen university might still offer you a place, so contact them as soon as you can.

OPTION TWO CONT. CLEARING

Call the institutions you are interested in and talk to them about your situation; they will be sympathetic! You can find out which ones have vacancies on the UCAS website or in the *Telegraph* newspaper. You will need to give them your Clearing number and UCAS Personal ID number, which will allow them to see your original application online.

We recommend having a reasonable explanation ready for missing your grades, and other credentials such as your mock exam results, as well as a copy of your personal statement printed and at hand so you can refer to it easily. If you change your mind about the type of degree you intend to study, then expect that the institution may want to know why – you'll have to be convincing because they will want you to demonstrate commitment!

Get a few informal offers from universities covering all the areas of interest, at institutions you can genuinely see yourself going to. Have a browse through their websites, and read more about what their specific course entails. Don't be disheartened if a few universities reject you, and certainly don't give up. You have the whole day to choose what to do, because UCAS won't accept Clearing entries until 5pm. We can't stress the importance of taking your time over this decision. Talk to teachers, friends, relatives, careers advisors… but, most importantly, ask yourself the pros and cons of your options.

5PM: ENTER YOUR CLEARING CHOICE

By entering a choice through Clearing, you are accepting the offer, so only do this when the final decision is made. If the course is still available, then you will be notified, and then you will receive a letter in the post shortly after to confirm your place. If the places are full, then you will be allowed to add another option, so wait until you have been accepted before leaving the computer screen!

OPTION THREE: RE-MARKING

You should find out from your school who the designated Examinations Officer is, and if they will be present on the day in case you want a re-mark. If they won't be there, find out their name, email and phone number in case you want to appeal. If your grade is much lower than you had expected, the Examinations Officer can ask the exam board to send your paper to be re-marked. This could be particularly important if you have fallen on a grade boundary and it could make the difference between getting into university or not.

Exam boards must receive your request (made on your behalf by your school) by the end of August. It is possible to ask for a priority re-mark. This applies if it is a matter of missing your existing university offer and your university will be able to hold your offer until you hear the results. It is important to be aware that there is a charge for re-marking A-Level papers. This is sometimes paid for by your school, but you must check this. If your grade changes, you will, of course, be refunded.

Each exam board has different re-mark options available, so you must check the relevant website to find out what your exam board's policies are. Most commonly, you will be offered a clerical check, which verifies whether your grade was calculated and entered into the system properly. If your teacher has concerns about several students' examination results, the exam board might well offer to re-mark 10% of the papers from your class. If, as a result of this check, several pupils are given higher grades, this could positively affect the rest of the class's marks.

PLEASE NOTE
The most important thing to remember is that your mark could also go down as well as up, so the process is a risky one. You should talk to your teacher to see whether he or she thinks that re-marking is the right option for you.

OPTION FOUR: RETAKING

It is also possible to resit your examinations in June the following year; the January resit option is no longer available. While this will involve a great deal of extra work, revision and taking a gap year, it could be less risky than asking for your papers to be re-marked because if you happen to do worse in your resits, you can keep your original grade.

Speak to your school about what they offer if you want to retake. You may also need to attend a different sixth form or further education college in the local area to do this. This option is particularly useful if, for any reason, you didn't have the chance to revise as much as you could have, or if there were any distracting circumstances at home that might have affected your exams.

PLEASE NOTE
You need to be sure that with extra hard work you can do significantly better – you may have to defer entry to university, so be sure that the extra time and commitment is likely to pay off.

OPTION FIVE: ADJUSTMENT

If you have done better in your A-Levels than you expected, congratulations! It is possible for you to apply for another university without losing your secure offer.

UCAS Adjustment allows students with better-than-expected results to effectively 'upgrade' their course and university.

HOW DOES IT WORK?

From the moment your offer is confirmed by your first choice university, you have five days to try to secure an offer from another university. You will be able to see exactly when your individual Adjustment period ends on the Track 'Choices' page on UCAS.

When you get your results, a 'Register for Adjustment' button will appear on your UCAS Track page. Registering will allow the universities that you decide to contact in the hope of a better offer to look at your whole application. In order to find out which universities are offering places through Adjustment, you need to visit their individual websites where they will list the courses they still have places for. If you are feeling confident about your exam performance, then it's worth doing some research in advance so you know who to target.

Once you shortlist suitable courses, you need to phone up the admissions department of those universities and discuss your application. You might have a short interview on the phone, in which case you will have to explain why you want to take this particular course and what it is about the university that attracted you to contact them. Don't be put off by this process! The interview will be informal, but make sure you've got a copy of your personal statement close by to refer to. Just be passionate about the course and confident in your results. Don't let them think it was a fluke – you got the grades because you deserved them and you worked hard!

If the university or college decides to give you an offer, they will phone you or send you an email, so ensure you have access to both of these throughout the next few days. Once you hear from them, keep checking your UCAS Track page so you can accept the offer when it comes through. Once you click accept, then your original offer will be affected, so make sure you've thought it through carefully and discussed the decision with teachers and family at length.

The best thing about the Adjustment process is that you can shop around at other universities without losing the offer you have already accepted at your first choice university. Adjustment is becoming a very successful system – each year thousands of students successfully find a place on a course they consider to be more suitable for them at universities such as Exeter, Durham, Warwick, Birmingham, Sheffield, UCL and King's College London.

THINGS TO KNOW

The Adjustment period only lasts five days, so you have a very short space of time to make a decision. UCAS and the careers service within each university will have trained advisors who will be available to help you.

Because you will be accepting a new university offer at such a late stage in the year, you might be at the back of the queue for student accommodation, and student finance might be affected too. It would be good to discuss accommodation and finance issues when you phone up the admissions department of the university you wish to apply to.

It is important not to make a spur of the moment decision. If you are happy with the course and university you originally chose, stick with it! Investigate the course content: a course with the same name could have a different structure, different assessment methods and cover completely different topics to your original course.

PLEASE NOTE

You may not be successful. You will not be judged on grades alone: your whole UCAS application will be taken into consideration, and you'll be up against competition from other students going through the process, so it isn't a guarantee.

OPTION SIX: DEFERRING

If, in between submitting your university application and receiving your results, you decide to take a gap year, you should contact the university that you have been accepted into on results day and check if you can defer your place for a year.

Explain to the university your reasons for deferring, such as a desire to travel, gain work experience, or become more independent.

PLEASE NOTE

Universities are not obliged to agree to this, but most do. If your university won't allow you to defer, but you have your heart set on a year off, then you still have the option of withdrawing from UCAS and reapplying the following year.

PURE POTENTIAL

PERSONAL STATEMENT MASTERCLASS

Your personal statement is an important part of your application and you need to do everything it takes to get it just right. You have a minimum of 1,000 and a maximum of 4,000 characters (including spaces) to show admissions tutors why they should pick you over other candidates.

Apart from your teacher's reference, this is the only section of the UCAS form where you will have a chance to show the 'real' you, the person beyond the grades. Don't listen to anyone who says universities don't look at personal statements any more, because they do. Apart from the main, first round of applications, they can be particularly useful in borderline cases if you're up against another candidate, or if you go through Clearing, so you need to give it your all.

You will need to have decided what you want to study before you start, as the main reason for writing the statement is to prove your suitability and passion for the course, so if you're still undecided, research how to choose your course first. You'll also need to have looked at the course structure at each of the universities you intend to apply to, as there can be significant variations between each course, and any inaccuracies on your statement could lead to you being put in the reject pile!

We have canvassed many admissions tutors to find out what they are looking for and the result is this masterclass on how to plan and write an outstanding personal statement. Don't forget that tutors will be reading a very large volume of personal statements and you need to make your application stand out from the rest. Assume that the reader is an academic who has devoted his or her life to their chosen subject.

What they really want to know is: have you chosen the right subject for the right reason?

HOW IT WORKS

The Pure Potential Personal Statement Masterclass will help you to write your statement if you follow it step by step and start by writing down as much as you possibly can. Your first few drafts are bound to be rubbish; it's the same for everyone! But it's much easier to cut down on material than it is to come up with it, so jot down everything you can think of in the boxes in bullet points as we go along. We'll edit it down later and turn the best bits into beautiful prose.

If you get stuck on any section then please just move on, as you can always come back to it, and we know there's nothing worse than having a mental block or getting stuck in a personal statement rut!

STRUCTURE
There are lots of ways to structure your statement, but Pure Potential's suggestion is for approximately 75% to be dedicated to academic study.

INTRODUCTION
Explain your motivation for studying the subject.

IN-SCHOOL EVIDENCE OF SKILLS & INTEREST
(optional)
Briefly mention any specific skills you are learning at school that will be relevant for your course.

EVIDENCE OF YOUR PASSION FOR THE SUBJECT
This must be outside of school so they can see it's a genuine interest!

GAP YEAR PLANS
If applicable.

WIDER SKILLS
What are you doing in or out of school that shows you are a mature, well-rounded person?

CONCLUSION
Remind them why they should pick you.

WRITING YOUR INTRODUCTION

You will need to provide a brief but convincing explanation as to why you want to study your subject at university. This should capture the reader's interest straight away so they are compelled to read on. Here are some suggestions of how to start your statement, but please don't use all of the suggestions below – choose one or two that are right for you, or come up with your own.

YOUR PERSONAL TRIGGER

What got you interested in the subject? Was it a book, a museum trip, a documentary, a film, a teacher, an inspirational mentor, a personal circumstance, a visit to a historical site, or perhaps work experience? Don't ever say 'I have always been interested in "INSERT SUBJECT"'. This is a cliché that admissions tutors are sick of reading, because it can't possibly be true! Nobody was born with a desire to be a doctor, lawyer or engineer. For example, an applicant might explain how their family holiday to the Somme gave them a genuine sense of the importance of history as a 'real life' phenomenon – something that exists beyond the pages of a textbook.

THE BIG PICTURE

Why is this subject important? Is it significant to the progression of society? What about our understanding of natural history and evolution? Will your subject lead to the betterment of lives of future generations? Does it shape the world we live in somehow? What's going on in the world right now that relates to your subject? This could be anything from cutting-edge scientific research or technology, grey areas in morality or justice, the state of the world's economy, or how looking at ancient civilisations or different cultures helps us to understand who we are. Why do you want to be part of the academic community researching this subject further?

SPECIFIC AREAS OF INTEREST

Having given a broad account of why you love your subject, focus on specific areas of interest within it. For example, if you want to study physics, you could go on to say how it's really the module on astrophysics that gets your pulse racing, and in what way you hope the degree course will develop your passion further. You will need to read the course prospectus for all the universities you are applying to before you write this!

USING QUOTES

We often get asked by students if it is a good idea to start the statement with a fancy quote from an expert in the field, famous author or scientist. Almost every admissions tutor we have spoken to would rather you didn't use one! It is only acceptable to do this if you directly relate it to your course and why you want to study it, show that you fully understand the concept of the quote and use it to enhance your own words instead of just using somebody else's, but if you can say it in your own words then do so.

CAREER PLANS

If you have a definite or even a rough idea of what you want to do when you graduate, and your university degree is a stepping stone towards that aspiration, then you may wish to write it here. If you have no idea, don't worry – many people don't. If you're a budding medic, dentist or similar, then you will need to go into further depth, but for all others remember that you are applying for an academic degree, not a job. So don't focus too much on your career.

FILL IN THE BOXES RELEVANT TO YOU:

WHAT WAS MY PERSONAL TRIGGER?
_____
_____
_____

HOW DOES MY SUBJECT RELATE TO SOCIETY OR CURRENT AFFAIRS? WHY IS THIS PARTICULARLY IMPORTANT TO ME?
_____
_____
_____
_____

WHICH ASPECT AM I REALLY LOOKING FORWARD TO STUDYING IN MORE DETAIL? WHY?
_____
_____
_____
_____

IS THERE A QUOTE I LIKE THE SOUND OF? COULD I EXPRESS THIS IN MY OWN WORDS?
_____
_____
_____

WHAT ARE MY CAREER PLANS? HOW MIGHT ACADEMIC STUDY FURTHER MY PLANS?
_____
_____
_____
_____

IN-SCHOOL EVIDENCE OF SKILLS & INTERESTS (optional)

WHY OPTIONAL?
This section is optional because you should only talk about current studies if you can talk about them impressively and academically. Not everyone will be able to, or should, relate their current studies to their chosen course and, in fact, this section pales in significance to evidence of what you've done out of school, so don't worry if you leave it blank!

Don't forget that every one of your fellow candidates (aka your competition) is studying A-Levels, BTECS, IBs or equivalent, so school work is not going to make you stand out unless you can truly demonstrate your understanding of how your current studies can specifically help your chosen degree course.

WHAT NOT TO DO
What they DON'T want to see is something like this: 'I currently study maths, English and biology at A-Level. Maths helps with my problem-solving skills, English helps with essay writing, and Biology has given me an understanding of human anatomy'. Firstly, they know what you study at A-Level from the rest of your application form, so don't waste precious words on repeating this information. Secondly, these examples linking your current studies to your degree course are hardly insightful. Far better examples of skills you have picked up during your school studies are critical analysis of evidence, laboratory work or the ability to study independently. Thirdly, don't feel you have to mention each and every one of your subjects; if you pick any, just pick the relevant ones.

SPRINGBOARD
We also suggest that you tell them how your current studies have been a springboard for further reading in your own time. If you take on further independent reading on a topic that interests you, and show enthusiasm for seeing how theories you learn apply to the real world, then you are exactly the type of student universities are looking for. It's not too late either – a quick Google search in your chosen area will open up a whole world of related topics for you to mention. Name-drop what you read, who wrote it and what was interesting. This leads nicely into the next paragraph.

A-LEVEL / BTEC / IB / etc.	RELEVANT SKILLS DEVELOPED
SUBJECT 1	
SUBJECT 2	
SUBJECT 3	
SUBJECT 4	
SUBJECT 5	
SUBJECT 6	
SUBJECT 7	
SUBJECT 8	

EVIDENCE OF YOUR PASSION FOR THE SUBJECT

This is by far the most important part of your statement where you can really shine because it's the things you've done in your own time that will show a genuine passion for the subject. Remember that one of the main differences between university and school is that there's no one looking over your shoulder, making sure you do your homework. You have to show that you are self-motivated to do things outside of the classroom or lecture theatre. For most students, these activities will come under the categories below. Tick all that apply to you and, crucially, are specifically relevant to the course you have chosen. First write down a list of things you've done, then write down what you learnt from that experience/book/documentary/trip that will directly help your degree course. Make sure you name all authors, directors, places, companies, books etc. We've given you a list of suggestions for each category, but don't worry — you're only expected to have done a few from each list!

You may end up with up to three paragraphs for this section – that's OK!

WIDER READING

One excellent way of demonstrating passion is through wider reading, and admissions tutors are looking for students who are willing to read around the subject in their own time. "But I don't know what to read?" we hear you ask! One of the best places to look for reading lists is on the university website. They usually have a list of suggested books for undergraduates, most of which will be available in your local library. If you can't find a reading list, then speak to your teachers, or even call the department of the university you want to apply for – they'll be more than happy to recommend a book or two!

	DETAILS	WHAT DID YOU LEARN?
Textbooks		
Plays		
Poetry		
Passages		
Articles		
Journals		
Newspapers		
Other		

OTHER RESEARCH

There are more interactive ways of researching your chosen subject that will convince the admission tutor you are truly interested. Many of these can be free of charge.

	DETAILS	WHAT DID YOU LEARN?
Theatre trips		
Art exhibitions		
Museum trips		
Historical sites		
Geographical landmarks		
Film documentaries		
Podcasts (e.g. TED)		
Other		

RELEVANT WORK EXPERIENCE

If you've undertaken any work experience that relates to your subject, then write it down here (save the casual weekend jobs for the next section). Did hands-on work reinforce any principles you have only learnt in theory, such as the importance of accuracy, trustworthiness, efficiency, collaboration, empathy, or any number of things that show how you deepened your understanding of the subject? We're NOT looking for generic skills like time management and general communication here. And don't forget to name-drop the companies.

	DETAILS	WHAT DID YOU LEARN?
Voluntary work		
Work experience		
Paid employment		
Internships		
Community activities		
Work shadowing		
Other		

COURSE-RELATED PROGRAMMES

Many universities and other organisations offer you the chance to sample your chosen subject through taster opportunities. These tend to get fully booked quickly, so find out what's going on and where, as early on as possible. We advise a scattergun approach – apply to lots of programmes; you'll learn a lot even if they are at a university you don't intend to apply to.

	DETAILS	WHAT DID YOU LEARN?
Webinars		
Workshops		
Laboratory work		
Lectures		
Masterclasses		
Residential courses		
Summer school		
Taster days		
Other		

OTHER ACTIVITIES

What else have you done that shows you're interested in the subject?

	DETAILS	WHAT DID YOU LEARN?
Competitions		
Prizes		
Awards		
Published work		
Hobbies		
Collections		
Other		

GAP YEAR PLANS

If you are taking a gap year and applying for deferred entry, then you should explain what you plan to do briefly in this section – give details and don't be ashamed of backpacking with friends around some far-flung land. Telling the admissions tutor about your plans for the year ahead shows that you are organised, and want to pursue interests outside of your studies, which is healthy and makes you a well-rounded person. If you can relate it to the course, or university life, that's even better. It is an academic application, so don't bang on about this too much, even if you're secretly more excited about travelling than starting university!

Plans for my gap year:
How will I fund them?
What am I hoping to achieve or get out of the experience?
How will this help me with my degree, university life or career?

WIDER SKILLS

This is where you will give an account of your non-academic achievements and the skills you picked up along the way through your interests and hobbies either in or out of school. Cover any extracurricular activities not necessarily related to your course to give the admissions tutor a glimpse of the kind of person you are outside of the classroom.

The table below has a list of skills you may have developed. Alongside each skill, enter the most relevant activity – try to pick just one activity per skill, even if you learnt more than one skill from it. Here are some examples: if you have volunteered as a reading mentor for younger students, this would definitely have developed your communication skills; you developed an efficient approach to solving problems during your work experience and you also showed great initiative; if you're on the football team, you would have developed teamwork skills; becoming a prefect might have given you a sense of responsibility; living abroad will make you more adaptable; directing a play would give you leadership skills.

What kind of things have you done? Sports, school plays, volunteering, fundraising, organising events, community work, a part-time job, other hobbies – this list will be endless because you're all doing such diverse things…

Remember to make yourself stand out. Juggling a Saturday job with studies isn't going to achieve that because thousands of sixth formers do it. You need to demonstrate you've gone the extra mile.

In the box below, fill in the top one or two skills you learnt along the way. Here are some examples:

	DETAILS	WHAT DID YOU LEARN?
Communication		
Commitment		
Time management		
Teamwork		
Using initiative		
Public speaking		
Adaptability		
Organisation		
Leadership		
Research & analysis		
Maturity		
Responsibility		
Other		

CONCLUSION

People often struggle with this, but it should be an easy paragraph once you've written the rest. Simply finish the personal statement with a one- or two-line summary of why you are a suitable candidate and what you hope to get out of, and give to, the university community. Make sure this sentence convinces the tutor of how much you're looking forward to it all, so use really aspirational language!

EXAMPLES

"Overall, I am a hardworking, active person and I am enthusiastic about achieving my goals and becoming a primary school teacher. I am looking forward to university life, both academically and socially."

"I am mature, confident and self-motivated - all qualities that I believe are critical to a successful university experience. I relish the opportunity to study Accountancy and Finance to degree level and hopefully beyond."

"I feel certain that this subject will provide me with the intellectual challenge best suited to my personality and ambition of pursuing an academic career in the social sciences. The prospect of studying a stimulating and dynamic course truly excites me."

WRITE YOUR OWN

_____

_____

_____

_____

_____

_____

YOUR FIRST DRAFT

Look back at the tables you've filled in – it might not look like it at the moment but this is your first draft! The next step is to choose which points are the most important ones to include.

So what are the admissions tutors looking for? Well, first and foremost, it is the things you have done that show passion for the course; the more 'outside of school' evidence, the better. Skills such as time management and teamwork are great, but are secondary to evidence of a desire to study a subject. If you can 'double up' on skills and talk about things you have learnt and what you have done to demonstrate your interest in the subject at the same time as one of these skills, then great!

For example, you did work experience at your local medical centre and learnt the importance of patient confidentiality, as well as developing an interest in a health-related career. You may well have also developed excellent communication skills by answering the telephone, contributing to meetings, and interacting with staff and patients.

Go back and look at all that you wrote down, and highlight or circle the aspects that you think an admissions tutor will find most impressive, and re-write them as brief bullet points in the space opposite.

Introduction

In-school evidence of skills & interest (optional)

Evidence of your passion for the subject

Wider skills

Conclusion

TURNING IT INTO PROSE

We can't teach you how to write well, but we can give you examples of positive phrases and key words that can help you link sentences together, and combine your experiences with skills. Choose some of these positive phrases and start putting sentences together, crossing each phrase off as you go along to avoid repetition. Add some phrases of your own too for originality.

FINAL NOTES

- Transfer the activities you have deemed worthy of your personal statement to a Word document. If in doubt, include it because you can always edit it out later. Don't worry about going over the word count at this stage. And don't forget to save regularly!

- Many people find it easier to work on the introduction last. It doesn't matter which order you do it in, as long as you keep the structure of your statement – subheadings can work well here to maintain order. Choose the activity or topic you feel most comfortable talking about first.

- Give enough detail, but don't bore them; two to three sentences on any topic should be enough.

- Illustrate your skills and abilities rather than state them. There is nothing worse than ending a good sentence with 'and this shows I have communication skills'.

- Do not state facts about the subject such as 'Geography is the subject that studies the lands, the features, the inhabitants, and the phenomena of the Earth'.

- Do not say lofty, important-sounding things you cannot back up – for example, 'The complexity of life and the Universe itself shows that the human race has only scratched the surface of knowledge'.

- Do not use negative words like never, hate, useless, mistake, tiring, stressful, etc.

- Personal statement advice can seem conflicting: be yourself but don't use humour, demonstrate a good vocabulary but don't overuse the thesaurus, be confident but not cocky, show your passion but don't use the word 'passion', show your skills but don't list them! We know it is hard, but try to find a balance once you get to the proofreading stage.

Furthermore
Enable me
Of particular interest to me
On reflection
Intellectual exploration
Additionally
Used my initiative
Strengthen
Explore my interests
Skills I have gained through
Thrive under pressure
As well as
Commitment
Reinforced
This has furthered my
I learnt from
Moreover
My pursuits
Taking part in
Creatively
Benefit
Efficiently
In addition
Hard work
I undertook
I aspire to
My interest in
Responsibility
I particularly enjoyed
I continue to develop
Through regular attending
To improve my
Combining... with... has taught me
This has expanded my knowledge of
Challenging
Immensely rewarding
Brought to my attention
Thought-provoking
Learnt to prioritise
Highly competitive

- Be ruthless! Get rid of any repetition or waffle.

- Don't have any 'don't's or 'I'll's or 'I'm's! This is a formal document.

- Spelling and grammar must be perfect! NO EXCUSES.

- Don't TRY and sound clever! You are clever and this will shine through; have faith in your achievements.

- Be careful with capitals! Make sure you are correct, and consistent.

- Don't send it out to everyone all at once, otherwise you'll get lots of different versions back, which can be overwhelming. Send it to one person, get their feedback, apply the feedback, then send it on again.

- Don't be surprised if you get conflicting advice from different people – sometimes there is no right or wrong, so if this happens, go with your gut instinct.

- Be sure to say please and thank you – so many people forget to ask nicely and show their appreciation!

PERSONAL STATEMENT CHECKLIST

Give this checklist to the readers when you ask them to proof it for you.

- ○ 1. Does my introduction hold your attention?
- ○ 2. Can you see clearly why I have chosen my course?
- ○ 3. Have I demonstrated at least once that I know what the course actually entails?
- ○ 4. Have I talked about my reading around the subject and shown I have understood what I read?
- ○ 5. Do I show the skills I have developed through my extracurricular and in-school activities?
- ○ 6. Have I given an indication of my future plans beyond university?
- ○ 7. Are my sentences either too short or too long?
- ○ 8. How is my grammar?
- ○ 9. Have I backed up everything I have said with evidence?
- ○ 10. Is my conclusion positive and does it encompass university life beyond academia?

FINALLY, RUN IT BY YOUR TEACHER

Listen carefully to their advice - they go through this process every year and can draw on valuable experience.
Make sure you give them plenty of time to give it proper attention, not five minutes before the school deadline!

EXAMPLE PERSONAL STATEMENT
Here is a model personal statement for the fictional subject of comedy studies:

I believe that laughter is fundamental to human experience. Basil Fawlty, John Cleese's comic creation in *Fawlty Towers*, once said, 'Still, you've got to laugh, haven't you?'. We have to laugh because, far from being a distraction or mere entertainment, comedy represents our attempt to reconcile ourselves to some of the deepest human truths, like death and love. I want to study this course to further my understanding both of the history and evolution of comedy, and to improve my critical skills so that I can unravel the whole meaning of each joke and scene.

[Here the student clearly explains what inspires him to study the course. He included a quote, but it is short, embedded in the text, and its meaning is clearly explained. He also demonstrates he understands what the course entails, and expresses enthusiasm.]

Comedy Studies A-Level has revealed the potential of comedy to create social change: we studied *Bremner, Bird and Fortune*, which opened my eyes to politics and the hypocrisies of government in a way conventional news never could. Theoretical study of political satire has led me to research this further in my own time by watching current and historical television shows such as *Spitting Image*, *Have I got News for You* and *Mock the Week*. I set myself the task of writing my own show *Politically Correct?* which was turned into a school play that I also directed.

[The student discusses his current studies, but briefly and using an insightful example of what he has learnt. He goes on to use this as a springboard to talk about independent study, name-dropping the shows he watched and throwing in his achievement of directing a play too.]

Having studied the television show *The Office* in my own time, I became interested in the idea that the conventional sitcom is dead, and documentary realism is the future of televised comedy. To further my understanding of cultural and national differences in humour, I watched the American version of the same show. I found there to be significant changes to the script – for example, the famous cringe-worthy scene in the British version where David Brent dances has been completely rewritten for American audiences; perhaps the different use of sarcasm between the two countries means that the timing of punch lines must be adapted.

I completed work experience helping to write scripts for television shows *People Like Us* and *Human Remains*. These two series chart the development of this comic genre, which, unlike the older cheerful sitcoms, deliberately confronts the depths of human despair and failure. Seeing the difference between a line that seemed funny on paper and how it was delivered by the actors on set showed me how objective comedy can be, and the challenges that face scriptwriters. To obtain an alternative point of view, I also booked tickets to see Channel 4's comedy *The Graham Norton Show* being filmed live in London. The experience showed me that comedy can have a vital and performative quality when filmed in front of a live studio audience, and the differences between scripted and off-the-cuff humour.

I have been a regular television reviewer for the local magazine, *The Pieshop*. Writing reviews has helped me to hone my critical style, and to appraise programmes in a lively and concise way. I also took on the challenge of playing Caliban in the school play of *The Tempest*, an experience which helped me to gain an insight into comedy from the performer's point of view as well as develop my confidence immensely. I also founded the comedy club at school. We have weekly meetings to discuss programmes and I enjoy having heated debates with my peers on what they find funny.

[He has divided his out-of-school experiences into three neat paragraphs that illustrate a broad understanding of various elements of comedy. He talks about what he learnt in a way that shows he is genuinely interested in the subject and engaged with each experience. He has clearly done a range of experience so his third paragraph covers a few experiences in less detail.]

I am in the school football team; I enjoy the regular team meetings to improve our performance, and it was immensely rewarding when we won the county cup. I also mentor students at a local primary school and teach them to read. I also ran for, and was elected for, the Head Boy position on the Sixth Form Student Council. We regularly liaise with the Upper School students on a range of non-academic issues, and present our findings to the School Governors monthly. These roles have taught me how to balance my studies and extracurricular responsibilities, which is important because I hope to continue both my sporting and voluntary activities while at university.

[This paragraph is brief but paints a picture of the type of person he is. Also, teamwork, leadership and time management are included in this paragraph without stating them.]

Comedy is something I have come back to, inside and outside of the classroom, throughout my life. I think I have the intellectual curiosity, the ability and, most importantly, the sense of humour to gain a much deeper understanding of this subject at university, and would love the opportunity to do so.

[Brief, enthusiastic, positive and a summary of why they should pick him.]

USEFUL RESOURCE purepotential.org — Read over 100 past personal statements annotated by the Pure Potential team.

ENRICHMENT

With thanks to Nuala Burgess

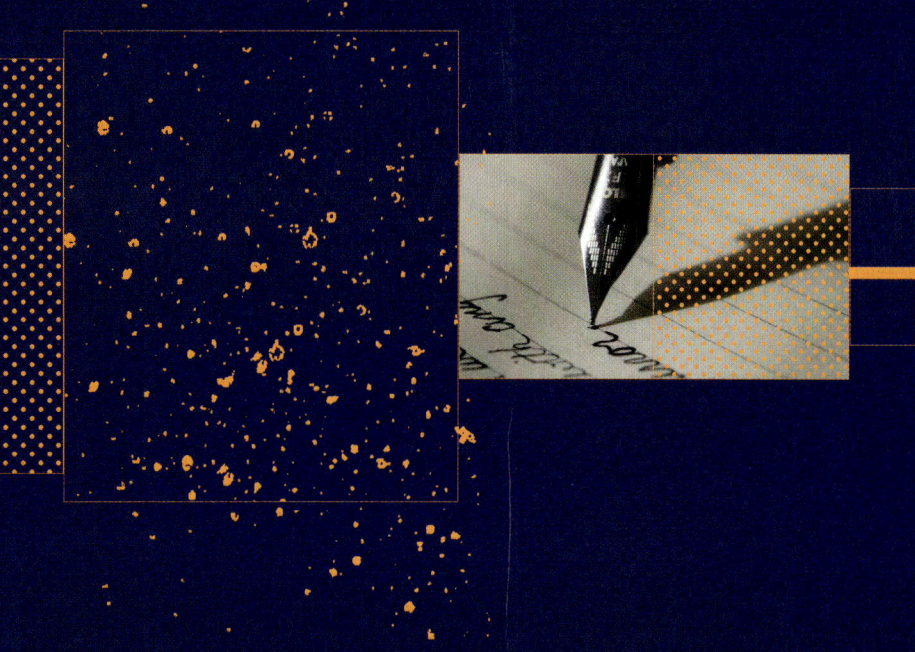

Everyone can write a personal statement that sparkles - it's just a matter of knowing how. Whether you are a scientist, a linguist, a student of the humanities, a mathematician or a potential lawyer or a medic, the trick is to think creatively about ways to enrich your personal statement.

Our most prestigious universities are looking for intellectual curiosity that goes beyond A-Level subjects.

It is especially impressive if you have discovered an author, or followed a political commentator or a science journalist, or kept up to date with a significant court case in the news, and become a 'specialist' in something that you have made your own. Perhaps you have discovered the social commentary contained in Willkie Collins' Victorian novels or in the slick American detective novels of Raymond Chandler? Perhaps in reading the legal arguments of a significant court case in the news you have begun to question whether law and justice are the same thing? Do you feel particularly strongly about environmental or human rights issues – why? Are you an historian interested in how past revolutions shed light on contemporary social upheavals? Perhaps you are a potential medic with something to say about the ethics of animal testing? Are languages where you shine? Do you relish the challenge of translating the sensibilities of Pablo Neruda's love poetry into English, or are you someone who has discovered the power of Italian neorealist film or French cinéma vérité? Whatever it is, find a specialist area of cultural interest and be an expert in your chosen field. Aim for discussing in their personal statement – make your section about your extracurricular interests the most interesting the admissions tutor will read.

If you can't think where to start, try a Saturday or Sunday newspaper – ideally, a paper with a good reputation for its journalism. Both *The Guardian* and the *Daily Telegraph* have recently won awards for their investigative and political journalism and both papers contain excellent reviews of literature, art, theatre and film. Skim your chosen paper and notice which sections really interest you. Avoiding football scores and celebrity gossip, which headlines grabbed your attention? Was it a news story about a space expedition or the political situation in a particular country, or was it a book review or interview with a film director? Why did your chosen article grab you? What questions did it make you ask? Why did you want to know more?

The serious student of economics, politics and the arts should also check out their school or local library for: *The Economist*, the *New Statesman*, the *London Review of Books*, the *Times Literary Supplement* and *The Spectator*. For online political commentary, google *The Huffington Post*.

BOOST YOUR PERSONAL STATEMENT

ARCHITECTURE
· Visit inspiring buildings and make notes on why you find them interesting
· Keep up to date with new architectural methods and building techniques
· Study the work of one or two famous architects in great detail
Useful resources: The Architects' Journal, Architectural Review and the RIBA Journal

ART & DESIGN
· Visit art exhibitions and design shows frequently
· Choose a few favourite artists and designers both past and present and familiarise yourself with their body of work
· Get your family or friends to set you extra-curricular projects
· Learn how to use programmes such as InDesign and Photoshop
Useful resource: www.creativereview.co.uk

BIOLOGICAL SCIENCES
· Read the New Scientist and National Geographic regularly
· Attend events such as the Cambridge Science Festival
· Research the work of at least three famous biological scientists
Useful resource: www.societyofbiology.org

BUSINESS/MANAGEMENT
· Read the Economist and the Financial Times regularly; follow two or three stories in detail
· Participate in business challenges such as Young Enterprise or the ICAEW BASE competition
· Apply for placements at small companies and get experience in a range of fields within a business (family or local is fine)
Useful resource: www.managementtoday.co.uk

CHEMISTRY
· Check the Royal Society of Chemistry website for updates on lectures and events you could attend
· Discuss how advances in chemistry affect our day-to-day lives
· Read Chemical Week for the latest news
Useful resources: www.rsc.org/chemistryworld
www.chem-ilp.net

CLASSICS
· Read books such as The Iliad by Homer and The Aeneid by Virgil
· Learn basic Greek and Latin in your spare time
· Visit Hadrian's Wall or a similar historical site
· Listen to BBC Radio 4's programmes on Ancient Greece and Ancient Rome
Useful resource: classics.mit.edu

COMPUTER SCIENCE
· Set up your own website, even if it is just for fun
· Read Computational Fairy Tales by Jeremy Kubica
· Research a famous computer scientist such as Alan Turing and discuss their influence on the world today
· Look up and understand the four main concepts of computer science
Useful resources: www.livescience.com
www.cs.ox.ac.uk/geomlab/home.html

DENTISTRY
· Apply for work experience at a dental surgery
· Volunteer to teach younger children about dental hygiene
· Practise an activity that will demonstrate excellent manual dexterity, such as painting, embroidery, playing a musical instrument or even having a go with electrical soldering kits!
· Read journals such as the Dental Update or Dentistry Mag
Useful resource: www.gdc-uk.org
www.healthcareers.nhs.uk

DRAMA & PERFORMING ARTS
· Try to get a prominent role in your school productions, whether onstage or offstage
· Visit the theatre as many times as you can, and compare the productions to film adaptations
· Read a different play every week and make notes on how you would direct key scenes
· Ensure you have knowledge of all genres, eras and styles of theatre
· Read reviews and understand how to critique them
Useful resources: www.thestage.co.uk   www.doollee.com

ECONOMICS
· Make notes on stories about the economy, both national and global, that interest you
· Research the potential economic consequences of Brexit
· Try to get work experience or attend an insight day at a leading financial firm
· Read the Financial Times and The Economist
Useful resource: www.res.org.uk

ENGINEERING
· Study five structures that you admire in great detail, and ensure you fully understand how and why they work
· Think about your favourite gadgets and what problem they solve
· Try and invent something that solves a problem, however small
Useful resources:
www.tomorrowsengineers.org.uk
www.raeng.org.uk
Engineering Education
or Applied Sciences,
Engineering Technology publications

ENGLISH LITERATURE
· Read, read, read, read; not just novels, read plays and poetry too, of all eras and genres
· Watch theatre, television and film adaptations of the books you read
· Start your own book club at school
Useful resources:
www.literaryreview.co.uk
The Times Literary Supplement

GEOGRAPHY
· Research current global issues such as the environment and population – be able to discuss your findings in depth
· Become a member of the Royal Geographical Society
Useful resources:
Geographical Association
www.nationalgeographic.com www.rgs.org

HISTORY
· Visit historical sites, museums and exhibitions
· Read books, watch documentaries and even films set in historical times
· Demonstrate your understanding of biased and flawed evidence
· Carefully read the course syllabus: will you be studying ancient or modern history, British or international history, or a bit of everything?
Useful resources:
www.historytoday.com
www.royalhistoricalsociety.org

HISTORY OF ART
· Read Critical Terms for Art History by Nelson and Shiff
· Listen to BBC Radio 4s' 'In Our Time' Culture archive online
· Visit art galleries and make notes on the artists and their place in history
Useful resource:
www.metmuseum.org/toah

LAW
· Attend insight days run by law firms
· Volunteer to help out at your local solicitor's office
· Follow stories in the news of high-profile cases in a variety of areas (criminal, commercial, property, family, etc.)
Useful resources:
The Lawyer, The Law Journal UK

LINGUISTICS
· Ensure that you understand the difference between linguistics and languages
· Read Noam Chomsky's Syntactic Structures and Steven Pinker's The Language Instinct
· Practise some basic phonetics by writing down sentences in the phonetic alphabet
Useful resource:
www.sil.org

MATHEMATICS
· Research mathematical theory that is outside the A-Level curriculum, e.g. Fermat's Last Theorem, Euclid's Proof of the Infinitude of Primes, Pythagorean Triples and Jordan Normal Form Theorem
· Enter the UKMT Maths Challenge and take part in MENSA tests
· Make notes on the ways in which mathematics can be applied in society, such as engineering, economics and computer science
Useful resources:
www.lms.ac.uk
www.plus.maths.org.uk

MUSIC
· Read Marcus du Sautoy's The Music of the Primes
· Research how music relates to mathematics; BBC Radio 4 has an archive programme on this
· Read Scales, Intervals, Keys, Triads, Rhythm, and Meter by John Clough
Useful resource:
www.musictheory.net

PHARMACY
· Get work experience at your local pharmacy or GP surgery
· Keep up to date on new drugs and advancements in the industry
· Read articles in journals such as The Pharmaceutical Journal and The British Journal of Clinical Pharmacy
Useful resource: www.abpi.org.uk

PHILOSOPHY
· Read Think by Simon Blackburn and The Problems of Philosophy by Bertrand Russell
· Watch TED talks online on the subject of philosophy
· Read up on the history of philosophy and the great philosophers
Useful resource: www.pfalondon.org

PHYSICS
· Regularly read the University of Oxford's science blog
· Keep up with developments from NASA and CERN
· Read and make notes on Lee Smolin's Three Roads to Quantum Gravity
Useful resources:
www.physics.org

POLITICS
· Read articles from Politics Review and The Economist
· Show interest in local politics by volunteering at your local assembly and join your local Youth Parliament
· Set up a debating society at school
· Get a global perspective by reading international newspapers
· Keep up to date with global current affairs on a daily basis
Useful resources:
www.spectator.co.uk
www.theweek.co.uk

PSYCHOLOGY
· Read articles from the British Journal of Social Psychology and The Psychologist
· Join The British Psychological Societys' Student Members Group
· Attend lectures such as 'Psychology 4 Students' or attend a summer school for psychology at a leading university
Useful resource:
www.bps.org.uk

RELIGIOUS STUDIES
· Watch TED talks online on the subject of religion
· Ensure you can fluently discuss the beliefs and practices of all the main world religions
· Stay up to date on current affairs and how news stories have been affected by religious beliefs
Useful resources: www.ted.com/read/ted-studies/religion

SOCIOLOGY
· Read up on theories such as Marxism, functionalism and postmodernism
· Attend student lectures organised by the British Sociological Association
· Read articles from the British Journal of Sociology, as well as journals that relate directly to your interests
Useful resources:
www.sociologyonline.co.uk
www.britsoc.co.uk

VETERINARY MEDICINE
· Read Eckert: Animal Physiology by David Randall
· Attend events such as the London Vet Show or RCVS Question Time
· Volunteer for work experience with animals at your local vet or pet shop
Useful resources:
www.rcvs.org.uk
www.vetnetlln.ac.uk

For any student taking any subject, you must call your chosen universities and find out if they are running any summer schools, access programmes or open days for your subject. This will give you the chance to really see what the course is like, and conveniently boosts your personal statement too.

UNIVERSITY INTERVIEWS

Will you have an interview? You need to do your research. Some universities interview, others don't, and within individual universities, some faculties interview and others don't. Confusing!

Your university will inform you through UCAS if they want to call you for an interview, but if you want some advanced warning, you can phone the admissions office to check up on the general policy. For any future doctors out there, pretty much all medicine courses want an interview, and the same goes for drama.

Whichever course you are planning to study, Pure Potential will show you what the interviewers are looking for and how you can best portray yourself as a student the universities should be fighting over!

We've divided the interview into two parts: the easy bits and the tough bits.

THE EASY BITS

WHAT TO WEAR

You want to feel comfortable but also look formal, but you don't want to be the only one wearing a three-piece suit! Most universities will inform you of the dress code in the letter you receive with information about the interview, but adhering to the 'business casual' dress code is a safe option. No denim, no trainers, no caps, no sportswear! You need to look like you're taking the interview seriously.

PLAN YOUR ROUTE AND ARRIVE EARLY

You'll be nervous enough, so don't add any stress to your day. Plan your journey the night before so you know exactly where to go and how to get there. Remember to leave yourself plenty of time for travel. You are better off being early than late! Make a note of the department's telephone number in case of an emergency that causes you a delay.

READ UP

Go over your personal statement a few times. The interviewer is likely to base questions on it, as well as any academic work you may have submitted. You've effectively invited the interviewer to ask you questions on anything specific you mentioned, so you should revise any books, theories or other areas of interest thoroughly. Next thing is to look over the course syllabus for the university you are going to for interview (don't get the same course at different unis mixed up) and be as fluent as you can about the modules and how they are assessed.

SMILE

Sounds easy, but when we are nervous we lose our ability to control even the most simple facial expressions! Make sure you start the interview off with a nice big smile (not a demonic grin). Professors want bright students first and foremost, but they also want people who are friendly and will be a pleasure to teach.

SHAKE HANDS

A firm handshake goes a long way so practise this with friends at school – you want to come across as confident and not too weak or too forceful.

SMALL TALK

Your interviewer is likely to ask you some simple questions to break the ice, such as 'How was your journey here?'. Go into a little detail; it will help make you feel at ease and will hopefully build a rapport with your interviewer. Did you travel a long way? Say so! Did you get to see any of the campus on your journey in? If yes, tell them what you saw! Have you been to the university before, perhaps on an open day? Give us some detail! Don't be afraid of the old clichés about the weather either – that is absolutely fine and allows the conversation to flow – but whatever you do, don't give a one-word answer.

HAND MOVEMENTS

Playing with your hair, pushing your sleeves up and down and up again, fiddling with jewellery and biting your nails are all very common things people do when they're nervous. Worst of all, they have no idea they are doing it… and it doesn't come across well. Practise what we call 'the window'. Imagine a box the size of a laptop screen in front of your lap. Your hands must either stay on your lap, or occasionally go through the window and back again. This not only controls involuntary nervous twitches but actually helps you to convey passion and emphasise points.

BODY LANGUAGE

A great way to get comfortable is to practise sitting down. We know it sounds ridiculous, but bear with us. Sit on a chair in front of a mirror. Observe yourself. Where are your hands? How are your feet positioned? Are your legs crossed? Are you hunched over? Are your shoulders back, and is your chin up high? Are you sitting far back in the seat or right on the edge? What feels comfortable to you?

Do you look like a confident student looking forward to discussing your future studies, or do you look like a bag of nerves? Getting your seated position right before you go into the interview will help you to look and feel more self-assured when the big day comes.

Once you've established a comfortable position, start practising some of the answers to the common questions – speak out loud. Having an answer prepared in your head is a great start but it's easy to get tongue-tied…

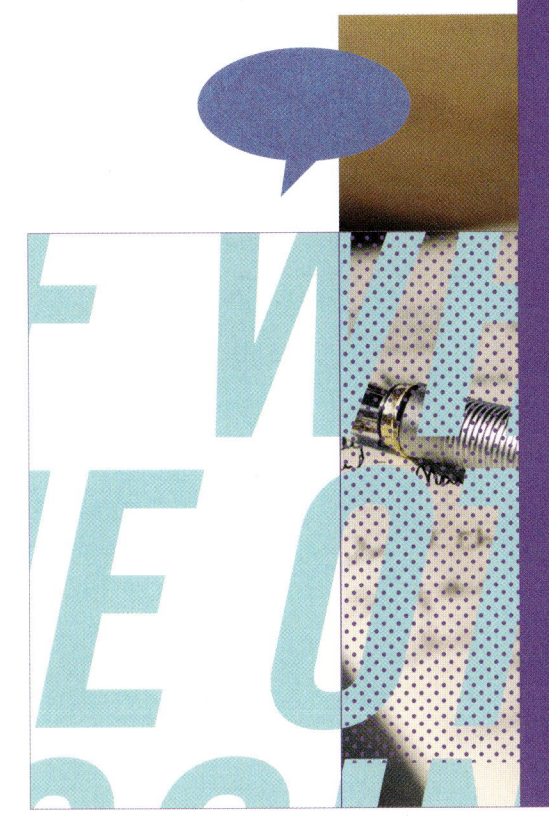

QUESTIONS TO EXPECT

There are certain questions you can predict, and you should be ready for these. No one should be surprised when they are asked why they want to study the subject, or why they think the course at that university is particularly good. Then there is the stuff you put down in your personal statement. The same goes for anything on the A-Level syllabus. It's not a test of knowledge – but you should brush up on any relevant current affairs, and have your own well-informed opinions.

"TELL ME ABOUT YOURSELF"

Remember, this is an academic interview, not a psychological evaluation. The interviewer is interested in information about you that relates to your degree choice. An obvious, but good place to start is your current educational situation, any hobbies that you have that relate particularly to the course, work experience and extra curricular activities. Use your personal statement to help you to summarise yourself. You only need to give four to five sentences and it is definitely a good idea to have this answer prepared.

"WHY DO YOU WANT TO COME TO THIS UNIVERSITY?"

Before you head to the interview, you must do your research on the university, the town itself, the accommodation, the nightlife and societies and sports clubs that you can join. This will preferably have been done at the open day, but if, for any reason, you did not attend, then you need to make up for it by showing the interviewer you know what you are letting yourself in for and have really thought about committing to three years or more at that particular institution.

"WHAT ARE YOUR STRENGTHS AND WEAKNESSES?"

It is highly likely this question comes up and it's one of the most important ones to be prepared in advance for, as you do not want to blurt out any undesirable traits in the interview! Really, the interviewer is looking for your strengths to relate to your course and that you do not have any fundamental weaknesses that would rule you out from studying it. For your strengths, think of skills such as communication, ability to adapt, determination, and organisation – and have an example of something you have done for each and every one of these. When answering the question on your weaknesses choose something that will not hurt you as a candidate, and explain what you are doing to work on it… For example, "sometimes I am shy when meeting new people, but I have recently joined a local youth club which is quickly helping me to improve this".

"ANY QUESTIONS?"

At the end of the interview, you may well be asked if you have any questions for the interviewer. Have some prepared. If you want to look like you are interested in the course and the university, there really is no better person to quiz than your interviewer, and this will convey passion and enthusiasm. Here are some topics you could cover: how the course is taught, when examinations take place, the number of lectures per week, how many students will be in the classes, is there support outside of lectures, what it is like living in the university city, the interviewers' backgrounds – did they attend the university? Make sure you don't ask any questions that should have been answered by the course prospectus, as this will make you look like you have not done any research!

THE TOUGH BITS

It's really important to make sure you master all of the easy bits, and practise those as much as you can, because the real challenge lies in the bit that is harder to practise – the difficult, unexpected questions designed to test your ability to think on your feet.

It really helps to understand what your interviewer is looking for, because the answer is often that they aren't just looking for the answer! Read on to find out what we mean.

LISTEN

It is amazing how many candidates do not listen to the question being put to them. It is also amazing how many students simply answer the question they would LIKE to have been asked. You will not be given credit for this and will give the impression of being a weak candidate with a few well-rehearsed answers. Once you've answered the question, you can then steer the conversation onto topics you are most confident in, if relevant.

ASK

If there are any terms or words that you do not understand, do not try to guess, but ask for clarification. Often, if you are working through a complex problem, an interviewer will give you hints and tips to guide you towards a possible solution. If your interviewer makes a particularly forceful or intelligent point, incorporate it into your own argument or use it as a launch pad for further ideas. Try to make the experience as interactive as possible. Asking questions and asking for clarification on things you don't understand is a sign of confidence and shows a level of humility appreciated by admissions tutors.

BE HONEST

The interviewer might ask you a question for which you don't know the answer – don't panic! Ask them to repeat the question and if you still do not understand, then be honest and explain to them that you don't know. If you make a point you later wish to correct or take back, let the interviewer know. Sometimes, there is no right or wrong answer and the interviewer just wants to gauge the way in which you think, or the methods you use to come to an answer. You will be respected far more if you are honest about what you do and don't know. Also, a moment spent clarifying what is being asked of you will generally result in a better response to the question.

BE ENTHUSIASTIC

If you obviously relish the opportunity to discuss your area of interest with an expert in the field, it will be taken as a good sign of the genuine pleasure you take in your subject. So even if you get asked a question that truly stumps you, make it look like solving it is an enjoyable challenge!

BE CRITICAL

An ability to think logically and give concise, rational arguments will impress your interviewer, so take a measured and intelligent approach to answering the question. How? Firstly, break it down into its component parts, if possible. Secondly, appreciate and acknowledge different sides of an argument. Thirdly, sit back and try to see why the question has been asked and where the interviewer is leading you. Don't be afraid to take your time and put your ideas in an ordered form before you begin to answer the question.

BE ORIGINAL

Throughout the course of your interview, you should be seeking not only to demonstrate what you know, but also to generate new ideas. Don't be too rehearsed; it's more about demonstrating potential than being polished. Use the questions as a stimulus to your imagination, and be bold in offering new solutions, suggestions or perspectives. As long as they are based on either facts or a logical argument, it does not matter whether your comments are ultimately 'right or wrong'. Feel confident in what you have to say, as you will never know everything (which is impossible!) but you can certainly use what you do know in a clever and original way.

WHAT ARE THEY LOOKING FOR?

MOTIVATION

How much do you really want to study your subject? Remember, your interviewer may have devoted his or her professional life to the subject you want to study for three years or more, so they want to meet people whose passion reflects their own. Speaking with enthusiasm and discussing the variety of things you've done that are linked to your subject – both inside and outside the classroom – will make a good impression. Remember that nothing conveys passion as much as independent research and reading done in your own time.

POTENTIAL

Will you be better tomorrow than you are today? How about the day after that? And the day… you get the idea. Interviewers know that everyone has had different opportunities during their education, and they're going to try to look past your current level of ability into the future. The best way of showing this potential is by trying to respond intelligently to all the questions you're asked, especially the ones that you've never considered before or don't know the answer to straight away. Don't worry about gaps in your knowledge; just try to be logical and clear in your thinking.

TEACHABILITY

Are you going to benefit from the university course? Will you turn up to lectures and tutorials and, more importantly, will you learn anything while you're there? Will your lecturer find it interesting to teach you? Interviewers want to see someone with an inquisitive mind that's open and hungry for new ideas. Ask questions during the interview – it's a two-way process, and if you come out knowing something you didn't know before you went in, the chances are you will have proved your teachability.

PERSONALITY

Who are you? Are you going to be an asset to the university, and a fun and interesting person to spend three years or more with? Pretty obvious stuff: just let your natural charm shine through, and don't let the formality of the occasion intimidate you into clamming up. It may be of some comfort to know that very few interviewees manage to 'be themselves' in an interview situation, and nerves are the norm.

KNOWLEDGE

Most people think this is the most important thing you can possibly show at the interview, but we find it's the least important of the criteria. The interview is NOT an exam. No one is going to just test you on what you know. Remember that the interviewer knows that everyone has experienced different standards of teaching: it wouldn't be fair or helpful to expect the same levels of knowledge from all candidates, or to use it as the sole measure of ability. However, remember that you must show the most important quality – motivation – through your love of the A-Level course, your outside reading, and further investigation of the subject. What would you make of someone who claimed to be a Liverpool fan but had never heard of Steven Gerrard? If an interviewer meets someone with a total lack of knowledge, they are likely to interpret that as an absence of real passion for the subject.

USEFUL RESOURCES

Visit purepotential.org for a list of example academic interview questions to practise.

YOU CAN AFFORD TO GO TO UNI

Ignore newspaper headlines about students leaving university with £50,000 of debt. That's a mostly meaningless figure. What counts is how much you'll repay – for some that's far more, for others it's free. This guide by me is written to bust common myths about student loans, grants and finance, including key facts every potential student, parent and grandparent should know.

Before we start, I'd just like to say: for 23 years, we educated our youth into debt when they go to university, but never about debt.

It was for this reason, and while no fan of them, when massive changes were announced to student finance for those starting in 2012 or beyond – including the trebling of tuition fees – I agreed to head up a Student Finance Taskforce working with the NUS, universities and colleges to ensure we busted the myths and misunderstandings that resulted from so much political spittle flying.

For me, what really counts is that no student is wrongly put off going to university thinking they can't afford it. Some may rightly be put off, but unless you understand the true cost, how can you decide? I hope this guide helps achieve that.

Thankfully, since then, we've also won a separate campaign to get financial education on the senior school National Curriculum in England. Yet, it'll be a long time before that truly pays dividends, so there's still a lot of nonsense spoken about student loans.

The aim of this booklet is to give you enough information to understand how much YOU will repay. After all, if you don't know how much it costs – how can you work out if it's worth it?

MARTIN LEWIS

MONEY SAVING EXPERT

INFORMATION CORRECT AT TIME OF GOING TO PRINT. VISIT www.gov.uk/student.finance FOR THE MOST UP-TO-DATE FIGURES

BEFORE YOU GO TO UNIVERSITY

Whether to go to university or not will be one of the biggest decisions of your life. And, like all big decisions, it can seem pretty scary. You need to think about what to study and where to go – and if you can afford it. While we can't help you decide about the first two questions, we can give you a quick answer to the third…

YES.
IF YOU WANT TO GO TO UNIVERSITY, THEN YOU CAN AFFORD TO GO.

OK, some of the costs seem pretty huge – up to £9,250 in tuition fees per year, before you even begin to think about living costs. However, before you start worrying about where you're going to find the money, remember two big facts:

NO ONE HAS TO PAY FEES UPFRONT

The government will provide loans for your time at university so it's not like you or your parents have to save up all the money beforehand.

YOU ONLY REPAY WHEN YOU EARN ENOUGH

Once you leave university, you only repay the loan if you earn more than £21,000 a year. If not, you don't repay. And if you never earn enough (although we hope for you that you do), you never repay a thing.

WHAT LOANS ARE AVAILABLE?

1. TUITION FEE LOANS

These cover the full cost of tuition fees and are available to all eligible first-time students. They are paid directly to your university every year by the Student Loans Company.

2. MAINTENANCE LOANS

Money is also available for eligible full-time students to pay for things such as rent, food and bills. The way some of this is decided is by means testing, which is where they look at how much your household earns each year, usually based on your parents' income (see the Q&A for exact details). In general, the less your parents earn, the more funding you're entitled to.

Applications for loans need to be done separately to your UCAS application. You can normally apply in spring before you go to university and you don't have to wait until you've got a confirmed place to apply. But make sure you don't miss the deadlines, which are usually the end of May. Remember the earlier you apply, the better, as it means your money will be available at the beginning of term. Applications are made to the Student Loans Company through the gov.uk website: www.gov.uk/student-finance.

WHAT DO TUITION FEES PAY FOR?

Universities and colleges need to be paid for. They have to pay staff to teach and assess you, keep buildings in good condition and provide facilities such as libraries and laboratories. Over recent years, it has been decided that, rather than the taxpayer paying, students should pay if they earn enough after graduating.

A £9,000 COURSE WON'T ALWAYS COST MORE THAN A £6,000 ONE

It sounds odd, but it's true. If you're planning to go for a course just because it's cheap, it's important you understand this first. Once you add in maintenance loans, many students who AREN'T higher earners after university won't repay in full even on £6,000 courses, which means there's no additional cost in going for a £9,000 course. Try www.studentfinancecalc.com, which allows you to see whether it's likely you'll be someone who repays or not and see the 'How do I repay the loans?' section.

THE LOAN IS WIPED 30 YEARS AFTER YOU GRADUATE

Whatever you borrow, regardless of what you've repaid, in the April 30 years after you graduate/leave university, the loan is wiped. You won't owe another penny. So even if you haven't repaid everything you borrowed, the rest of the debt is gone.

PART-TIME STUDENTS REPAY TUITION FEES IN THE SAME WAY

Universities can charge up to £6,935 a year for a part-time course. Part-time students can get a tuition fee loan that works exactly the same way as for full-time students, but not a maintenance loan, so they have to think about saving up to cover their living costs. See the Q&A section at the end for more information.

YOU DON'T HAVE TO TAKE A LOAN

You don't have to take a loan if you already have the money to pay for your tuition fees and living costs. But you could actually end up spending more than needed if you pay upfront because, if you do take out a loan, you might not have to pay it all back before the debt is wiped. Of course, paying for the fees isn't everything. As well as finding innovative ways to cook baked beans – and whatever you're there to study – managing your money is one of the most important things you'll learn at university, especially if you don't want to eat those beans EVERY night of the week.

WHILE YOU'RE AT UNIVERSITY

SO THE BIG QUESTION IS WHERE DOES THE MONEY FOR DAY-TO-DAY LIFE COME FROM?

Like everyone else, students should not spend more than they earn, and knowing how much income you'll have is essential. Once you get the information back from Student Finance England, you should know exactly how much you'll be getting each year, making it easier to plan your spending. Most of your income will come from one of four places.

1. MAINTENANCE LOANS ARE TO HELP YOU PAY FOR FOOD, RENT AND OTHER LIVING COSTS.

They are paid into your student bank account in three instalments – one at the start of each term – and are repaid just like tuition fee loans. The amount you can borrow depends on your household income, your course and where you live and study.

THE MAXIMUM AMOUNTS ARE:

£11,002
FOR STUDENTS LIVING AWAY FROM HOME INSIDE LONDON

£8,430
FOR STUDENTS LIVING AWAY FROM HOME OUTSIDE OF LONDON

£7,097
FOR STUDENTS LIVING AT HOME

£9,654
IF YOU SPEND A YEAR ABROAD AS PART OF YOUR COURSE

2. BURSARIES AND SCHOLARSHIPS ARE EXTRA CASH PROVIDED BY UNIVERSITIES AND COLLEGES OR OTHER ORGANISATIONS LIKE CHARITIES AND BUSINESSES, WHICH YOU DON'T HAVE TO PAY BACK.

Not everybody can get a bursary or scholarship, and they are awarded to different students for different reasons – like your household income and how well you've done in your exams. Ask your choice of university what extra funding they provide and how you can apply.

Some universities might offer you a reduction on their fees – or a fee waiver – instead. If you are given a choice, with everything else being equal, it is usually better to go for a bursary, as that's cash in your hand, rather than a reduction in a fee you may not have to repay.

3. PART-TIME JOB

Many students supplement their cash when studying by getting a part-time job or working in the summer holidays. This can make a big difference to the lifestyle you can afford – and many also provide valuable skills that are helpful for getting a job later. Do think realistically about how much time you will have for work though, so that it won't damage your studies.

4. CONTRIBUTIONS FROM PARENTS

Your parents may also decide to give you money if they can afford it. However, it's also worth noting that the amount of maintenance loan you get depends, for most people, on their parents' income; those who come from wealthier homes get a smaller loan. This is done because your parents are expected to contribute. So if you don't get the full loan, while there is no way to force them and they are not legally required to give you money, it is certainly worth having the conversation with them in advance about whether they'll contribute. Feel free to show them this paragraph if it helps.

WHAT DOESN'T COUNT AS YOUR INCOME?

DON'T include things like 'interest-free overdrafts', or, far worse, credit cards as part of your income (i.e. money you can plan to spend). They are debt and will need paying back. So while they may help get over any minor cash flow problems in the short term if you know money is coming soon, it's important not to see these as part of your income.

NOT ALL DEBT IS THE SAME

It's easy to think "I've got to get a student loan, why not borrow a little more?" but you have to understand how special student loans are. No other loan only needs you to repay if you're earning enough. With others, it'll never go away; they'll chase you even if you can't afford it – the interest is higher and will multiply at speed. Be very careful about taking any other form of borrowing.

DOING A BUDGET IS CRUCIAL

This is where you match up what money is coming in with what is going out. It's incredibly important or you may end up having a great first week splashing the cash – then spend the rest of term struggling to survive. Of course, it's tough right now to know exactly what you'll need to spend on things like books, transport, course equipment and partying. Plus, there are other costs people often forget, like TV licence or toilet roll (none of which are much fun to buy, but are even less fun if you're caught without them at the wrong time). Once you know what your situation is, try www.studentcalculator.org.uk, a free interactive tool to help you.

AFTER UNIVERSITY

HOW DO I REPAY THE LOANS?

This is a long time away, but it's worth understanding now. Once you've graduated (or even if you didn't complete your course), you may worry that you've got an enormous debt hanging over you. But don't panic! You don't have to repay a penny until you get a job and are earning more than £21,000 a year. Once you're past that point, you'll pay back 9% of everything you earn above £21,000. So if you earn £22,000, as it is one grand over the threshold, you'll pay £90 of it a year.

WHAT YOU'LL PAY BACK

SALARY	MONTHLY REPAYMENTS	YEARLY REPAYMENTS
£20K	£0	£0
£25K	£30	£360
£30K	£67	£810
£35K	£105	£1,260

It's worth thinking about this for a second. It means the amount you repay each month ONLY depends on what you earn, not on how much you borrowed in the first place (though borrow more and it may mean you repay more in total and over a longer time). So whether you're on a £6,000 or £9,000 course, the amount to repay is the SAME.

Actually you won't even see this cash. Unlike normal borrowing, where you have to hand over the cash, with student loans, if you've got a job your employer takes the amount you owe from your salary each month (it's called a 'payroll deduction') in the same way they do with any tax you need to pay (see the Q&A section at the end for what happens if you're self-employed).

So you might not even notice the money has gone, since you'll never actually have it in the first place – you'll just take home less each month than someone who doesn't have to make loan repayments. This is a very important point, because it means the rather scary debt collectors who normally enforce loan repayments won't come knocking at your door for student loans.

YOU WILL BE CHARGED INTEREST THOUGH

You will pay interest on your student loan as soon as you take it out, at the rate of inflation plus an extra 3% a year. How much interest you pay after studying depends on how much you earn. Afterwards, interest starts at the inflation rate (when you earn less than £21,000) and goes up to inflation plus 3% (when you earn more than £41,000). Interest is added to what you owe: it's not an upfront fee and it won't affect how much you pay each month. The interest cost will only affect you if you repay all you owe before the debt wipes after 30 years; otherwise you'll never repay it. Yet if you do earn enough to repay fully, it's likely to mean you repay more overall and you'll be paying for longer.

WHAT IS INFLATION?

Inflation is a measure of the rate at which prices change over time. Usually, though not always, they are increasing. So if inflation is 4%, then a basket of shopping costing £100 this year will cost £104 next year.

Therefore, if the interest on a loan is set at the rate of inflation, it's like saying you were lent a 'basket of shopping's worth' of money this year, but when it comes to repaying you'd only have to give the cash that'd buy that same basket back. This means your actual spending power hasn't been diminished by taking out the loan so it hasn't cost you anything.

WHAT IS INTEREST?

Interest is the price you pay for borrowing money. It's based on how much you owe and how long you have the loan for. So if you borrowed £1,000 with 10% annual interest, you'd owe £1,100 at the end of the year if you didn't pay anything back.

WHAT HAPPENS IF I DON'T GET A JOB, LOSE MY JOB OR TAKE A CAREER BREAK?

If your income ever falls below £21,000 a year, or if you don't get a job, lose your job or decide to take a career break, your repayments will simply stop. For more information on any aspect of student loan repayment, see www.studentloanrepayment.co.uk.

QUESTIONS & ANSWERS

HOW DOES MEANS TESTING WORK?

Means testing is used to decide how much financial help you are entitled to. For most students, it's based on the joint income of your parent(s) before tax (they are allowed to take off their pension contributions and some allowances for each of your younger siblings, if you have any). If you have a lot of savings in your own name, this will also be taken into account. There are a few situations that mean the testing is based on your own income (and your husband, wife or civil partner, if you have one) including if you are over 25, or have financially supported yourself for more than three years, have no living parents or are caring for a child. See the Student Finance England link for more information.

IF MY PARENTS ARE DIVORCED / SEPARATED, WHOSE INCOME IS MEANS TESTED?

If this is the case in your family, the income of the parent you live with most of the time will be used (if that's not clear, this is normally the parent who claimed child benefit for you before university). If the parent you mainly live with remarries or has a cohabiting partner, their joint income will then be looked at.

WILL THE STUDENT LOAN GO ON MY CREDIT FILE?

Whenever you apply for a financial product which involves lending you money, be it a bank account, contract mobile phone or monthly paid car insurance, the company you're applying to will check your credit file to help decide if they want to lend to you. Your file is a record of things like how much debt you already have and whether you have missed payments on credit cards or utility bills. Having a lot of outstanding debt on your file can make it hard to get a loan or credit card. Unlike other loans, student loans won't appear on your credit file, so lenders won't know about it unless they ask – and they often won't. Even if they do though, in the bigger scheme of things (due to how it's repaid), it's only likely to have a limited impact on your ability to borrow.

Once you're earning enough to repay the student loan, you'll have less income than if you didn't have it, so this will have a minor impact on your ability to get a mortgage. However, it's worth noting that this has always been the case. One of the few advantages of the new system should be, because you repay at £21,000 compared to current graduates who have to start repaying when they earn £16,365, you'll actually have more money in your pocket.

IF WE'VE GOT THE MONEY, SHOULD WE SIMPLY PAY AND NOT TAKE THE LOAN?

If you or your parents decide to pay your tuition fees without taking a loan, there's a few things to bear in mind. It's definitely a bad idea if you or your parents are borrowing the money elsewhere to do it – as student loans are a very cheap long-term form of borrowing and you only have to repay them if you earn enough. Even if you used savings, it's worth remembering that if, as an extreme example, you never earned over £21,000, you'd have effectively paid that cash for no reason – as you'd never have needed to repay the loan. This is a complex subject though, so if you're serious about doing it, for more information on the pros and cons, see www.moneysavingexpert.com/students.

WHY DOES A BURSARY BEAT A FEE WAIVER?

Unless you earn a higher salary on graduation, a fee waiver is unlikely to reduce the amount you repay at all. So while it may feel like your fee and debt is lower, there may well be no material impact on your pocket. Yet a bursary will provide cash now, which could reduce the need for any commercial borrowing. So as one is a certain gain and the other a 'you may benefit in the future but might not', the choice is a no brainer.

HOW DO I PAY BACK THE DEBT IF I AM SELF-EMPLOYED?

If you set up your own business or work for yourself, your repayments will be collected via HMRC's Self Assessment scheme. This means you will need to make payments at the appropriate deadline to fulfil your legal obligations. If you do not pay, HMRC will pursue you for any amount overdue.

IF I'VE GOT SAVINGS OR OTHER EARNINGS AFTER I GRADUATE, DO THEY COUNT?

If you have additional income of £2,000 or more from savings interest, pensions or shares and dividends, this will also be treated as part of your income for repayment purposes and you'll need to repay 9% of that, again via Self Assessment.

DO I STILL HAVE TO PAY IF I MOVE ABROAD?

Yes is the simple answer. You're still obliged to repay the student loan based on 9% of all earnings above the equivalent of £21,000 in the country you are in and can face a fine if you don't. By taking out the loan, you have a contractual relationship to repay it. You may have heard that some people don't repay loans when they move abroad. If that happens, it's because there are practical difficulties in the government pursuing them for the money – but that doesn't stop them being responsible for paying it back.

WHAT HAPPENS IF I DROP OUT OF UNIVERSITY?

If you don't complete your course, any tuition or maintenance loans you have taken up to that point will still need repaying. The repayments and interest work in the same way as if you had done the course – in other words, you repay 9% of everything earned above £21,000 from the April following the three years after you started.

WHAT HAPPENS TO THE LOAN IF I DIE?

While it sounds morbid, it's worth knowing that if you die or are permanently injured, the rest of your loan is wiped, meaning your kids or parents will never have to pay it on your behalf.

CAN I PAY BACK THE LOAN MORE QUICKLY?

Yes, the government has said that you will be able to repay the loan early without penalty charges, although this doesn't mean you should pay off early. While, in general, it's better to repay debts as quickly as possible, student loans are one of the rare cases where it may be a bad decision because you might not repay the full amount before it's wiped after 30 years.

IS THE THRESHOLD FIXED?

Yes, the repayment threshold for any student starting in HE from 2012 onwards has been frozen by the government at £21,000 until at least 2021, when it will be reviewed again.

WALES

All Welsh applicants will be charged up to £9,250 per year for all full-time courses, irrespective of whether you study in Wales or not. The amount charged may vary between courses, as well as between universities or colleges – check the amount your university or college will charge on their websites. Two important things to note here: you will never have to repay anything until you earn over £21,000 a year; and there is nothing to pay upfront. A tuition fee loan and grant is available from the Welsh Government via Student Finance Wales and they will send the money directly to your university.

TUITION FEE LOAN

You may choose to take out a Tuition Fee Loan of up to £4,296 to cover the initial tuition fee costs. This is a loan so you will have repay this amount once you earn over £21,000 per year. If you're sharp when it comes to maths, you'll probably have worked out there is a shortfall – if universities are charging you £9,250 per year, then where is the rest of the money going to come from?! Welsh students also have access to a Fee Grant, where you can apply for a grant of up to £4,954 to cover the difference. This is money that you do not have to repay. Your fees will be paid directly to your university or college on your behalf so you don't have to worry about anything.

MAINTENANCE

On top of the support you receive to help with tuition fees, you will also receive help with funding your living costs. Maintenance loans are designed to help with the cost of living while you are at university. The amount of loan you receive is dependent on household income, but the maximum loans available are listed below.

£9,697
IF YOU LIVE AWAY FROM HOME AND STUDY IN LONDON

£6,922
IF YOU LIVE AWAY FROM HOME AND STUDY AT A UNIVERSITY OR COLLEGE OUTSIDE OF LONDON

£5,358
IF YOU LIVE AT HOME

£8,253
IF YOU SPEND A YEAR ABROAD AS PART OF YOUR COURSE

You can also apply for a Welsh Government Learning Grant, which is non-repayable money (free money) from the Welsh Government and is dependent on your household income. You can receive up to £5,161 if your household income is below £18,370; and a partial grant if your household income is between £18,370 and £50,020.

If you have children or dependent adults, or you have a disability, you may qualify for extra help on top of your main student finance package. Part-time students may also apply for grants to help with the cost of study. The amount of support you receive is dependent on your circumstances and household income, but it's worth enquiring with your university and Student Finance Wales to check how much you could receive.

You do not need to have a confirmed place at university to apply for student finance: you can enter your first choice university on the form, and update once you know exactly where you will be going.

The quickest and easiest way to apply for financial support is online at www.studentfinancewales.co.uk. Applications should be completed as soon as possible to avoid any delays in processing your form and making your payments. You can also ring Student Finance Wales on 0300 200 4050.

NORTHERN IRELAND

SCOTLAND

At the time of going to print, the exact details of student finance for 2017-18 had not been released by the Department for the Economy, but will be online from Spring 2017. However, they did state that it was likely that non-means tested tuition fee loans of up to £5,500 will be available to help with course costs, and that students will be able to apply from Summer 2017.

For more information on student finance for Northern Ireland, please visit: www.studentfinanceni.co.uk.

If you are a Scottish applicant wanting to study at a Scottish university, you will not be charged a tuition fee. You can still apply for a maintenance loan to help fund your living costs while at university. The amount you receive is dependent on your household income and whether you choose to live at home.

If you are a Scottish applicant but want to study at a university anywhere else in the UK, you will be charged up to £9,250 per year. You are eligible to apply for tuition fee and maintenance loans, and there are various grants available to support you with living costs.

If you are from anywhere else in the UK and you want to study at a Scottish university, you will be charged up to £9,250 per year. You will need to apply for student finance via the same process for all other universities and you will be eligible for a loan and/or a maintenance grant depending on your household income.

Further information can be found on the Student Awards Agency for Scotland (see website: www.saas.gov.uk).

FRESHERS' WEEK

By Megan Walsh

Megan studied English at the University of Manchester, and then went on to write for The Times. She is currently doing a Masters in Chinese Studies at SOAS.

For some, Freshers' Week is an exhilarating seven days sparkling with new faces and fizzing with the taste of freedom. For others, it can feature people and experiences you spend the remaining three years trying to avoid. Your first week at university is an exciting, bizarre time; there is a lot that can – and should – be crammed in. Here are a few tips to live it out to its full potential.

PEOPLE

OK, so you don't know anyone. Everyone else seems to have made loads of friends already and you worry you will never make any. You see yourself eating alone in the canteen every day and they'll all point and laugh… The first thing you need to know about Freshers' Week is that no one really knows anyone very well and no one knows what to expect or whmo to talk to. But everyone is keen to look like they do. Try to talk to as many people as you can, even if you hate small talk. Go with the flow and try to keep an open mind. University is a melting pot and there is every chance that you'll befriend people very different to those you would have expected to before you arrived. Don't expect meaningful relationships to blossom immediately but enjoy the panoply of personalities and their quirks.

EVENTS

Your social calendar will be awash with parties, fairs and events. Go to as many as possible; they are an excellent way to meet people. You may have to put up with cheesy student anthems and wear some oversized T-shirts but it'll be fun.

REGISTRATION

You will queue for hours to have a mug shot taken for your student card. Use your student card liberally. It gains you entry to all student nights, and discounts on tickets, clothes and music – among other things. When in doubt, flash it.

LECTURES & TUTORIALS

Yes, you'll have to go to some of these in the first week. They are important in terms of getting your bearings, establishing what you'll be studying and catching a glimpse of your fellow classmates. Some more progressive tutors like to play 'ice breaker' games, so if you dread the thought of being caught on the spot, you best know what to say about yourself when it's your turn in the introduction circle. If you're nervous about your academic ability compared to others, don't be. You are there because the university wants you there.

THE FRESHERS' FAIR

All universities have clubs and societies that use the fair to sell themselves to you. They offer a mind-boggling array of extracurricular activities for you to follow up on old hobbies, beliefs and activities, or to branch out and try something new. There is no time after university in which you will have such eclectic opportunities – make the most of them. They, too, are a great way to make friends.

HALLS

Halls are noisy. People like to crank up their stereos, sing, play games and shout about their crazy antics. In Freshers' Week, the fire alarm might go off every five minutes; burnt toast and drunken fools the likely culprits. It's annoying, but if the alarm sounds, make sure you still leave the building. And it's not unusual for traffic cones and street signs to appear in the common room. (This is illegal though, so try to bring home some legitimate mementos instead.)

LOVE

You will probably not find it in the first week (although there are always couples who meet on day one and are together three years later). Enjoy it, with all its bumps and potholes. It's all part of the experience.

YOUR ROOM

The rooms in halls can be a bit spartan. The Freshers' Fair will probably have on offer innumerable posters and potted plants to spice up your domain (remember to water the plant). And the bed linen provided will look less than inviting so, if you can, bring your own.

WASHING

The same rules apply as at home. You have to wash (yourself and your clothes). There'll be a laundrette nearby, and some halls will have washing machines so there is no excuse!

HYGIENE & HEALTH

Take care with what you eat, try to have a balanced diet and remember that basic health and safety precautions in the kitchen are as essential at university as in the wider world, if not more. Make sure you look after yourself – especially during the first couple of weeks if you want to avoid getting struck down by 'Freshers' Flu'. To stay feeling your best, try to get plenty of sleep and fit in some exercise. Oh, and try to get ahead of others by registering with the doctors during Freshers' Week; there is usually one on campus.

FEELING LONELY

Everyone will experience this in the first few weeks of term at least once. It's perfectly normal, but if you feel like it's getting too much, then speak to Student Services – if you have trouble coping with anything at university, there are many resources to help you, no matter what the problem. Find out what they are and where they are.

And finally – your family misses you. Call them from time to time.

MAKING THE MOST OF YOUR TIME AT UNI

It's tempting to laze your free afternoons, weekends and summer holidays away, but beware – the job market is competitive and you're going to have to do something to show that you're worth employing when graduation comes around. Here are some tips to help you maximise your spare time at university and set you apart from other graduates when you are looking for your first full-time job.

DURING TERM TIME

While at university, there are services set up to support you to develop a career plan and gain new skills. Usually, they are free (which they may not be once you graduate) so make the most of them while you can.

Visit the careers guidance team

Use all the resources available and don't leave it until your final year – you will be much too busy doing your final exams to think seriously about it then. A significant number of employers now offer spring weeks to first years, open days and internship programmes that can all be accessed before your final year.

Set yourself regular career-related objectives

This includes exploring potential career opportunities, understanding your strengths, finding relevant work experience, developing a draft CV and gaining practical interview skills.

Learn to sell yourself

Marketing your own skills often doesn't come naturally but is a critical skill that you need to develop. Use every opportunity to build these skills – for example, join your debating society or do a presentation skills course. Use the language that employers speak. You don't have to approve of business jargon but you do need to know what employers are talking about when the time comes to start job hunting.

Develop your skills

Employers want to see real skills that you can apply in their business. These may be people skills such as leadership or self-reliance skills such as networking. Sign up for as many skills workshops as possible. Look out for any careers-related modules or options.

Embrace the opportunity to join clubs and societies

Take part in new activities, sports, clubs and societies. It will give you a chance to meet new people, build your self-confidence and develop key skills. In today's competitive world, you need much more than just qualifications.

DURING SUMMER HOLIDAYS

Use your summers wisely. They are the longest holidays you'll ever get. Most students have up to four months off – this is plenty of time to get some work experience or an internship, and have time to work to save the pennies for the year ahead, travelling or your future plans.

Work experience and internships

Work experience will show employers that you are proactive, diligent and, above all, serious about a career. Try to seek out paid internship opportunities, or a structured volunteering programme. You will develop skills by meeting new people and being in a working environment. You will be able to add career-relevant, bright, sparkling experience to your CV while learning more about your career options.

Travel

Students often use their long holidays to travel. If you are interested in seeing more of the world and experiencing different cultures and environments, then grab your passport and venture off the beaten track. This world of ours has a million and one things for you to see and do beyond our shores. Travelling can be expensive, but you could fund it through part-time work, or by working for half of your holiday and saving your pennies. You could also look into volunteering opportunities abroad; save turtles in the Galapagos, help build a village in Africa or teach English in Indonesia – this is rewarding, useful and impressive.

Employers want to hire people who are motivated, passionate about what they do and have the intellect and skills to get things done. By focusing on your studies and your extracurricular activities in a meaningful way, you will get the career opportunities you seek.

agr

With thanks to Stephen Isherwood, CEO of Association of Graduate Recruiters

CHANGING YOUR COURSE OR DROPPING OUT

CHANGING YOUR COURSE

You applied to do the course, spent hours agonising over getting your personal statement just right, celebrated when you got an offer and have finally arrived at your university, excited to begin the first of three or more years studying a course you thought would inspire you and take your knowledge and understanding of the subject to dizzying heights.

But you don't think you like it, it's not what you thought it would be and you're feeling about as inspired as a wet blanket. Don't worry – each year 16% of students across the UK decide to change their course or university.

If you are not enjoying your chosen university subject because it is too difficult, assessed in the wrong way for you or not what you had expected, you might be considering changing course. Some students find that once they start university, they change their mind about their future career path, and require a different subject.

Make sure that you speak to a careers advisor or tutor at your university to get their advice on the options available to you. They might have a way of solving your problems without having to go through the difficulties of changing your course.

If you decide to change course, you will usually have to restart your degree from year one, and so you will be at university for longer and will rack up more debt in tuition fees. It will also be longer before you get a job. Some courses will have specific grade requirements for entry into their department, so you will need to check this before you contact the relevant professors.

DROPPING OUT

Students drop out of university for various reasons. It is a very serious decision to take, particularly in terms of the financial implications, and therefore one that you should consider carefully. Just like changing a course, it is very important to contact your careers advisor and tutor to ask their advice. Are there any courses that you would prefer doing instead of this one? If your decision to drop out is due to health or personal reasons, would you consider returning to university after a year? After discussion with your tutor, it is usually possible to take some time out to reconsider your options.

If you have made the decision to drop out of university, there are two main options available to you:

– Reapply to a different university to start the following year. This would be a good idea if you like the idea of university, but were not enjoying life at your particular institution.

– Get a job or apprenticeship. There are many exciting career opportunities available for school leavers. Visit the 'School Leaver' section for more information on alternatives to university.

THINGS TO CONSIDER

Enquire
Speak to Student Services and find out what your options are – they will have heard this all before so don't feel that they will judge you or that you are inconveniencing them. Whether you want to change course, university or even take a year out, they will be able to help you with all aspects, including student finance as your loan or grant may be affected.

Research
You will need to do your due diligence and research the new course you have in mind thoroughly. Go and find the faculty, speak to staff as well as students and get a very clear idea of what it entails. Be prepared to defend your decision. You will have to explain why you have chosen your new subject and why you think that it is a good idea for you to change.

Make a list
It is a good idea to draw up a list of all the things that you like about your course, and the things you dislike. Then write a list of all the things you like about the university in general, and the things you dislike. Compare them and see where there is an overlap – this will enable you to see if it is the course or the university that you want to change.

Are you 100% sure?
If university life is not what you expected, changing the course may not help. It's very important that it is the course itself you are not enjoying. Be careful not to confuse homesickness, loneliness, stress, or poor time management with wanting to change your course. If these issues are what's on your mind, then speak to Student Services who will be able to help you.

Don't delay!
After you have made a definite decision, you need to get the changes made quickly so that you can start your new course as soon as possible – the longer you leave it, the more catching up you'll have to do.

STUDYING ABROAD

WHICH COURSE? WHICH UNI? WHICH COUNTRY?

Packing your belongings, saying farewell to friends and family and immersing yourself in a new culture, environment and even language to study your degree is a brave move indeed, but one that will be recognised and rewarded in years to come.

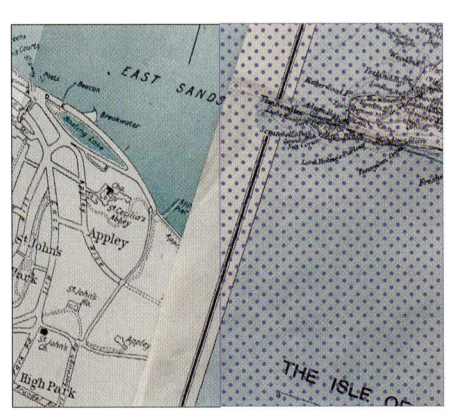

By taking on such a challenge, you will be demonstrating that you are adaptable, culturally aware and resilient. You will also be opening yourself up to unique and exciting international opportunities, perhaps learning a new language, making friends from all over the world and expanding your employment opportunities upon graduation infinitely.

If you are interested in studying abroad, there are lots of different options; you don't have to go away for the full duration of your undergraduate degree. It might be that you would prefer to be based in the UK but travel abroad for just one year of your degree. We've explained some of the options below to help you decide which might suit you best.

FULL DEGREE (3 – 4 YEARS)

Studying at a university abroad for the full duration of your degree will bring huge benefits. You'll live in the city you study in, immerse yourself in the culture, speak the language and make lifelong friendships over the course of three years. The first step of the challenge is to find out which course you want to study and where. Most other countries don't have a central system like UCAS to make it easier for you, so you will have to apply to the universities individually. If you are applying to study a course that will be in another language, you will have to show proficiency in that language, so just like with UCAS personal statements, make sure your applications have no mistakes. There are many organisations out there to help you.

TERM/SEMESTER (5 MONTHS)

You can choose to study abroad for one semester of your degree; this will be around five to six months. This will still give you an enriched experience, but your main degree will be awarded by a UK based university. Your classes for that semester are conducted abroad and you live in the city you've chosen for the entire semester. This option is great for students who want to test the waters of studying abroad.

SUMMER SCHOOL (1 – 2 MONTHS)

Lots of universities offer summer schools for anything between three to eight weeks. There is often a charge for these summer schools, but they will give you a chance to use your summer wisely by studying in a different country and meeting people from all over the world. These aren't tied into your undergraduate degree and you can study any subject that you are interested in.

SANDWICH COURSES (1 YEAR)

If you like the idea of studying abroad, but going away for your entire degree seems a bit much, then you should consider sandwich courses, where you spend only part of your degree course in another country.

Depending on the course you choose at university, some students will also have the opportunity to take a year out as part of their degree – this is particularly true for language students, joint honours degrees and many business courses. You can take time out independently or as part of a scheme.

ERASMUS (1 YEAR)

The Erasmus Programme is an EU exchange student programme that has been in existence since the late 1980s. Its purpose is to provide foreign exchange options for students from within the EU and it involves many of the best universities and seats of learning on the continent.

The programme is aimed at cross-border cooperation between states to aid the growth of international studying and, with over 4,000 students involved in the programme at any one time, it offers an excellent chance of experience abroad.

Students must be registered in a higher education institution and enrolled in studies leading to a recognised degree or other recognised tertiary-level qualification (up to and including the level of doctorate). There is no immediate change to the UK's participation in the Erasmus+ programme following the EU referendum result and the UK National Agency will continue to manage and deliver the programme across the UK.

All participants and beneficiaries should continue with their Erasmus+ funded activities and preparation for the published application deadlines in 2016 and 2017.

HOW WILL I FUND IT?

Once you've decided you'd like to study abroad, the next hurdle that you need to overcome is funding. Student loans are not available from the Student Loans Company for students who wish to study outside of the UK. Students from the EU pay the same fees regardless of which EU country they are from – however, individual countries do not have to give financial help unless the student in question has been living in the country for at least five years. If you wish to study outside of the EU, tuition fees are generally much higher and will need to be paid upfront.

So, how should you tackle the funding issue? Firstly, check the tuition fees at the university you wish to attend, and then approach the appropriate agency in the country you wish to study. Make sure that you know exactly how you are going to fund your studies before you apply, and take the time to research bursaries and scholarships that may be available to you. You'll also have to think about how you fund your accommodation, food, social life, and all the other expenses that students incur. You should definitely consider getting a part-time job while you study, or working during the holidays in between terms. You could also take out a personal loan from your UK bank, but it is important to bear in mind that you will have to repay the loan immediately and that your bank will charge you interest.

If you are planning on studying outside of the EU, you must check whether you will be permitted to work while studying as this is not always the case. Please ensure you look into funding as soon as possible; if you have even a small inkling that international study could be for you, then start researching straight away to find out where you could go.

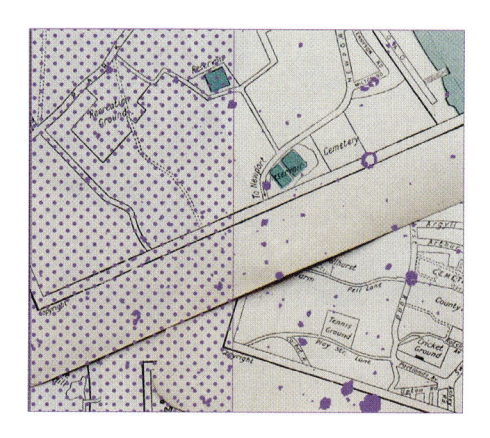

THINGS TO CONSIDER

VISA – Will you need a visa to study in your chosen country and how much does it cost?

LANGUAGE – Will the course be taught in English, or will you need to demonstrate proficiency in another language?

ACCOMMODATION – Will the university help you find accommodation or will you have to organise this yourself?

LEAGUE TABLES – Have you looked at the international university rankings?

COSTS – What are the average costs of living in your chosen country?

VISITING HOME – If you are studying on the other side of the world, it might not be easy to travel home during the holidays, so consider how often you might want to come home and include the cost of flights home in your budget.

USEFUL RESOURCES

STUDY IN EUROPE:
ec.europa.eu

STUDY IN THE US:
fulbright.co.uk

STUDY IN AUSTRALIA & NEW ZEALAND:
studyoptions.com

FOR ALL OTHER COUNTRIES:
idp.com

BURSARIES & SCHOLARSHIPS:
ukcisa.org.uk

ERASMUS FUNDING:
www.erasmusprogramme.com

FUNDING FOR STUDYING IN EUROPE:
european-funding-guide.eu

STUDYING IN THE USA

FULBRIGHT COMMISSION

Have you ever considered studying in the US? You're not alone: 2015-16 saw the largest year-on-year increase in UK students going to the US in over 30 years. There are many options to fit your interests and finances, from a full bachelor's degree to a summer internship or study abroad programme. Read on for more information about these options and ways the US-UK Fulbright Commission can help you join the 11,600 British students in the USA.

WHY GO ABROAD?

Why do so many students cross the Atlantic? In a recent survey, we found British students were most attracted to the availability of funding for undergraduate study in the US, as well as the reputation and flexibility of its degrees – you don't have to choose a field of study until your second year. Studying or working abroad for a summer or semester is also a fun and exciting way to learn about a new culture, all the while expanding your CV and developing the international perspective and skills employers seek.

YOUR OPTIONS: A BACHELOR'S DEGREE

You may have heard US study is expensive or that it is difficult to apply. First, keep in mind that Fulbright's advising team has many free resources and events on American university admissions. Also, millions of dollars in scholarships and financial aid are offered each year on the basis of your academic success, financial need or for being an international student. Over 200 alumni of the Sutton Trust US Programme have access to $50 million in funding.

STUDY ABROAD AND INTERNSHIPS

If you complete your degree in the UK, there are still plenty of opportunities to go to the US. Most UK universities have programmes set up for you to spend a semester or year abroad at an American university. You'll be able to use your UK loans, and your tuition fees are discounted for the time you are abroad.

If you're interested in a summer programme, Fulbright offers two Study of the US Institutes, hosted by American universities for UK undergraduates. Another option is to explore short-term work opportunities during your UK degree, such as a summer camp or internship programme.

WHAT ARE YOU WAITING FOR?

Check out the Fulbright website – www.fulbright.org.uk – for step-by-step guides on US undergraduate admissions, internship programmes and Summer Institutes. If you are planning to study in the US for a full degree, come along to our USA College Day Fair on 29th-30th September 2017 and meet reps from over 180 US universities, or attend a Fulbright seminar on undergraduate study.

The Fulbright Commission also partners with the Sutton Trust US Programme (us.suttontrust.com), which helps British state school students apply to American universities through support, advice and a one-week summer school in the USA. It is free to take part in the programme.

USEFUL RESOURCE: www.fulbright.org.uk

STUDYING IN AUSTRALIA AND NEW ZEALAND

Australia and New Zealand share much with the UK – a language, a history, and an education model. While universities there are a long way away, being a student down under is much the same as it is here.

Their degrees are directly equivalent to a UK degree. They take the same time to complete and are taught in the same ways. Australian and New Zealand universities have all the facilities you'd expect at a good UK campus, including libraries, cafes, laboratories, bookshops, bars, student unions, sports facilities and student clubs and societies.

For all these reassuring similarities, however, there are key differences. It is usually these that attract UK students.

BROAD, FLEXIBLE DEGREES

Undergraduate degrees in Australia and New Zealand are broader than UK degrees. When you enrol on a general degree (a Bachelor of Arts, Bachelor of Science or Bachelor of Business), you will choose a 'major'. This is your specialist subject. You can also study subjects from outside your major ('electives'). This allows you to construct a degree that is unique to your interests and tailored to your goals.

TEACHING CULTURE

Contact teaching hours in New Zealand and Australia are higher than at universities in the UK and the teaching atmosphere is relaxed and informal. UK students in Australia and New Zealand report that academics are accessible and easily approachable if they have questions or problems.

STUDENT LIFE

The universities offer a huge range of opportunities for you to make the most of your student years. You can go on an academic exchange, do an internship, join a community project, get involved with a student society, or take part in a leadership programme. Or all the above!

PRESTIGIOUS, WORLD-RANKED UNIVERSITIES

Many students are drawn to studying in Australia and New Zealand because of the reputation of their universities. In the 2014-15 QS World University Rankings, 9 Australian and New Zealand universities were ranked in the world's top 100, compared to 19 from the UK. There are only 42 universities in Australia and 8 in New Zealand, compared to around 120 in the UK.

Australian and New Zealand universities are seen as world leaders in a diverse range of subjects including, sport science, physiotherapy, geology, physical geography, social work, environmental science, and marine studies. They also offer amazing opportunities for fieldwork. Marine scientists in Australia, for example, can use the Great Barrier Reef as a living laboratory…

THE PRACTICALITIES

COSTS AND FUNDING – You will need to budget for tuition fees and living expenses for the duration of your course.

Each university sets its own tuition fees for each course, so universities charge different amounts for the same degree. Check tuition fees carefully. The least expensive courses are lecture-based (for example, history or English literature). The most expensive are medicine and dentistry. Fees start at around £9,000 per year.

For more information on Australian and New Zealand universities, see:
www.studyoptions.com/scholarships-and-funding.

To find out what degrees cost, contact Study Options and request a course list:
www.studyoptions.com/contact
www.studyoptions.com/costs-and-practicalities

HOW AND WHEN TO APPLY – Applications to Australian and New Zealand universities should be made through Study Options, not via UCAS. Applications to overseas universities should not be listed on the UCAS form, and do not impact your chances of getting a university place in the UK.

You can apply to up to five universities in Australia and New Zealand via Study Options. These are in addition to your UCAS choices.

You can apply at any time after you get predicted grades for A-Levels (or the equivalent). The majority of students apply between November and May of Year 13 for a conditional offer of place.

USEFUL RESOURCES: www.studyoptions.com www.studyingdownunder.co.uk

STUDYING IN EUROPE

Despite being closer geographically, and certainly much cheaper to get to, than the US, New Zealand or Australia, the main consideration when studying in Europe will be language. If you aren't already proficient in the local language of your chosen destination, you may view this as an exciting challenge to acquire an excellent new skill, or it may raise concerns about settling in. Some unis offer what is called 'English Medium Tuition' courses, which means you will learn your degree in English; alternatively, you can throw yourself in the deep end and learn alongside local students in the local language.

CULTURE

You will be hard-pressed to find a place more rich in culture than Europe! Art, music, literature, architecture, ancient history and modern politics can all be explored with relative ease and low cost. Many students spend their holidays interrailing – adventures by train across the continent. What better place to study history then in the very places it happened?!

FUNDING & ENTRY REQUIREMENTS

The good news is that many countries in the EU charge much less for their degree programmes than on home turf.
The even better news is that the entry requirements for many courses are lower than UK universities. This isn't necessarily a reflection of quality – the UK university system is disproportionately over-subscribed, but make sure you don't choose a course just because the grade requirements are low! You'll need to research the institutions individually, and see how they do on league tables, as well as get some insight into the university experience from UK alumni – the uni should be able to put you in touch.

WHICH COUNTRY?

If you already have an affiliation with a European country, perhaps family roots, an interest in their history or culture, or you have already begun learning the language, then that may help to sway your decision. If you are just keen on exploring Europe and don't have a preference, then let the course and quality of the institution be your guide. Although you will, no doubt, have many wonderful experiences and meet lifelong friends wherever you go, when the course is finished, you will want a quality degree from an internationally recognised institution to show for it.

USEFUL RESOURCES

eunicas.co.uk
interrail.eu

MY EXPERIENCE

STEF SILVESTER
studies in New Zealand

"I am studying a Bachelor of Science, majoring in biochemistry, at the University of Otago in New Zealand. I decided to study in New Zealand because of their similar education system and because I'd always dreamed of travelling here!

Dunedin has a student population of 25,000 and there is always something to do with so many students about. There is a great range of clubs and activities, from tramping and kayaking to dancing and knitting. Nightlife is a huge part of student life here. Most weekends a good party can be found by following the music!

My classes are great. I can access all my lectures online as well as via podcasts. The labs are really well equipped and there is plenty of help available if needed, through study groups or one-on-one tutor sessions.

Coming to New Zealand is one of the best decisions I ever made and I'd urge anyone to make the same jump!"

OLIVER BROOM
lived in France for a year during his degree

"I chose to spend the third year of my Durham University French degree course in Grenoble, France. It seemed the perfect opportunity for me to experience living abroad at the same time as trying to become a fluent French speaker.

I organised it through my university. I had to fill out some forms requesting to go to university in Grenoble and Student Services gave me guidance on the whole process. I spent the summer before working hard and saving to supplement my student loan. In September, I moved into an apartment that was found for me by my host university, Université Stendhal.

I had an amazing time and met people from all over the world, English speaking, French speaking and many others, and I am still in touch with many. Studying French at a university in England is all very well, but it is no substitute for immersing yourself in another culture, language and way of life day in, day out.

So it was fantastic socially and did wonders for my French, but I have also since found out that employers look very favourably on graduates who have spent time living abroad, and since graduating I have found it comes up again and again in interviews. I would definitely recommend the experience to anyone."

IBRAHIM BUTT
studies in the USA at Duke University

Two years ago, I started an incredible journey with the Sutton Trust US Programme that culminated in my acceptance to Duke University in Durham, North Carolina. Studying abroad was always going to be a priority during my undergraduate degree and the programme inspired me to contemplate completing my whole degree in the USA. I was given expert advice and support on all aspects of the challenging USA university application, and have never regretted my decision to study in the USA!

The main attraction of the USA was the liberal arts system of education on offer, which is completely different to the UK system. I've been able to take classes ranging from foreign languages to theology, allowing me to discover my interests before committing to a degree path. When submitting my applications, I had no idea which degree subject I wanted to do, so the US system and its flexibility has allowed me to engage in different subject areas before choosing my degree!

My experience in the US has been unbelievable, from hiking in the Appalachian Mountains as part of an orientation programme to being served breakfast at midnight before our final exams by my professors – the sense of community on campus is inspiring. I am surrounded by diverse individuals from over 70 countries who are involved in all parts of campus life.

There's much more than just academics at an American university, especially so at Duke. Students are encouraged to change their campus, community and country. Opportunities include fully funded summer trips around the world to engage in community service projects, from environmental conservation to volunteering in schools.

My time in the USA has been phenomenal; the academic freedom and school spirit offered at US universities are unrivalled and I cannot wait for what the next three and a half years have to offer!

Yale University

LOCATION

Yale is in New Haven, Connecticut, about 90 minutes by train from New York City. New Haven is a small city with a big cultural scene and a rich history spanning more than 375 years. New Haven residents lovingly refer to their home as #GSCIA: "Greatest Small City in America."

ACADEMICS

Yale offers a liberal arts curriculum with depth and breadth across the arts and sciences. Over 2,000 classes and 80 major fields of study are on offer at Yale College, along with opportunities at Yale's 13 graduate and professional schools. International experiences are a key part of life at Yale and the University provides over $6 million a year to support Yale College students in research, study and volunteer opportunities overseas.

ADVISING AND UNDERGRADUATE FOCUS

With a student/faculty ratio of 6:1, close interaction with world-class professors is a key part of the Yale experience. 75% of classes enroll fewer than 20 students.

RESIDENTIAL HOUSING SYSTEM

Every student is assigned to one of 14 residential colleges. Microcosms of the larger student body, the colleges encourage students to meet peers of all different ages, backgrounds, and interests. The colleges are small communities of 400–450 students each and are an integral part of the Yale experience.

EXTRACURRICULARS

The list of opportunities is endless – sport, music, theatre, improv comedy groups, political and debate societies, multicultural organisations, community service, and newspapers and publications are but a few of the opportunities Yale has to offer outside of the classroom.

TRADITION

There is more to Yale than academics and beautiful buildings. A wonderful array of rich and quirky traditions, including 'College Teas' with famous speakers, celebrations at every Yale Football game, 'Spring Fling' (Yale's largest campus-wide party), Yale Winter Ball and many others make the experience a memorable one.

APPLYING TO YALE

Information, forms, and deadlines can be found at:
admissions.yale.edu/

Specific advice for international students can be found at:
admissions.yale.edu/international

Begin the process early – the final deadline for applications is January 1 for entry in September of the following year.

FINANCIAL AID

Yale admits students on the basis of academic and personal promise. We want to admit the best students from around the world regardless of economic background (need-blind) and will meet 100% of any accepted student's demonstrated financial need with grants that do not need to be paid back. This covers tuition, room and board, books, and travel. Yale's financial aid budget is over $120 million a year.

For more details, please visit:
admissions.yale.edu/financial-aid

www.yale.edu

HARVARD UNIVERSITY

You have probably heard of Harvard College, located in the USA in Cambridge, Massachusetts, but do you know how to prepare for and apply to an American university?

Harvard has created a website especially for British students, teachers, and parents/guardians – all the information you need to educate yourself about US unis, about how to apply, what kinds of students go there, and especially about Harvard.

Just go to *www.harvard-ukadmissions.co.uk* and find out for yourself what the opportunities are!

And don't be put off by the US uni fees – make sure you read the 'Financial Aid' page and see how the generous Harvard scholarships programme can often provide enough support so that the costs are actually competitive with the UK. Below are some of the typical questions Harvard often hears from British students – we answer them more fully on the website, where some current and former students give their views and comments too.

What does a 'Liberal Arts' programme mean?

Liberal arts is an American term for an academic programme that recognizes the need for both broad education across the spectrum of the arts and sciences and depth of education in one specific field. You do not apply to a specific programme, but instead just 'apply to Harvard' and then choose your particular field of interest, or 'concentration' during the second year of the four year-programme.

What are some benefits of the American college experience?

Student diversity: You can expect to find classmates from all across North America and around the world, coming from every conceivable socioeconomic, geographic, religious, ethnic, and political background. The diversity of experience and belief and the resulting exchange of ideas add to the lively mix of campus life, both in the classroom and outside. After graduation, you'll have friends and contacts all over the globe.

Extracurriculars: Most colleges in the US encourage a balance between your academic and extracurricular lives. Schoolwork is primary, but your outside interests are equally important. Make friends, practice organizational skills, learn the fine arts of teamwork, diplomacy, and compromise – all while having fun!

Residential life: Harvard, like many US colleges, provides on-campus housing for all students for all four years, which means that 24/7 you are surrounded by the social and academic life of the school.

Timeline: Start your search for information early!

There is a degree of forward planning involved in order to assemble all the required information in time for the deadlines, so it is helpful to think about this process as early as Year 11 or even before. The application deadline is January 1st for entry the following September. You will also need to take some standardised tests called the SATS (no relation to the UK ones!) or ACT, and because they are in multiple-choice format, it is a good idea to practice them in advance. Have a look at the website that discusses the application process and the application requirements, such as the SAT or ACT tests.

Getting the application together

Grades: There are no set grade cut-offs for admission, but for the most selective colleges in the US, such as Harvard, usually GCSEs would be mostly A or A*, and predicted A-Levels would be AAB or better. This past year, we had over 37,000 applications for about 2,000 places...you do the maths! But also remember that Harvard is not just about grades, but seeks out exceptional all-rounders.

Essays: You will need to write personal essays as part of the application. The website offers you some good examples of US-style writing.

Recommendations: Two teachers plus your housemaster or careers advisor should write letters of recommendation on your behalf. Ask them to include as many details and anecdotes as possible to help bring you alive to the reader. There are samples of good 'Teacher Reports' on the website too!

Interview: You will have the chance to meet informally with a graduate of Harvard. The dual purpose is to let you ask questions of someone familiar with our campus and community, and for us to learn more about you. We talk more about this on the website.

Uni costs and Harvard's financial assistance

It's true that Harvard is more expensive than uni in the UK, but in many cases financial assistance will be sufficient to make the 'net price' affordable. Harvard is fortunate to be able to admit all students, even international students, without regard to whether they need financial assistance. We have a generous financial assistance programme that awards bursaries based entirely on need and not merit, and takes into account all costs (tuition, fees, room, board, books, and travel). We want to be sure that the best students, no matter what their economic background, are able to enrol at Harvard. More details about our financial assistance programme, including typical aid awards for UK families and a link to our easy-to-use Net Price Calculator can be found on our website.

Net Price Calculator: college.harvard.edu/financial-aid/net-price-calculator
Admissions: college.harvard.edu/admissions
Financial aid: college.harvard.edu/financial-aid

www.harvard.edu

GAP YEARS

We are asked again and again what universities and employers think of students taking gap years. The majority of universities and employers we work with really don't mind either way and some actually prefer for students to take gap years as it helps students to develop a wealth of life skills. That said, it's worth noting that there are a select few academic departments within universities that would advise against taking a gap year, so have a conversation with your potential universities before you launch into planning your year out.

In most cases, students consciously plan to take a gap year, but for some it might be unanticipated.

Here are some of the top reasons why students take a year out.

1. TRAVEL

Whether you are interested in seeing the pyramids, want to work on a conservation project in South America or you plan on exploring the Great Barrier Reef, a gap year is the perfect chance to satisfy the travel bug within. The time between school and university provides a really great opportunity to go and do these things before you're committed to longer-term education or careers.

2. RESULTS

You might be forced to take a gap year because your A-Level results weren't quite as good as you had expected, and you now need to retake some of your exams and reapply to university. Don't worry – this is not uncommon and your school or college will be able to offer support.

3. WORK

If you're career-minded, a gap year can be a great way to gain a valuable placement to add to your CV. There are plenty of employers offering gap year work placements but you need to start researching these in Year 12, as most employers will expect you to apply during Year 13. You should receive a salary, which is great as it means you start university with some extra cash in your bank account or have some money to spend on travel, a car, or anything else you might need.

4. TIME TO REFLECT

You have been in full-time education since the age of five, which can take its toll. Some students need to take time out to think about what it is they want to do next, be it university, a school leaver programme or entering full-time employment. A gap year can offer you the time you need to think about your options, rather than jumping too fast into something that isn't right for you.

Whatever your reasons for taking a gap year, bear in mind that universities and employers will expect students to be productive with their time, so don't just think that you can spend a year glued to your parents' sofa. Speaking of parents, we suggest you have a chat with your family before you plan your gap year – although it is your choice, it's worth asking for their advice and keeping them in the loop. They might have already planned on turning your bedroom into an office, gym or walk-in wardrobe, so you might want to let them know that you will be sticking around for an extra year! If they need more advice on gap years and post-sixth form options in general, check out our gap year section at www.purepotential.org.

Some students we speak to are concerned about taking a gap year and being left behind when the rest of their friends head off to university. But it is worth considering that this is your chance to do something for yourself; to take a year out to do things that interest you, and that help you develop your skills and give you life stories that you will want to share with your grandchildren!

USEFUL RESOURCES

volunteerics.org   etrust.org.uk/the-year-in-industry   realgap.co.uk   vsointernational.org   projects-abroad.co.uk

MY EXPERIENCE

STEPHEN SPENT HIS GAP YEAR GAINING EXPERIENCE IN INDUSTRY:

"After my original gap year plans to go travelling didn't come to fruition, I knew I still wanted to do something exciting and worthwhile with my year out. Having already deferred my place at the University of Southampton to study engineering, I wanted to do something related to that field. I wrote to and called a number of companies but all were a bit reluctant to take someone on with limited professional experience and qualifications.

For any STEM subject, one of the best ways to find a worthwhile year of experience is through the 'Year in Industry' scheme. I filled out a single application form, which was then sent off to all kinds of big-name employers in the engineering sector including: Rolls-Royce, Aero Engine Controls, BAE Systems, etc. A few weeks later, there was an interview day in which all these kinds of companies were present and they invite you to attend a 15-minute interview. If they're interested in you, then they'll contact you for another interview at their own offices and from there they'll send out offers.

I was offered a placement with Rolls-Royce, working on their gas turbine engines. The scheme is designed to ensure you get the most out of your placement and you are therefore given target-focused projects that make a real contribution to the department you are in. A lot of my work focused on improving manufacturing processes and saving costs; this meant I was often presenting to high-level management and suppliers. Although this can be very daunting at first, it was undoubtedly the most worthwhile experience I have had for developing my personal and professional skills.

I was worried that the year out may affect my ability to go back to university the year after and study again. However, I believe the year in industry gave me a better focus and an insight into the area I want to go into in the future. In my summer holidays, I've been able to go back and work at Rolls-Royce, proving my placement to be useful for making contacts in the industry and securing further work to contribute towards my CV. Overall, I would thoroughly recommend a year in industry before going to university as it has given me a massive head start compared to my course mates, whose first taste of industry will be in their first real job."

JO SPENT HER GAP YEAR TEACHING ENGLISH IN A SECONDARY SCHOOL IN TANZANIA:

"Between my first and second year of A-Levels, I was able to travel with my school to volunteer in Costa Rica for one month. During that trip, I realised how much I enjoyed travelling; seeing new places, meeting new people and learning about different cultures and traditions and, as soon as I got back, I knew I wanted to see more of the world before going to university so I decided to take a gap year. I still went through the usual university application process in Year 13, going to university open days, writing my personal statement and applying through UCAS, but I chose to defer my entry by one year on my application form. At the same time as applying to university, I also had to decide where to go and what to do during my gap year – at that point, the world really was my oyster! I knew I wanted to go somewhere different from home, where I could volunteer and feel part of a community so I chose to volunteer as an English teacher in Tanzania, East Africa. As soon as I finished my A-Levels, I worked full time for five months to save up all the money I needed to go away. Before my placement, I was matched up with another volunteer and we travelled out together to a secondary school in the foothills of Mount Kilimanjaro that would become our home for the next eight months. The teaching was very rewarding and being able to learn about the education system in a different country was really eye-opening. Although it was a huge challenge, I learnt so much from a different way of life – we had no running water in our house, only had electricity for a couple of hours a night, we had to hand-wash all of our clothes, cook on a small paraffin stove and had a one-hour walk to get to the weekly food market! During the school holidays, we travelled around Tanzania and other parts of East Africa and I even got to take a group of 15 students to the top of Mount Kilimanjaro as a geography field trip! The experience changed my outlook on life and education forever, and I would urge anyone who is thinking about volunteering abroad to get out there and do it – you won't regret it!"

INTERNATIONAL CITIZEN SERVICE

THE ULTIMATE OPPORTUNITY TO VOLUNTEER OVERSEAS

Danial Williams and Takyiwa Danso both from London volunteered with the government funded International Citizen Service (ICS) programme, which is run by leading international development charity, VSO. Not only did Danial and Takyiwa contribute to projects that have a positive impact in developing countries, but they gained loads of great skills and experience too. Hear what they have to say about this once-in-a-lifetime opportunity for young people.

Danial, 20, was volunteering in Nepal with ICS VSO, he says;

"I had never been abroad before. The whole build up to going away was terrifying. I was scared about the jetlag, about getting homesick being so far away. With my dyslexia, I was also worried about being put into a situation where I couldn't teach the kids. However, when I got there it was one of the best experiences of my life."

"Our project was based on community development and livelihoods. We made 400 bins out of weaving baskets, painting them and distributing them. We got a doctor to give free checkups to women with prolapsed uteruses. My favourite moment was when I built a pull up bar out of wood, originally for myself. The paint hadn't even dried when the whole school came out to have fun on it."

"I want to show people that your background can't determine your future. I'm like them. I've gone through the criminal justice system but I've still got amazing opportunities. It's such a great programme that I've recommended it to all my friends."

UK volunteer Danial with his host family and in-country counterpart Bzay Bhital

Danial testing out his pull up bar with the local children

UK and in-country volunteers stand for photo after their community action day

Takyiwa is now working as a mentor through the IVO4ALL scheme, (International Volunteering Opportunities for All) and a VSO Development Advocate since completing the ICS programme. She says;

"From spending three months in Kenya volunteering with the ICS programme, I saw first-hand the enthusiasm, creativity and willpower to create a better future from both my fellow UK volunteers and the inspiring young Kenyans we worked alongside. We have the right mix of passion, determination and optimism to push for the change we believe in.

It is our responsibility as members of civil society to enact change and I'd love to be a part of this change in championing strong female leaders who are actively improving the participation of women and girls in society.

Now that I've returned, I also hope to keep the momentum going and work to narrow the gap in young people's perception and understanding of what the UN does and how they can influence this."

UK volunteer Takyiwa (centre) is all smiles with the children from the village of her host home

ICS — international citizen service

WHO CAN TAKE PART?
VSO's International Citizen Service (ICS) is a once-in-a-lifetime volunteering opportunity open to all 18 to 25-year-olds, funded by the UK government, regardless of cash, qualifications or work history. All you need is the drive to make a difference.

HOW MUCH DOES IT COST?
You will be supported by a dedicated fundraising officer to fundraise a minimum of £800 that is put back into the programme to help others benefit from the ICS programme. The cost of flights, visas, travel and medical insurance, vaccinations, food and accommodation are all covered.

HOW DOES IT WORK?
You'll work side-by-side with local 'in-country' volunteers in developing countries on 12 week placements, to make a meaningful contribution to fighting poverty while gaining valuable skills.

ICS is led by VSO, in partnership with 9 respected development organisations and has placements across Asia, Africa and Latin America. On your return to the UK, you'll complete an Action at Home activity, using your new skills in your local community.

YOU CAN FIND OUT MORE AND APPLY ONLINE AT:
www.volunteerics.org

THE CAREERS SECTION

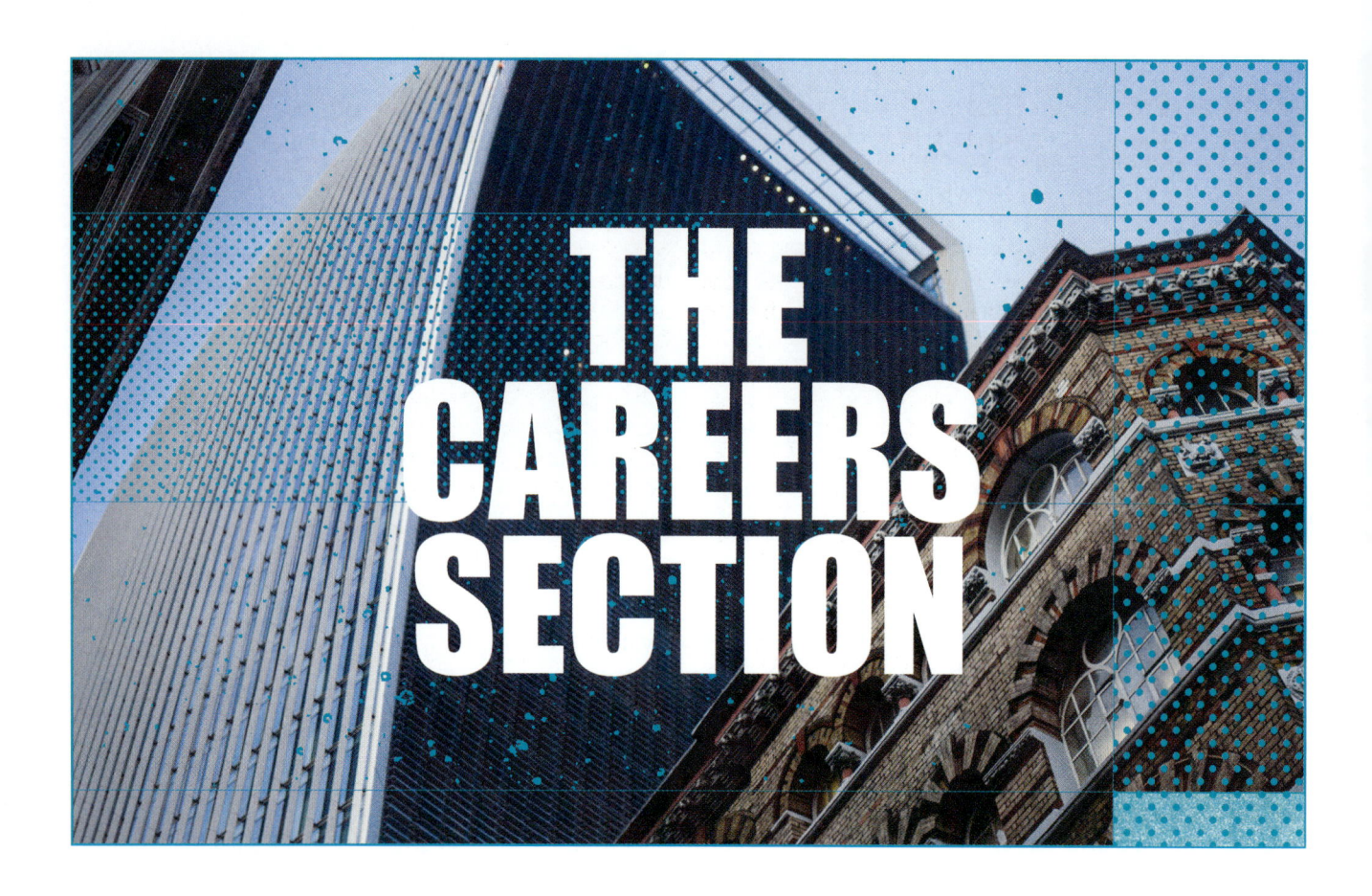

'What are you going to do with your life?'

is a question you have no doubt been asked a thousand times by teachers, parents, family friends, and relatives who think you should have mapped out your future by now and be able to summarise it in a sentence. In reality, not many people know what they're going to want to do in two years, let alone 10 years down the line – but it is something to start thinking about. Now a decade into our careers, the Pure Potential Team have some advice to pass on…

When our grandparents embarked on their careers, times were very different. The old-fashioned, traditional roles of husband going out to work while housewife looks after the house and children is only one of a plethora of lifestyle options that we can choose today. And when these husbands of yesteryear chose their career path, they would usually stick to it, often staying within the same company throughout their entire working life, gradually rising up the ranks until retirement. Oh, how times have changed.

So next time someone asks you 'what are you going to do with your life?', translate the question to 'what's your next step?'. These days, it is much more common for people to try out several different careers throughout their lifetime, taking sidesteps into different industries and retraining to gain new skills. When choosing which career path to take, it is so much more daunting if you feel like you are being forced to decide the rest of your life. So, instead, think of it one step at a time, each step giving you more experiences to find out what it is you really enjoy. Trust me, you will find it eventually, if you don't get complacent and stay in a job that doesn't inspire you.

I have friends who are over 30 who still aren't sure, but they try different roles and, with each new experience, they are fine-tuning what it is they really want to do, and they are enjoying the journey of discovery. Take my friend Sophie for example – she went to university, did her law conversion course, got a training contract with a top law firm, worked there successfully for several years … until her 29th birthday, when she decided after all that that her real passion lay in film. She did some work experience, met as many people working in the industry as she could, then quit her job and is now working for an independent film production company and loving it. Best of all, she is able to use her legal knowledge to look after the legal side of the business, such as drawing up contracts with actors and film crew.

Sophie's story is a great example of how the skills you learn in one job can be transferred to the next. So don't worry that embarking on a career will mean that you are stuck in it for life. The most important thing is that you pick up skills such as working well with people and getting along with clients and colleagues (communication skills), getting on with your work without your boss having to keep asking you (self-motivation), working out what can be improved – from the filing systems to the sales strategy to the day-to-day efficiency of the rest of your team – and acting on it (taking initiative), being willing to work late sometimes or cover for a sick colleague or take on new responsibilities (flexibility), not forgetting what you need to do, or losing important documents (organisational skills) and knowing how to use a computer (IT skills). Any job from doctor to fireman to marketing manager to PR officer to lawyer to banker to entrepreneur will need every single one of these skills.

Don't forget also that your life outside of work will change with the years, and so too will your needs. In your twenties, you might want to work in a fast-paced environment, with the opportunity to travel, meet new people and live in the city surrounded by bars, restaurants and nightlife. If you get married and have children, you may decide that you want a quieter life, and that travelling isn't going to be practical. Everyone is different so don't do what your peers do, or what your parents expect. There is a job out there for you that you will love. Maybe not every minute, but something that you fundamentally enjoy and gives you a sense of achievement and fulfilment, whatever that may mean to you.

So, during which moments do you feel most fulfilled? Is it when you score a goal in football? What about when you hand in your big coursework project? Or when you are out with friends and making them laugh? Is it offering advice to someone in the year below you? Or helping a friend during a difficult time? Reading a brilliant novel? Performing or speaking in assembly? Think about those moments and then think laterally, not literally. If you enjoy scoring a goal in football, it doesn't necessarily mean you should become a professional footballer, but it could mean that you enjoy working in a team, thinking on your feet and getting results in high-pressure environments, so you could be suited to a role in sales. If you really relished the moment you handed in your coursework after months of working on it, then perhaps you are more suited to a more research-based role, such as investment management or law. If you enjoy being the centre of attention amongst friends, then maybe you'd be suited to a job where you have to charm clients – something like equity sales at an investment bank, or as a management consultant gaining the confidence of CEOs. Do you see where we are going with this? Think about what you enjoy and then apply it to job roles, in a 'big picture' way... and this can literally be anything. If at this time in your life, the only time you feel happy is when you are at home on your sofa watching boxsets on Netflix (you'd be amazed at how many students we meet who say stuff like this), then you are likely to be suited to a role based in an office, which doesn't have to be boring! When you wake up every day and go to work from 9–6 or beyond, you need to be sure that your job is giving you a sense of personal fulfilment and satisfaction. We don't mean that every day you spring out of bed, desperate to get back to your desk and sing good morning to your boss, but we do mean that when you get asked if you enjoy your job, you can reply 'YES' with conviction. Take our jobs at Pure Potential, for example; helping state-educated students to pursue their dream careers and get into the world's best universities makes us happy. This feeling of achievement doesn't have to be charitable though; it could be that you get a real buzz from problem solving, creativity, adventure, justice or the advancement of science and technology. Only you know what is important to you, so have a think about what you believe in and what your values are.

> **We don't expect that after reading this article, you will now have a definite idea of what you want to do next, but we hope that you will start to have a sense of yourself and your skills and a clearer understanding of what sort of things you should be thinking about when deciding on the next stages in your life.**

What we will say is that the good grades you get now will stand you in good stead for future job security and a higher salary. So work hard, even if you're not sure what you're working for and keep your options open.

As your life twists and turns through the remainder of school, possibly a gap year, a university degree, a school leaver programme or apprenticeship, keep an eye out for careers that might suit you. Everything in life, from taking transport to school, the food you eat, the magazines and books you read, the television programmes you enjoy, the money you spend, the shops you spend them in, the home and community you live in, the countries you visit, has hundreds, no, thousands of jobs supporting them... one of which will be right for you.

What CAREER LIVE?

APPRENTICESHIP

FREE ENTRY

Meet the UK's top employers and universities

Meet over 100 exhibitors including*:

Civil Service Fast Track Apprenticeship · J.P.Morgan · EY Building a better working world · VINCI Construction UK · Direct Line Group · Health Education England · NHS · ALDI · Mercedes-Benz

KPMG · KAPLAN · Rolls-Royce · RSM · IBM · AON · Network Rail · McDonald's

Stannah · Superdrug · HSBC · Schneider Electric · dpd · hellmann Worldwide Logistics

What Career Live? in association with: The Telegraph · Apprenticeships

*Correct at time of print

What UNIVERSITY LIVE?

UNIVERSITY →

WHAT WILL YOU DO NEXT?

3 & 4 MARCH | NEC, BIRMINGHAM
6 & 7 OCTOBER | OLYMPIA, LONDON

Book free tickets at **WhatCareerLive.co.uk**

UNIVERSITY OF BIRMINGHAM · The University of Nottingham · MANCHEstER 1824 · WARWICK · UNIVERSITY OF EXETER · UNIVERSITY OF LEEDS · UNIVERSITY OF Southampton · CITY UNIVERSITY LONDON · UNIVERSITY of DERBY · Keele University · University of HUDDERSFIELD · Swansea University Prifysgol Abertawe · Teesside University · University of Roehampton London · Aston University Birmingham · UNIVERSITY of Hull · Coventry University College · Brunel University London · UNIVERSITY OF WOLVERHAMPTON KNOWLEDGE · INNOVATION · ENTERPRISE · DE MONTFORT UNIVERSITY LEICESTER · LIVERPOOL JOHN MOORES UNIVERSITY · DISCOVER WITH PLYMOUTH UNIVERSITY · FULBRIGHT COMMISSION

f What Next? 🐦 @whatcareerlive 📷 whatcareerlive

What University Live? in association with: UNIVERSITY OF BIRMINGHAM · Aston University Birmingham · WARWICK

WORK EXPERIENCE

Work experience is an important way to work out what you might like to do as a future career, develop skills that will be of use in any working environment and potentially supplement your income while you are studying. In today's competitive job market, it's a necessity to have work experience on your CV, but finding relevant work experience (either paid or unpaid) is not an easy task. And just how 'relevant' does it need to be? Read about some of the different types of work experience, and how to get your foot in the door.

INSIGHT EVENTS OR WEBINARS

Although not strictly work experience, these are fantastic opportunities to get involved in. The selection criteria is generally less strict than for formal programmes, so you have a higher chance of getting in – you just have to ensure you're on the right mailing lists so that you get notified of them when they launch. You can sign up for alerts about these sorts of events on the Pure Potential website (www.purepotential.org). They are usually short and snappy – designed to give you an idea of what the career entails and the kind of candidates they are looking for, and to entice you to apply!

VOLUNTEERING

Doing voluntary work with a registered charity or non-governmental organisation shows passion and integrity, as well as motivation, because you will be doing it without being paid, although your expenses will be reimbursed. The experience will be rewarding, and will provide you with an opportunity to develop skills that are important to future employers too. Charities are always looking for people to help out, so this kind of experience is easier to get than others.

WORK SHADOWING

Observing someone in their role can be an effective way to decide whether a certain career is really for you, in just a few days. You will gain experience of real, high-level work and be able to talk about a role and industry with someone on the job. Shadowing is a more informal type of work experience, and tends to be the norm in creative industries where there is a looser and smaller structure to the business, such as film and television production, publishing, journalism or marketing. The downside to this type of placement is that it can be unstructured, so could involve a lot of administrative work without much 'real' experience. However, even if you don't get that much responsibility, these placements can be great in terms of the contacts you make and people you meet and getting an idea of what the job entails.

HOW TO SUCCESSFULLY SECURE WORK EXPERIENCE

DO THE RESEARCH
Identify the industry in which you wish to sample through work experience; be sure that any company you write to offers the role that appeals to you and is a place you'd like to work.

CALL
Telephone the organisation and ask if they need any temporary help. Send a CV with a covering letter or covering email.

PERSEVERE
You might not succeed at finding a volunteering opportunity straight away, but don't be put off. Keep persevering to find a placement that suits you and that is in a field you are interested in.

BE SPECIFIC
Always try to address your letters to a person rather than a 'Dear Sir/Madam'. You are much more likely to get a response.

ASK AROUND
What do your parents, friends' parents, teachers, tutors do? Can they help or put you in touch with someone? State your availability. Give a potential start date and indicate how long you can work for.

BE WILLING
Offer to volunteer, even for just a few hours. If that doesn't work, ask if you can buy them a coffee, or even just have a 15-minute phone conversation – who knows what doors this might open?

INTERNSHIPS

This kind of work experience is structured and paid, though often involves a highly competitive application process. Internships consist of a fixed period of work within a company, during which you may be given quite a high degree of personal responsibility. Investment banks, for example, tend to run programmes in the spring and summer holidays, and the bigger law firms have an equivalent programme called a 'vacation scheme'. Application deadlines tend to be several months in advance, so don't leave things too late. They will also want to see evidence of other work experience.

GAP YEAR PROGRAMMES

Some firms offer programmes where you can work in your gap year, enabling you to earn some money, acquire new skills and get a taste of the working world over a prolonged period before you start university. These programmes are not only an excellent addition to your personal statement, but also will stand you in good stead when it comes to finding a job once you have graduated if you decide to go to university. Participating in one of these programmes will show you have ambition, are motivated and take your career seriously, and who knows – if you excel during the programme, the firm may offer you a job. Nobody forgets a keen and enthusiastic employee!

HOW RELEVANT DOES IT NEED TO BE?

Many students worry about finding work experience that is relevant to their university course or future career; however, we all know that finding these opportunities can be difficult, and that you might change your mind later down the line – does that mean the work experience you've done is irrelevant? NO! Finding any type of work experience that builds upon your key skills is far better than nothing at all. It's about the skills you develop while on your work experience that counts more than the companies you did work experience at.

MAKE CONTACTS

After any work experience you do, make sure you take down the contact details of all the people you met – you never know when these might come in handy, or when your paths may cross again. During the placement, be a pleasure to work with and always go the extra mile by being proactive, staying that little bit later, offering your assistance to everyone you meet, and being somebody they would want to see again in the future. At the end, thank them for giving you the opportunity and, if anyone has been particularly kind or useful, then a box of chocolates or bunch of flowers will ensure they remember you.

THE PURE POTENTIAL CV WRITING MASTERCLASS

Curriculum Vitae means 'the course of one's life' in Latin and is one of several methods used by employers to select candidates.

We like to think of a CV as a personal marketing document – it offers employers a snapshot of who you are and sells your strengths, achievements and any relevant work experience you've gained. It doesn't matter how amazing you are or how much of an asset you would be to a company – if you can't communicate it through your CV, you certainly won't get very far. This is exactly why you must spend time creating a high-quality CV, which you regularly update.

The majority of employers will ask for a CV, along with a supporting covering letter that clearly outlines exactly why you are applying for a particular role, why you want to work for that firm and what makes you the perfect candidate. There's plenty of advice on writing a covering letter later on, but let's focus on the CV to begin with…

WHAT GOES IN YOUR CV?

A concise CV is extremely important when it comes to making a positive first impression – no recruiter wants to read pages and pages of information. Never let your CV expand beyond two sides of A4, preferably one side (yes, we are being serious). In fact, even the CVs of middle-aged professionals with a lot more experience under their belts than trainees are often kept to just one side of A4. Your CV should include only the most important bits of relevant information about you that relate to the job in question – check out the CV template for a breakdown of the core sections.

There are many good ways of structuring a CV, and this will vary depending on how much experience you have and what stage of your career you're at. The rules are to be clear, concise but comprehensive.

SECTION ONE: THE BASICS

Include your name, address, contact number and email. Don't include a photo or your date of birth, and there is no need to provide a middle name unless you use it. Make sure your email address sounds professional; 'funkyfairy@' or 'gangsta_lolz@' is not going to impress. Your name should be the title, not 'CV'.

SECTION TWO: SUMMARISE WHO YOU ARE

Some people like to have a two to four sentence summary that outlines their key skills and attributes, but some prefer not to. Either way it is a good exercise to get you thinking about what you have to offer and what makes you unique.

EXERCISE: Ask a good friend or family member to think of up to five words to describe you. We're talking positive words here! We are not looking for things like 'hilarious' or a 'good sport', but more along the lines of the following:

Hard-working, Reliable, Patient, Trustworthy, Committed, Determined, Meticulous, Well-presented, Professional, Effective communicator, Efficient, Adaptable, Independent, Confident, Mature

Once you've finalised a few words you feel truly represent you, then turn this into sentences, and add what you hope to do. For example:

'I am a hard-working, determined person with a professional attitude. My ability to communicate effectively makes me an asset to any team. I am looking for a role within the retail sector to gain valuable work experience.'

SECTION THREE: EDUCATION

The employer only wants to see your secondary education, so no nursery or primary school information please! Enter your education in reverse chronological order, so put what you're doing now first, and work your way backwards. Always include the date, and if you're still studying, put the date as e.g. '2014–present'. If you are currently taking A-Levels or equivalent, then list each subject and the grade achieved. If you haven't got any grades yet, then you may wish to enter your predicted grades, followed by '(predicted)', but this is not compulsory.

Unless they have specified any particular subjects for GCSE (sometimes they want to know your maths and English grade), you don't need to tell them all your subjects; just a summary such as '5As, 3Bs and 1C' should suffice. If you have taken any other qualifications that would count under education, then enter them here too.

SECTION FOUR: WORK EXPERIENCE

Again, list your work experience in reverse chronological order. It can be hard to decide what to put down here. Much of the work experience you have done already may not be at all relevant to the job you are applying to, but that's absolutely fine. As a sixth former, you are not expected to have done industry-specific work, but what you do want to show is that you are willing to work hard. Have confidence in the character building work you've done and don't dismiss valuable work experience because you don't think it will make you stand out. Employers value young people who are willing to do unglamorous work – it shows you have tenacity, commitment and drive, and are willing to start at the bottom. Start by including everything you've ever done! You can always edit things out later.

Many young people complete work experience immediately after their GCSEs; this can be a good place to start. If you've helped a family member in some way, then you can include that too, any menial work or manual labour could count, so jot down everything you've done, from paper boy/girl, assisting at a baker or butcher, stacking shelves, mowing lawns, dog-walking and baby-sitting to making tea and photocopying in an office – it could all count! Don't go too far back though – it should not include anything before Year 10 unless it is particularly relevant.

EXERCISE: Once you have listed the work experiences you have done, you need to make whatever you did sound as professional and worthwhile as possible by using what we call 'Power Verbs'. These tell the recruiter what you are doing, or did – make sure you get the tense right! It can feel odd to use these words to describe something you consider easy but it shows the prospective employer that you recognise the skills you have picked up – a sure sign of maturity. Here are some examples to get you started:

Organising, Consulting, Negotiating, Presenting, Managing, Booking, Attending, Writing, Working, Liaising, Assisting, Creating, Producing, Helping Ensuring, Participating, Communicating, Shadowing, Transferring, Analysing, Reading, Overseeing

SECTION FIVE: PERSONAL DEVELOPMENT

Anything that isn't employment, but is helping you to develop as a young adult should go in this section. Mention any voluntary work you do, awards you have won, or positions of responsibility you hold. For example, if you have a mentor, or even a mentee, this is where you talk about it briefly.

SECTION SIX: SKILLS & INTERESTS

Include IT skills (be clear about skills in Excel, PowerPoint and Word – they are essential for the workplace), your driver's licence if you have one, a first aid certificate, additional languages you may speak (even if you're not fluent). Under your list of interests, remember that you are not looking for new friends, you're looking for a job, so they only want to know the wholesome, well-rounded hobbies you take part in such as sports (even cycling and going to the gym can count), theatre, cinema, reading books and listening to music.

SECTION SEVEN: REFERENCES

Contact your referees in advance to check that they are happy to provide a reference, send them your CV and give them some basic information about the job you have applied for. You don't need to give their details at this stage; just put 'REFERENCES AVAILABLE ON REQUEST' at the bottom of your CV.

STYLE

When it comes to the style of a CV, we've seen it all – the good, the bad and the ugly! Here are some basic points you should consider if you want your CV to stand out in the right way.

Font: Use an easy-to-read, professional-looking font such as Arial, Times New Roman or Cambria in font size 10–12.

Subheadings: Break up the information using subheadings and have clear divisions, but don't make your format too fussy by using lots of boxes or borders.

Bullet points: The information should be easy to read quickly so use bullet points instead of continuous sentences.

Spacing: Add line breaks and spaces in between your subheadings so it's not too cramped.

CREATE YOUR OWN

Now that you understand what a CV should include and how this information should be presented, the next step is to work on creating your own.

JOE BLOGGS

1 Education Street, Schoolton, UN1 1PP   Joe.bloggs@unimail.com / 07123 456 789

EDUCATION

University of Anywhere   2:1 expected in Name Subject (BA)
St Whatever High School   3 A-Levels in Subject 1 (A), Subject 2 (B),
                            and Subject 3 (C), 10 GCSEs (1A*, 2As, 3Bs
                            and 4Cs including an A in both Mathematics and English)

WORK EXPERIENCE

Company & Co. – *Part-Time Marketing Assistant*   (January '15–present)

- Organising…
- Consulting…
- Negotiating…
- Presenting…

Organisation Ltd. – *Events Assistant*   (June–July '14)

- Managed…
- Booked…
- Attended…
- Wrote…

Fashion Clothing Store – *Shop Assistant*   (Jan–March '14)

- Worked…
- Liaised…
- Assisted…
- Created…

PERSONAL DEVELOPMENT

Charitable Charity – *Volunteer*   (June–August '12)

- Helped…
- Ensured…
- Worked…
- Participated…

School Award for Excellence – *Silver Award*   (June '14)

- For excelling at…

OTHER

- Excellent knowledge of Microsoft Office
- Proficient in French and Spanish
- First aid certificate holder
- Full, clean driving licence
- Hobbies include football, cycling and attending music festivals

REFERENCES AVAILABLE ON REQUEST

You can download a free CV template from www.purepotential.org

USING LINKEDIN

LinkedIn isn't just about creating your 'online CV' and making work-related connections – it also has features and information that can help you choose the right course and right university for your future aspirations. These tools provide access to information about real graduates from these universities and courses, and insights into what jobs they have gone on to do after university.

There are over 450 million people on LinkedIn and many have entered their education details, and then their subsequent career path, so the data is very robust.

EXPLORE UNIVERSITIES

Every university has a home on LinkedIn, and on that page (accessed via the main search bar), you can tap into the 'Career Insights' feature. This tool pulls together information on thousands of graduates on LinkedIn who went to specific universities, and enables you to explore where they work and what they do.

Select a subject area and see where graduates from that course work. Select a company and see what courses are most likely to lead to a job there, and which are the top listed skills for people working there. In short, there is lots of information on real careers to help you make decisions about yours.

EXPLORE EMPLOYERS

Most companies have pages on LinkedIn. Use the main search bar to find ones you are interested in. Once on their page, you can elect to 'follow' the organisation, meaning that you will receive their updates, news and job alerts into your own newsfeed. You can also explore the people who work there – what they do, how they have developed their careers to reach their current roles and what they say about working there. Companies often have included further information about careers and working there. Look for the 'Careers' or 'Life at….' sub-pages for cultural insights and employee testimonials.

Then, of course, there are jobs – either from the Company page or via the link in the top menu, you can search for the jobs you are interested in. When you view a job, you'll find more useful information on LinkedIn than anywhere else – not just the job description, but also information about the company, about people who are doing that job already, the top skills needed, and also similar jobs to the one you're looking at (maybe at companies you haven't heard of).

LinkedIn and these features are free to all registered users. Set up your professional profile (your online CV), including your work experience and educational qualifications, plus other awards and skills; add connections from your school/college/university, and your work experience; and get ahead with real insights on different careers, employers and jobs.

Download the LinkedIn App, or visit www.linkedin.com

**Charles Hardy,
Client Relationship Manager,
Higher Education**

THE COVERING LETTER

You will usually need to send a one-page letter with your CV called the covering letter. This is where you can discuss the skills and achievements most relevant to the position you are applying for in more detail. The covering letter, like your CV, is a very important document and could be the first thing a potential employer will read, so it must be unique to that company and impactful.

THE PLANNING & RESEARCH STAGE

A well thought-out letter is exactly what your future employer is looking for. Once you have spotted a vacancy that interests you, read the job description carefully and find out what they are looking for in their ideal candidate. Highlight which aspects of the job you feel, or know, you are capable of doing and the aspects that appeal to you, then look at the skills required and highlight which of those you have gained from past work experience or your education. You should have gone through a similar process when you updated your CV so keep your notes and use this as a starting point for this exercise.

STRUCTURE

INTRODUCTION

Start off by stating which position you are applying for, where you saw the vacancy and briefly explain your current circumstances, i.e. 'I saw the role of Marketing Assistant advertised on GradJobs.com, and attach my CV for your consideration. I have just completed my A-Levels and will be starting university after a gap year...'.

HOW DO MY SKILLS AND PERSONAL ATTRIBUTES SUIT THIS ROLE?

Discuss how you became interested in the industry and support your points with examples of past work experience, knowledge you've gained from your course, or any extracurricular activities that sparked your interest. Remember to reference any similar placements you've undertaken that will show the employer that you've got the relevant experience. If there were any skills mentioned in the job description that you have not yet developed, express a willingness to learn.

WHY HAVE I CHOSEN TO APPLY TO THIS PARTICULAR COMPANY?

Never, ever think a generic letter will do. It must be about the company you're applying to. Discuss aspects of the company that you find particularly interesting. This does not mean cut and paste information from the company website! Show that you have researched the firm and the sector – read newspapers (broadsheets, with business sections), company annual reports and research their competitors. You need to be able to say why you have been inspired by what the company has done and why you want to be a part of it.

SIGNING OFF

A weak, half-hearted ending to a covering letter can leave the employer wondering whether you even really want the job, so make sure you sound enthusiastic and super keen. The final paragraph should include a word of thanks, details of your availability, and how you're looking forward to hearing from them.

A. Student
1 Student Street
Megatown
City
X1 Z23
a.student@abc.com

20th July 2017

Mrs M Smith
Personnel Manager
Choice Supermarket
Any Road
Thistown
AB1 2CD

Dear Mrs Smith,

RE: Store Manager - Starting Sep 2017

I would like to apply for the role of Store Manager with Choice Supermarket that I saw advertised on GreatJobs.com. I am currently in my final year at King's College London studying Mathematics with Management and Finance, and will be available to start work from September.

Working with Customer Services, Merchandisers and Buyers during my summer placement with Big Department Store, I have developed an understanding of the role of Store Manager, and how crucial this position is to help the business become more efficient and profitable. I have also studied in-depth the most effective marketing strategies for fast-moving consumer goods during my degree course, and I am keen to apply my experience to Choice Supermarket. Although I have yet to experience working at a supermarket specifically, I am a fast learner, and many of the skills I have developed will be useful for this role.

Choice Supermarket's market share has grown from 3% to 5% in the previous financial year, no doubt due in part to this year's brilliant advertising campaign. Targeting multiple market segments and highlighting the discounted prices of basic household products, and providing new niche goods and services has led to impressive growth, despite the economic downturn.

Choice Supermarket is an exciting place to work and I hope that the enthusiasm I can bring to the role, along with my relevant experience, make me a suitable candidate. I am available for interview for the next month, but will be on holiday between 8th and 15th August. I look forward to the opportunity to discuss my application further.

Yours sincerely,

A. Student

A. Student

APPLICATION FORMS

For some companies, the application form has replaced the traditional CV and covering letter because it is a standardised way for employers to collect key information from applicants without having to trawl through hundreds of CVs and covering letters in varying formats, lengths, font sizes and styles. Application forms work as a filtering process so employers can weed out unsuitable candidates before they go to the trouble of interviewing them. So, if you want to get through to the next stages, you need to put the time in and make sure your application form is up to scratch.

WHAT DO APPLICATIONS FORMS INCLUDE?

The application form will ask you to give much of the same information as on a CV, such as your name, address, your school and university, grades and employment history. This information should be easy for you to complete, but just be sure to check and double-check all the details are correct before you submit as you'd be very surprised at how many students put down an incorrect email address or mobile number!

There will normally be a section that asks you about your previous and current roles. Make sure that you complete this fully, listing all of the achievements and experiences that you would on the 'Work Experience' section of a CV and making sure to tailor it specifically for the role you're applying for.

TIPS AND ADVICE

Have a copy of the job description at hand to look at when filling in an application form. Take every opportunity you can to link what you're saying back to what it says in the job description and try to use any key words you can see.

Read each question carefully to make sure that you're answering it correctly and to the highest standard. This is especially true if you're saying anywhere that you've got 'good attention to detail'. If a box isn't relevant, put 'N/A' (not applicable) in the space provided.

If it's an online form, then draft your answer offline using something like Microsoft Word. This means you can do a spelling and grammar check. Save a hard copy and proofread the printed final version – it is easier to spot errors, and will help you avoid accidentally submitting an incomplete application.

If you're filling in a physical form by hand, write as neatly as you can in black ink and practise your answers before writing them onto the form.

Get someone to read over your application before submission.

Finally, make sure you check the application deadline and get your form completed and submitted in plenty of time. You won't be able to give it your all if you're rushing hours before the cut-off point, or, worse still, if you put your heart and soul into the application and miss it!

COMPETENCY-BASED QUESTIONS

Whether you're filling in an application form or sat in a job interview, it is incredibly likely that, at some point in the application process for a job, you will be asked some questions along the lines of "describe a time when you have worked as part of a team" or "tell us about a time that you put your organisational skills to good use". Known as competency questions, these are often tricky to answer as there is no clear right or wrong response, but the STAR model can help you reply to the question fully.

Star stands for Situation, Tasks, Action and Result/Relevance:

SITUATION
Open with a brief description of the situation and context of the story (who, what, where, when, how).

TASK
Explain the task you had to complete, highlighting any specific challenges or constraints (e.g. deadlines, costs, other issues).

ACTION
Describe the specific actions that you took to complete the task. These should highlight desirable traits without needing to state them (initiative, intelligence, dedication, leadership, understanding, etc.).

RESULT/RELEVANCE
Close with the result of your efforts and include figures to quantify the result if possible. Furthermore, and perhaps most importantly, what new skills have you learnt from the experience that are relevant to the role you are applying for?

When using the STAR model, be sure to concentrate most on the action taken and the result, and its relevance to the role you're applying for. See the inset graph as a rough guide.

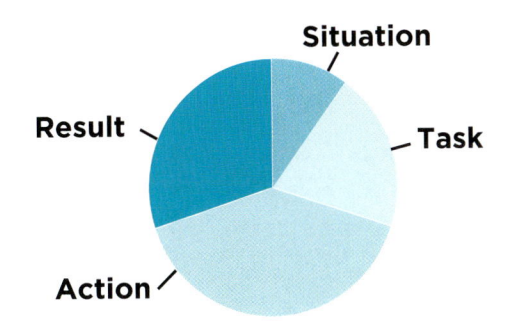

EXAMPLE QUESTIONS: WHAT IS YOUR GREATEST ACHIEVEMENT AND WHY?

The employer does not need to see that you've won an Olympic gold or found a solution to world peace, but a personal achievement that you can be proud of. If you have ever solved a problem, overcome a challenge or persevered with something, then you're on the right track. What the employer definitely doesn't need to know is that you fluked something! They want to see an example that shows hard work paying off or difficult challenges faced rationally and logically – and, above all, a process or work ethic you can apply to future situations that can allow you to achieve even greater things.

DESCRIBE A SITUATION WHERE YOU WORKED IN A TEAM

Almost any job you can think of will involve teamwork. You will have to report to someone, or present your findings to colleagues, so make sure you show that you understand how important being a team player is to maximise performance.

The challenge with this question is that everyone, and we mean EVERYONE, has experience of working in a team in some shape or form, so it won't be enough to simply describe the situation. The way to stand out is to show what you took from those experiences. The employer will be interested to know what role you took within that team, and will be looking out for evidence of your ability to listen to, and be listened to, by others. Don't fall into the trap of thinking that the 'best' role to take in a team is leader – if everyone did that, the workplace would be a nightmare, so be true to who you really are, and if you take a more passive role such as planning, executing or co-ordinating then talk about that and how effective communication between all the team players is the most important thing.

You could also mention that, because of your age, you started by taking a backseat, but in future, once you've learnt the ropes, you hope to lead a team.

When choosing which anecdote to discuss, think about any problems that arose, who tackled them, why and how. What observations have you made about teamwork going wrong? What about teamwork going right? Whether it was in your school sports team, a theatre production, academic project, or Duke of Edinburgh, you should be able to find common themes, but make sure you talk about how this can apply to the job you want!

EXAMPLE QUESTIONS TO PRACTISE

1. How do you go about solving a problem?

2. Have you ever influenced someone to do something or changed their mind?

3. Tell me about a time when you failed to complete a task or project on time, despite intending to do so.

MOTIVATION- OR STRENGTHS-BASED QUESTIONS

A newer line of interview questioning is focused on your motivations and strengths. These questions look at what you enjoy doing and what you do well. Sometimes they will be asked at speed to prompt you to answer quickly (and interviewers hope more honestly!). These questions aren't asking why you're applying for the job or what your career goals are; they're asking what motivates you in life in general. What makes you tick? What gets you out of bed? You can find some examples of these type of questions below:

- **What motivates you?**
- **Which tasks do you get the most satisfaction from?**
- **How would your manager motivate you?**
- **What would you do in life if money was no concern?**
- **What made you choose your current role?**
- **Do you need other people around to stimulate you or are you self-motivated?**
- **Do you enjoy working?**

HOW TO PREPARE

It is very important to prepare for these questions so you don't respond with something that sounds unconsidered. Do some soul-searching – what is your motivation? We are all different, and we shouldn't be ashamed of being motivated by success. Examples of what might motivate you are:

- **Achieving results**
- **Helping others**
- **Team collaboration**
- **Being rewarded**
- **Performing in public**
- **Thinking on your feet**
- **Researching a topic in-depth**
- **Discovering something new**
- **Being creative**
- **Travelling**
- **Meeting new people and networking**

The employer is looking for honesty here, so don't just say what you think they want to hear!

ASSESSMENT DAYS

Once you have applied for a job through a CV or application form, and maybe even after you've had a preliminary interview, you may be called to an assessment day. As the name suggests, they are a chance for the employer to assess your abilities through a range of activities, exercises and challenges. Examples of this include presentations, business challenges, team games and mock pitches.

PREPARATION

You may be given a rough outline of what's in store, or they may not give much away, so preparing for an assessment day can be difficult. The best thing you can do is research the company thoroughly – look at their website and their annual report for clues on their main revenue streams, their culture, and what sort of person they might be looking for.

As with any other important, potentially career-launching occasion, make sure you look the part, you're on time and you've had plenty of sleep the night before. The UK job market is more competitive than ever, so you need to give yourself every chance you can to show you've got what it takes.

TEAMWORK

Being friendly to your interviewers is a given, but what will make you stand out is if you are friendly and even helpful to your fellow interviewees. Everyone loves a team player, so encourage and support as well as put your own ideas forward during the activities and challenges. It will show a level of maturity and leadership far beyond being bossy and getting everyone to do what you want.

If you feel you have let yourself down on one part of the day, don't be disheartened – you are being assessed on your performance throughout the day, so don't let your disappointment affect the next challenge, and approach it with fresh energy.

ENJOY IT

Finally, don't forget that everyone will be as nervous as you are. The best thing you can do is try to enjoy it, engage with everyone you meet, and ask plenty of questions – it shows you're truly interested in the role.

JOB INTERVIEWS

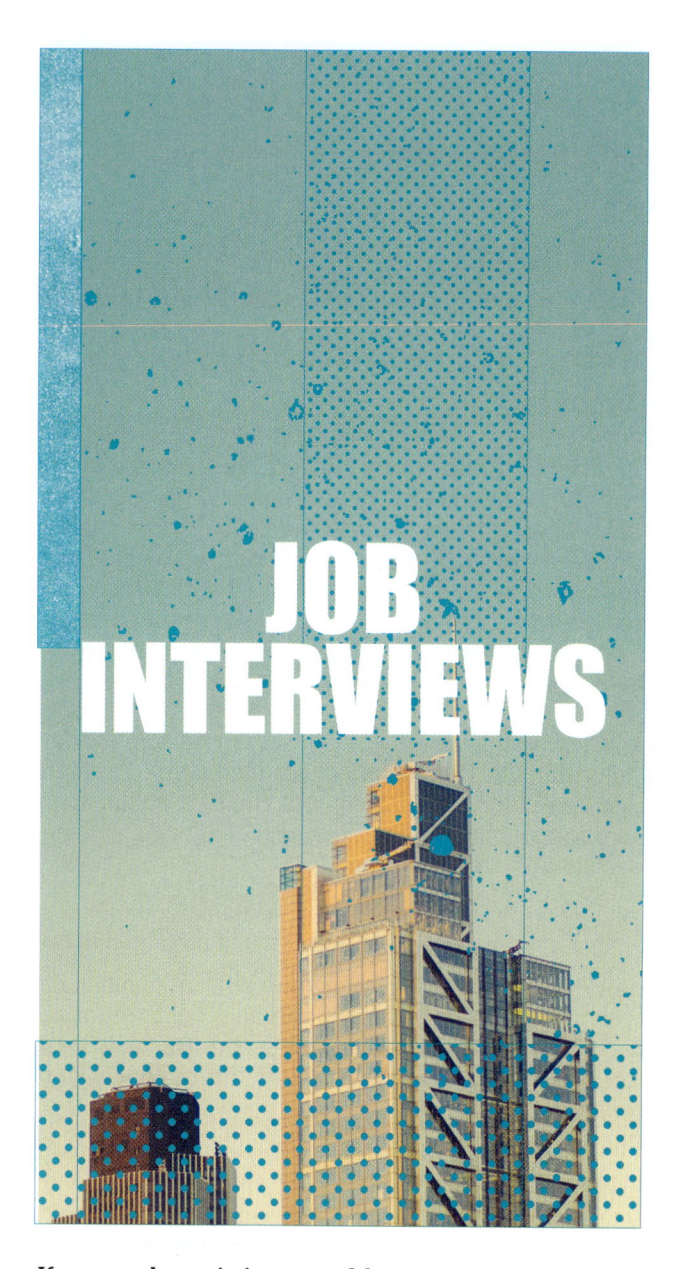

If an employer is impressed by your application, you may be asked for an interview. There are lots of different types of interviews; the standard interview with members of staff from the potential employer, telephone interviews (which are just as important and some people find more difficult), video interviews (often via Skype) or panel interviews with several people grilling you. You may even get several kinds of interviews with the same company as you progress through the application process. It's natural to feel nervous before an interview – in fact, it would be impossible not to! Here are some simple tips on how to appear confident, and employable:

Resist the urge to fiddle

Don't play with your hair, nails, sleeves or jewellery. Instead, use your hands to emphasise points.

Dress to impress

Try and find out the dress code of the office you're interviewing at. If in doubt, wear a smart suit. Gents: have neat and tidy hair, and make sure your clothes are clean and ironed. Ladies: don't over-do the make-up, have an elaborate hairdo, or wear heels you can't walk in.

Smile

Sounds easy, but when we are nervous, we lose our ability to control even the most simple facial expressions. Make sure you keep your smile in check to look friendly and confident.

Plan ahead

Plan your journey in advance so you know exactly where to go and how to get there. Find out if there are any delays on public transport or road works on your route.

Small talk

Don't be afraid of the old clichés about the weather or traffic; it's a great way to get started. Just allow the conversation to flow… and don't give a one-word answer to simple questions.

Prepare and read up

You should be fluent in the job description, the company and how you fit in.

Sit confidently

Shoulders back, legs together, chin up, feet pointing straight forward, hands in lap.

QUESTIONS TO EXPECT

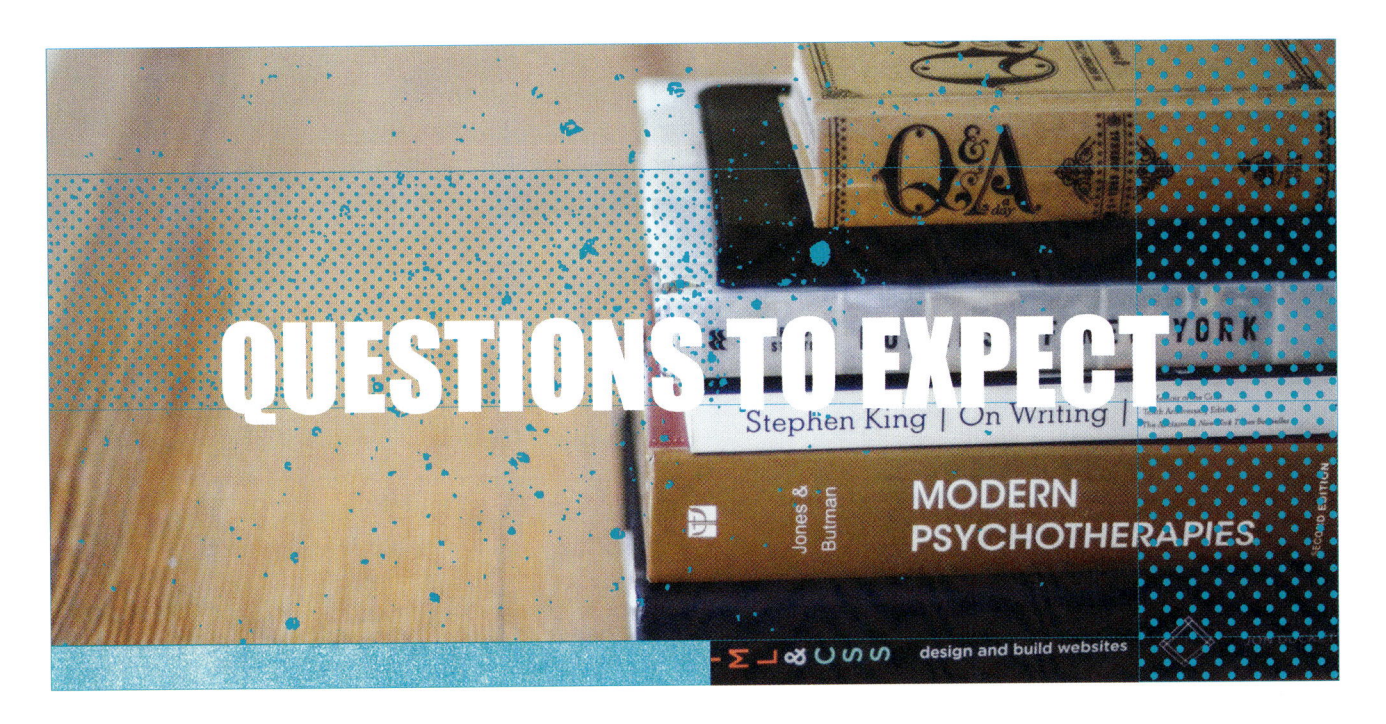

"TELL ME ABOUT YOURSELF."

This question gets asked a lot and can really throw people so it's a good idea to rehearse your answer beforehand. Make sure you keep it focused on the professional (not the personal) and keep your answer relevant to the job you're applying to. Start by talking about past achievements, give a little information on your current situation and end by stating what you're hoping to do in the future and how the job you're interviewing for fits into that plan.

"WHY DO YOU WANT TO WORK FOR THIS COMPANY?"

This is another question where preparation is key. Google the company before the interview and think about what it is that makes them attractive to you, what their values are as an organisation, what makes them stand out from their competitors and what exciting things they have on the horizon that you'd like to be part of.

"WHAT IS YOUR BIGGEST WEAKNESS?"

This feels like a scary question but it's not really so bad. The trick is to talk about a problem you've had in the past (which displays self-awareness) and what you did in order to manage or combat it – showing you can learn from experience is what they want to see evidence of. It helps to choose a weakness that wouldn't be a key requirement of the job you're applying to.

"HOW WILL YOUR PREVIOUS EXPERIENCES HELP WITH WORKING AT THIS COMPANY?"

Think about what work you would be doing if you secure the job and give examples of how previous experiences have prepared you to do those things well. Don't just list off everything you've ever done – try to give specific examples that link to what you know about the role you're interviewing for.

"WHAT APPEALS TO YOU ABOUT THE ROLE?"

In order to give a good answer to this question, you need to have done your research and be very familiar with the job description. Use the question to apply your strengths to the different elements of the job role and use positive words and body language to show that you're enthusiastic about the position on offer.

"WHAT CAN YOU BRING TO THE ROLE?"

This is a great opportunity to really sell yourself to your interviewer. Be confident in talking about your strengths and past achievements, and make sure you link them back to the role description. Don't forget to talk about your passion for the role (especially if you're at the start of your career and a bit thin on experience) – bringing positivity and enthusiasm will only be seen as a good thing and can help you to come across as motivated and committed.

"WHAT ARE YOUR GOALS?"

Talk about any ambitions or plans you have for the future and explain how the role you're applying for will help you get there. Be sure to give the impression you intend to stay in the role for some time – they might not want to employ someone for the short-term. If you're not exactly sure of what you would like to do in the future, don't worry – you can explain that your current goals are to learn and experience more to develop your skills and plans.

SPONSORED DEGREES

Sponsored degree programmes are becoming increasingly popular and it's no wonder why - they allow you to go to university and get a degree while having your tuition fees paid for and earning a salary. What's not to like?

What is a sponsored degree programme?

A sponsored degree acts as an alternative for those who wish to gain a degree qualification but do not necessarily want to attend higher education full time.

Sponsored degree programmes are made up of both employment and study. Your time will generally be split between attending university and working for the company that is sponsoring your degree – meaning you gain both a qualification and valuable work experience.

Are all programmes the same?

Sponsored degree programmes can really vary.

Depending on the programme, you might attend university in person or undertake a distance learning course remotely from home or your employer's office. For those courses where you will physically attend university, the amount of time you spend there will differ for each course. For some, you may do one or two days of the week at university and be in the office the rest of the time. For others, you might attend university on a full-time basis, and just spend holidays working for the company.

Some programmes will offer only a specific degree from a specific institution, whereas others provide some choice in where you study and what qualification you work towards.

There are also slightly different forms of sponsorship that act more like a scholarship, with universities sponsoring students irrespective of their course or university. Students might undertake work placements or graduate schemes with the employer in return. An example of this type of scheme is the EY Advisory Scholarship.

As you can see, sponsored degrees can differ greatly – so make sure you do your research and understand the structure and terms of any programme you're interested in.

What are the benefits of a sponsored degree scheme?

There are plenty!

- Getting to study towards and gain a degree, an internationally recognised qualification that you can refer to throughout the rest of your working life.

- Having your university fees paid for/contributed to and potentially avoiding thousands of pounds worth of student debt.

- Getting to earn a salary while you study.

- Access to work experience with a professional employer and an opportunity to develop valuable skills.

- The likelihood that once your sponsored degree programme reaches its conclusion, you'll be offered a graduate position with the company.

Where can I find out more about sponsored degree programmes?

Big companies are increasingly offering sponsored degree programmes. If you think you might be interested in sponsored degrees then have a look at the UCAS website.

Many of Pure Potential's partners offer sponsored degrees, so it's worth registering at www.purepotential.org for events where you can meet a sponsored degree programme provider.

USEFUL RESOURCES

purepotential.org
allaboutschoolleavers.co.uk
ratemyapprenticeship.co.uk

MY EXPERIENCE

Libby Horsley
Sponsored degree at KPMG Reading office

"I chose a sponsored degree as I wanted to go to university and earn money at the same time. Having no debt and also holding a degree was a definite winner! I wanted to kick-start my career, and the programme offers a great opportunity to do this – the qualification is recognised worldwide and you get all the perks of working for a major accounting firm!

I enjoy the mix of university and work life the most. Spending half the year at each means that neither gets boring.

Occasionally, the employment aspect of the programme meant I was at work when my friends at university were relaxing or enjoying long lie-ins! However, now I'm in the fourth year of the programme, most of my friends are busy trying to find graduate jobs, and they are really envious I don't need to worry about that. Things have definitely balanced out and worked to my advantage.

The advice I'd give to anyone thinking of applying is simple – GO FOR IT! The application process might put some people off, as it's not the usual UCAS application that your peers are doing... But ask questions and take advice from teachers, careers advisors and your parents; then the process does not feel as daunting as you might think."

Katie Forbes
Sponsored degree at KPMG Canary Wharf

"I chose a sponsored degree due to the importance of having practical work experience in addition to a degree. I believe that working in a real business environment is one of the best ways to gain different skills to those you learn at university, and better sets you up for success.

One of the most rewarding aspects is being given so much responsibility, and the opportunity to progress within a major accounting firm at such a young age. I love being able to work with a wide variety of people, from those on the same programme as myself to some of the most senior employees within the firm.

The programme involves a lot of studying and exams, some of which are very challenging. However, that is to be expected while working towards degree and professional qualification. We are very fortunate to be offered lots of support and it's great to mix teaching with work experience that brings the tuition to life.

As long as you are willing to work hard, it really is one of the best ways to learn about business and you'll be amazed how quickly you can progress. Don't be overwhelmed by the length of the programme – there is so much variety that time really does fly by. Good luck!"

Jack Dann
Sponsored degree at Rolls Royce

"I decided to join a sponsored degree programme after looking at the rising cost of living for students – on top of university fees themselves. Also, with a sponsored degree, I could earn money and learn how to stand on my own two feet while still being able to study at one of the country's top universities! I adore the programme I have chosen because it provides a great deal of variety and experience. I am gaining genuine experience in business – undertaking numerous real-world business improvement projects. I can see the difference my work makes, and I am picking up endless amounts of knowledge along the way. All this while undertaking a structured and recognised masters degree at a Russell Group university, which I never have to worry about paying for. Of course, being on a programme like this won't be for everyone. Personally, one of the biggest challenges has been just choosing a different path from many of my friends who went to university via the 'traditional' route. It has been difficult relocating and learning how to look after myself without the protective university bubble. The commitment is also much greater; you are given a great deal of responsibility to propel your own career – and this can be challenging. My advice to anyone considering a sponsored degree programme is to do some serious research and consider all your options. There are some outstanding programmes out there – but they are not always easy to find. Take all the opportunities that come your way and really take charge of your own future."

Kick start your career with an apprenticeship

Whether you have finished school or college, are about to start your final year or you are looking for a new career, have you considered an apprenticeship? There are lots of great options, each offering different benefits. There is no better, right or wrong choice - there are many options that could be right for you. Making a choice to go down one route also doesn't mean that you will be turning your back on another. University and college leavers can choose to start a higher or degree apprenticeship.

Apprenticeship:

An apprenticeship offers you education in the workplace, enabling you to gain invaluable experience right away while studying for a qualification up to masters level – plus you get paid! With hundreds of apprenticeships available, from digital marketing to law and engineering to hairdressing, there has never been a better time to follow this path.

College and university:

College and university will give you a stable environment in which to learn and develop your knowledge and specialise in your chosen area. There are some careers where university can be the only route, such as training to be a doctor or a vet.

Gap year:

A gap year is great for exploring the world and learning more about different cultures, learning a new language and life skills, even gaining some work experience if you work as you travel.

Full time work:

Going into full-time work will enable you to begin gaining work experience and life skills straight away while earning a wage.

Earn while you learn

Did you know that you can now do an apprenticeship in over 170 different industries?

You can progress your education all the way from leaving school – starting with an intermediate apprenticeship, and then moving on to an advanced, higher and even a degree or masters apprenticeship.

Study anything from business admin, IT, marketing and management, through to construction, finance and accounting, law, health and social care, engineering and even scientific research!

As an apprentice, you will work full time, usually 30–42 hours per week, get paid a wage and you will get all the same benefits as your colleagues, including paid holiday. You will do your training on the job, learning from other employees and have formal training that will be offered either online, in college or at a dedicated training centre or in the workplace.

Apprenticeships are respected by employers around the world and are a great way to start paving your way in the world of work in your chosen career. An apprenticeship can open doors for you with great companies and offers great future prospects. Often apprentices stay with the company they trained with and progress into senior management roles.

Apprenticeship section provided by

GetMyFirstJob
Where it all starts.

Visit getmyfirstjob.co.uk/apply2017 to search for apprenticeship vacancies in your area, learn more and apply for vacancies straight away.

Weighing your options

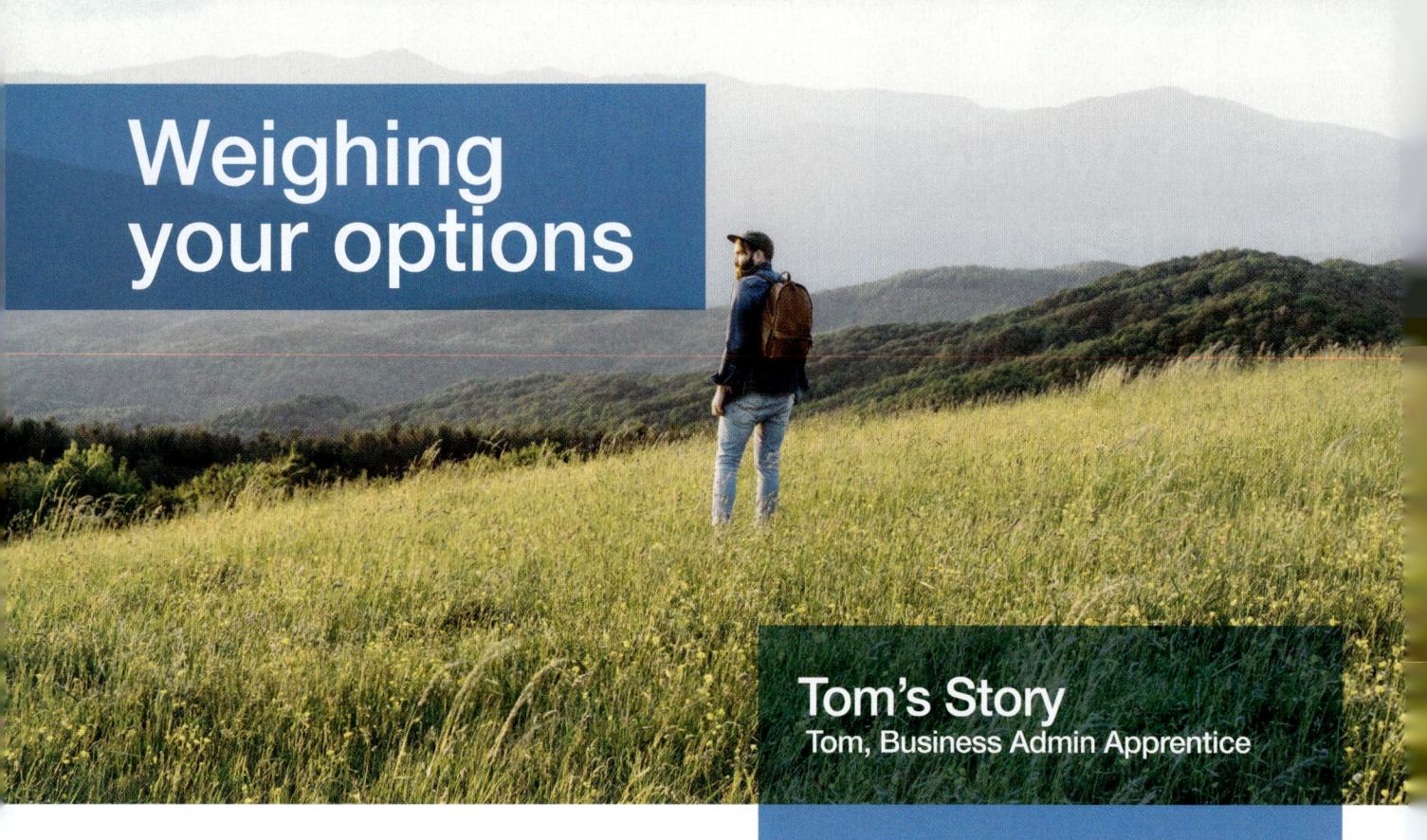

Tom's Story
Tom, Business Admin Apprentice

Choosing your next steps after school or college can be overwhelming and confusing. No doubt you have had multiple people talk to you about what you will do next, but often too many opinions can confuse the issue further. We have put together this quick unbiased comparison guide of some of the options available to you, so you can weigh up the benefits of each route to help you make an informed choice.

I chose an apprenticeship because you gain experience as well as a qualification. It is more valuable to me than gaining a qualification without the additional work experience.

I would highly recommend doing an apprenticeship, as it is a great opportunity to gain experience in a functional working environment. You're being trained to do a job while putting it into practice rather than learning how to do it. Due to having no work experience, an apprenticeship was the right path for me. With time, I have gained quite a high level of responsibility in my apprenticeship role. I started two months ago and, so far, I am really enjoying it. This is the right path to choose to build a career.

Using GetMyFirstJob was very simple, clear and easy to apply for jobs. I applied for my role and it took me less than a month to get a job. The website was very useful when trying to find a job. The application process was straightforward and the ability to track your application and see where it was in the process was also an added bonus.

	Apprenticeship	University	Work	Gap Year
Employability	Qualifications are recognised across the world and work experience will open many doors as you will have gained the specific skills and qualifications needed.	University qualifications are recognised across the world. For some careers a degree is the only route. Some employers will specify that you must have a degree or training to do certain roles.	Work experience counts for a lot when moving on through your career, but some jobs will require you to have a higher education qualification or job specific training.	Life skills and work experience will stand you in good stead to start a successful career but some jobs will require you to have a higher education qualification or job specific training.
Training	You will gain an internationally recognised qualification at level 2-7. Training will take place on the job with formal training in college or a training centre, online or in your place of work	You will gain a degree qualification. Training will take place in university, usually full time.	You may be offered training by an employer to further your skills but this is not guaranteed.	Although there won't be any formal training, you will be developing your life skills.
Work Experience	From the beginning of your training you will be working full time in your chosen role, learning on the job from your colleagues.	Some courses may include a period of work experience or a longer term work placement, but generally you will be learning in a class room environment.	You will gain work experience from the minute you start, building up your skills and increasing your knowledge.	If you choose to work during your gap year you will gain useful work experience and demonstrate to future employers that you have the life skills and experience needed to progress in the work place.
Cost	There are no costs to you, all of your training is paid for, so no student loans to worry about once you complete your qualification. You may have some travel expenses, which you will need to account for in your budget.	University currently costs up to £9k per year, which you will need to fund yourself or you can apply for student loan. You will begin paying your loan back once you are in full time employment and earning over £21k. If you are moving away from home, you will also need to consider accommodation and living costs.	You will need to consider commuting costs to and from your work place.	Travelling can be expensive so you may want to look into your rights to work in the countries that you visit to help fund your adventure.
Wage	As an apprentice you will be paid a wage as you work and learn, starting from £132 per week, up to £400 per week for 40 hours, depending on the role and qualification level. Qualified apprentices will more than likely be paid a higher wage than someone without any higher education qualifications, most netting a wage equal or even higher than their graduate colleagues.	You won't get paid a wage, so you may need to consider a part time job to help with living costs. Once leaving university you will most likely be paid a higher wage than someone who hasn't completed any further education qualifications	The minimum wage for under 18's is currently £3.87 rising as you get older to reach £7.20 for over 25s. However, depending on your experience and roles that you are applying for your wage could far exceed this.	If you are going to work and travel, the wage will vary greatly, each country has their own working and wage rules, so be sure to check that out
Time Frame	1-2 years is the average, some of the higher qualifications may take up to 7 years to complete.	A degree usually takes 3 years, but if your course includes a year's work placement it will more than likely be a 4-year course. For more specialist training such as medical training it could take up to 10 years including vocational training on a work placement.	As long as you're enjoying the job. The longer you can stay in a job the better it will look on your CV, especially if you are able to progress through the ranks. This shows commitment and your drive to succeed.	As long as you like, however staying out of full time employment for longer than a year or 2 could have a detrimental effect on your CV. Employers may see a long stint of travelling as a warning sign that you may not be able to commit to a long term role.
Career Prospects	Apprenticeships are recognised around the world and can open many doors. The fact that you have learnt on the job and therefore gained the exact skills needed for the role will mean that you're a highly skilled worker. Many apprentices move through the ranks of the business that they trained in and some move on to even bigger things.	University degrees are recognised the world over and will help you gain employment in more specialist and higher level roles within a business. For some specialist careers a degree is essential to gain employment in the sector.	Getting straight into work from the word go will really show your commitment and drive to succeed. If you work hard, show you're willing to learn and develop your skills you will open doors to new challenges or potential promotion.	Getting strong life skills and potentially some work experience under your belt, while seeing the world, can definitely set you on the right course to get stuck into a fulfilling career. Your experiences will be completely individual and will more than likely give a different perspective on life and work, which many innovative employers will love.
Social Life	As an apprentice you will be moving straight into a professional environment, but that doesn't mean it will be all work and no play. You will make new friends in your new job, plus earning a wage will give you more freedom to pursue your hobbies and doing things that you love.	University offers a varied social life. It's a great opportunity to meet new people and you will more than likely go on a night out or two! However, if you don't work whilst training you may find it hard to find the cash to go out with your new friends.	You will be moving straight into a professional environment, but that doesn't mean it will be all work and no play. You will most likely make new friends in your new job, plus earning a wage will give you more freedom to pursue your hobbies and do things that you love.	Travelling tends to be one big social gathering. You will meet loads of new friends along the way, but unless you have a large savings pot you will need to work in order to fund sight-seeing and evenings out.

Top 5 benefits of apprenticeships

1 Learn on the job

An apprenticeship is a real job. You'll be working alongside experienced people, supporting them and learning from them as you go. You'll gain most of the practical training you need in the work-place. Depending on the training provider or college delivering your training, you may go to college or a training centre or learn online to gain your qualification.

2 Training is free to you

You don't need to worry about funding your training; if you're aged between 16 and 24, the employer and the government cover the cost.

3 Earn a wage while you learn

For an apprentice, working hours are around 30–40 per week and you will get paid an hourly wage. Wages vary depending on the level and type of apprenticeship you are doing, but you must be paid at least the minimum apprenticeship wage, which is currently £3.40 per hour. In some job roles, your wages may increase as you progress and take on more responsibility. You will also get the same benefits as other employees, including a holiday allowance.

4 Lots of careers to choose from

You can now do an apprenticeship in over 170 industries, so there will definitely be something that fits your interests and chosen career path. Many people think that apprenticeships are aimed more at practical job roles, such as hairdressing, childcare and engineering, which of course, you can choose these careers, but you there are also lots of professional and business related apprenticeships on offer, such as management, law, finance and business administration.

5 Great future prospects

Once you complete your apprenticeship you will have lots of options open to you. Many apprentices stay with their current employer and progress through the business, while others move on to a new job confident in their new skills. There is even the option to continue your training by progressing on to a higher-level apprenticeship; you can train all the way up to degree and masters level! Apprenticeship qualifications are recognised by employers around the world, so the world literally is your oyster!

Go higher with your education

Apprenticeships offer more than just qualifications in manual jobs.

The apprenticeship scheme has grown to different sectors over the last five years and can now offer an excellent route into professional qualifications, including finance, management, law and business. Whether you've completed you're a-levels or BTEC, an apprenticeship can offer a great progression route with qualification starting from intermediate level 2 all the way up to a masters level 7. It's a great opportunity to get work-based learning giving you industry-standard skills, as well as being able to learn theoretical methods from your training provider.

Higher apprenticeships

Higher apprenticeships are the next step after you have completed A-levels or a further education vocational course and range from level 4 up to level 6, which is the vocational equivalent to a university degree. It's a real job and gives you the same great benefits as other apprenticeships including high quality-training while working, gaining skills on the job and getting paid.

Higher apprenticeships are now available in more than 40 job areas, so there are plenty to choose from. Respected by employers across the world, higher apprenticeships lead to a national qualification, with a network of support available to give you all the help you need to do well. It's in your employer's best interests to help you succeed. So you can relax in the knowledge that you're learning in order to get you ahead in your chosen career.

Degree and post graduate apprenticeships

As a degree or postgraduate apprentice, you will split your time between university study and the workplace – gaining a full bachelors or masters degree from a top university while getting real on-the-job experience in your chosen profession. Currently offered in 13 key industries including chartered surveying, law, aerospace engineering and nuclear, your degree apprenticeship will take you even further in your education and career. Degree apprenticeships are an alternative route to gaining a degree while getting straight into the world of work.

Focus on finance apprenticeships

Working in the finance industry can offer you a varied and fulfilling career.

Every business in the UK requires some form of financial workforce, whether that be a team that works internally or outside financial services, to keep their business going and to ensure that they meet their financial and tax obligations. There are many different roles within the industry, offering lots of pathways depending on your interests and your preferred route.

Working in finance could see you working as a qualified accountant, insurance broker or even an investment banker: You could be running pay roll, looking after pensions, tax or doing book-keeping.

Your skills

People who work in finance tend to be extremely organised and methodical with a good head for numbers. If you're offering financial advice, you will also need good communication and people skills and be trustworthy due to dealing with confidential and sensitive information. Most elements of finance are completed on a computer these days, so you will need to be good with technology and quick to learn new systems and software. You will also need to be able to grasp financial terms and stay up to date with the financial industry news. If that sounds like you, a career in finance could be the right path for you.

Finance apprenticeship programmes

- Accountancy
- Tax
- Management Accounting
- Insurance
- Banking and Investment Operations
- Bookkeeping
- Financial Services Administration & Customer Services
- Payroll
- Professional Services
- Pensions
- Auditing
- Mortgage Adviser

Training

GetMyFirstJob works with many training providers across the UK who offer the best financial apprenticeship programmes in the country, including BPP, Kaplan and Babington. Depending on your training provider, your training will take place in the workplace, online or in a classroom.

Salary

Doing an apprenticeship in finance is a financially smart decision in itself! You will be gaining a top-class qualification and work experience for free and being paid for your work, so you will have no debt from your training at the end. A career in finance can pay a lucrative salary ranging from around £12,000 to £40,000 per year, depending on the role, your experience and the business you work for.

Career progression

Finance offers great career progression with many qualifications overlapping or offering progression into new pathways within the industry. So you could be gaining skills in several areas of the finance industry at the same time, making you highly employable as well as offering lots of options, including running your own financial services business or working as a self-employed accountant or bookkeeper in the future.

Georgina's Story
Georgina, Accountancy Apprentice

I had always expected to go to university and actually had a place at University of Birmingham to study maths; however, as finance has always been my desired career sector, I couldn't turn down the opportunity to work for a FTSE 50 company and get a fast-track route into the finance world.

I felt that, with the majority of students choosing university, it would be hard to stand out with only a degree on my CV. When I looked into other options, I thought professional apprenticeships would definitely give me something different to offer employers – valuable experience in the finance sector, a good knowledge base and studying to become a chartered accountant.

I found GetMyFirstJob through a Google search. The system was easy to use and it was very simple to find the relevant apprenticeship opportunities. I was contacted by BPP who had seen my profile on GetMyFirstJob. I had a role within two to three months and that was with minimal effort. Simply putting your profile on this website seemed to be the key.

I am currently an apprentice at Experian, where I do four six-month rotations around different finance teams. Would I recommend doing an apprenticeship? If you are confident in the sector you want to work in, then yes. You will, in most cases and definitely mine, be guaranteed a job on completion, with real knowledge and experience. I am well on the way to becoming chartered, have built a considerable business network and all while earning. It's a fast-track route to where you want to be.

Focus on law apprenticeships

It is no longer essential to go to university to gain a qualification in law!

The new Legal Services apprenticeship programmes offer you the opportunity to study law as you gain real experience and you'll be getting paid!

Law apprenticeships offer a great progression route, taking you from a level 2 intermediate qualification all the way up to a level 7 masters degree to become a qualified solicitor. Working in finance could see you working as a qualified accountant, insurance broker or even an investment banker; you could be running payroll, looking after pensions, tax or doing bookkeeping.

Law apprenticeship programmes

You could be working in a variety of roles depending on the sector your employer covers and the level of your apprenticeship. The current legal apprenticeships available are:

Legal Advice
– Level 2 Intermediate & Level 3 Advanced
Legal Services
– Level 3 Advanced & Level 4 Higher
Paralegal
– Level 3 Advanced
Chartered Legal Executive
– Level 6 Higher
Solicitor
– Level 7 Masters Degree

Legal Advice:
Legal advisers are on hand to offer independent advice and guidance to members of the public on their rights, entitlements and responsibilities under the law.

Legal Services & Paralegal:
Paralegals or legal assistants have some legal training but are not qualified as either a lawyer, barrister or solicitor and form an important part of the legal team. They normally work for, or are under supervision of, a qualified legal practitioner to progress case files or specific parts of the legal process.

Chartered Legal Executive:
Chartered legal executives advise both internally within a business or externally for clients on legal matters. They help negotiate on behalf of clients and represent them in formal and informal proceedings.

Solicitor:
Solicitors are qualified to legally represent and act on behalf of a person in a court of law, providing expert legal advice and managing cases. They take instruction from clients and advise on the necessary course of legal action. Once qualified, solicitors can work in private practice, in-house for commercial or industrial organisations, in local or central government or in court services.

Training

Your training will depend on the level of your chosen apprenticeship. For level 3 to level 6 you would study with a private training provider, such as CILEx Law School. For degree apprenticeships, you would train at a university or a training provider who offers their own university facility such as BPP Professional Apprenticeships. Training may take place in your workplace, in a training centre or university and possibly some online learning - it will all depend on the training provider. Training can take from one to seven years and will be fully funded by the government and employer, so there will be no costly tuition fees.

Salary

Training in law can be a lengthy process so being able to earn a wage while you are learning is definitely a bonus. Your apprenticeship wage will vary based on job role, level and employer, but law apprenticeships generally pay well above the minimum apprenticeship wage, often rising as you progress and take on more responsibility. Your wage once qualified will vary depending on your role and employer, and tends to range from £15,000 to £50,000 per year.

Career progression

An apprenticeship in legal services will not lead to becoming a solicitor and barrister, but can lead to many exciting roles such as a paralegal, personal injury specialist, senior claims handler, litigation executive or a chartered legal executive within:

- Criminal prosecution
- Civil litigation
- Employment law
- Family law
- Property
- Working for private clients

Completing the degree apprenticeship will lead to becoming a fully qualified solicitor.

Laura Birks
Legal Apprentice, Kennedys Law

When I first started thinking about what I wanted to do for a career, I knew I wanted to work in law but never knew I'd be able to qualify as a solicitor without going from school to university. It's going to take longer but it will be a bigger achievement for me, and through my apprenticeship, I'm being paid to get my degree!

Everyone thought I'd go university. It would have been natural to go and do a law degree, but I chose not to do it because of the expense and I wanted to live at home. I decided to be an administrative assistant in a law firm, and was quickly promoted to a legal assistant. I missed the learning side of work so I wanted to do an apprenticeship, and was successfully recruited as a legal apprentice at Kennedys. It's a degree apprenticeship so I'm already three years ahead of my friends that went to uni – I have a job!

At Kennedys, they don't treat me as a tea maker. I get my own cases, and I'm involved in all the legal work. At first, I got to work on quite simple cases, but now I'm on high-value cases worth hundreds of thousands of pounds. They're quite complicated but they trust me to do them and it's a challenge I enjoy. I spend a lot of time on the telephone talking to the court or solicitors, I review legal documents and I write lots of letters to solicitors. The best thing is, I'm not just in the office - I even go to court and attend meetings.

When I compare myself to when I first started, I've progressed so much – I definitely made the right decision not to go to university.

Everyone should do an apprenticeship or at least seriously consider it as an option; don't rule it out. Look at all the options; the traditional route may not be the right one for you. If you're thinking of going to university, there might be firms out there that will fund you and you get to do a degree alongside working, which is a better route. Anything that offers you a qualification is worth doing as it is the best of both worlds.

HEALTHCARE

Working within the healthcare sector can be rewarding for those of you who are interested in making a difference to people's health and wellbeing. If you are interested in having an impact on some of the most important issues that society is facing, like the rise in obesity levels, cancer treatments and the increase in diabetes, then this could be the sector for you.

Whether you like caring for people, carrying out research and testing, dealing with emergencies or problem solving, but above all, working with people, then you can find a role that will suit your skill set. The NHS is the largest employer in Europe, with over 1.3 million staff across the UK. There are also many private companies that work within the healthcare sector. You could find yourself working in various settings within the community: hospitals, care homes, GP surgeries, sports clubs, or laboratories.

There are many different jobs within the healthcare sector and here are just a few to get you thinking:

Clinical Psychologist
Healthcare Scientist
Biomedical Scientist
Dental Health
Nurse
Optometrist
Pharmacists
GP
Social Carer
Radiographer
Sports and Exercise Scientist
Paramedic

We've picked a few interesting roles to explore in more detail...

CLINICAL PSYCHOLOGIST
The role of a clinical psychologist is to improve the psychological wellbeing of their clients. They use different types of therapy to support their clients to make positive changes to their lives. Their clients might be experiencing different mental or physical issues, such as anxiety, depression and eating disorders. To qualify as a clinical psychologist, you need to study an undergraduate degree, followed by three years of postgraduate training. Gaining voluntary or paid work experience is essential to access this career.

BIOMEDICAL SCIENTIST
Biomedical scientists work to diagnose disease and evaluate the effectiveness of treatment through the analysis of fluids and tissue samples from patients. They may work on understanding medical conditions, such as cancer, diabetes, AIDS and malaria. Most people who go into biomedical science have a relevant degree, and each individual needs to be registered with the Health and Care Professions Council. However, it is possible to enter the career with A-Levels and your employer will support you to study for a degree part time.

SOCIAL CARER
Care workers are the front-line staff who work with all types of people who need care and support. They are responsible for the individuals' overall comfort and wellbeing and they help people who need care and support to live as independently as possible. You don't need formal qualifications to be a carer and there will be plenty of opportunities to acquire more skills, training and qualifications depending on how far you want to take your career in the sector.

OPTOMETRIST
Optometry is the care of eyes and vision, identifying injuries and diseases, as well as prescribing glasses and contact lenses. Optometrists also work with other health professionals to help care for patients' general health. For example, conditions like diabetes can affect the eyes, and optometrists can both help to manage the resulting problems and will sometimes identify the diabetes in the first place. In order to qualify as an optometrist, you need to study an optometry degree which is offered at 11 universities across the UK.

USEFUL RESOURCES

www.brightknowledge.org/knowledge-bank/medicine-and-healthcare

www.healthcareers.nhs.uk

MEDICAL APPLICANTS

Medicine is an incredibly rewarding and respected career. Although it is exciting and dynamic, it is ultimately about helping people, about being willing to put someone else's needs first and doing all that you can to improve their health and wellbeing.

It is far from an easy option – it takes years of study and hard work, but if you want to push yourself and also have a passion to improve people's lives, it could be the right thing for you.

Medicine is a challenging career, but the two most important things you must have to succeed are an enquiring mind and the ability to relate to people as individuals, each with their own health needs. Very few areas of work can match the variety of medicine – it will confront you with something new every day. The profession is also concerned with integrity and is committed to uphold a number of timeless values.

APPLYING TO MEDICAL SCHOOL

Undergraduate medicine courses last approximately five years and the course can vary significantly depending on which university you attend. Some universities offer a problem-based learning (PBL) course, which allows students to set their own learning goals and working through various clinical problems with the help of an experienced tutor. This is becoming a very popular form of teaching and is something you should think about when selecting your university. Work experience is a really important part of the medical profession and it is essential to try and get as much experience under your belt before you reach medical school. Although it is often difficult to find work experience opportunities in hospitals, there are plenty of alternatives that demonstrate your compassion and ability to care for others, e.g. shadowing a district nurse, care homes or centres for the homeless. Universities now require students to take aptitude tests, such as the UKCAT and BMAT. These tests help support your application and they are used in conjunction with your personal statement and A-Level grades.

MEDICAL SCHOOL AND BEYOND

After graduation from medical school, doctors undertake a clinical apprenticeship and learning is undertaken while actually doing the job. The apprenticeship begins at the foundation house officer grade and continues until you become a consultant or a GP. It is also important to remember that doctors have to update their knowledge and skills throughout their career.

To a certain extent, doctors are able to choose in which area of medicine they practise. Within the practice of medicine, there are over 60 different specialities, each with their own particular characteristics. For example, community-based doctors like GPs have daily face-to-face contact with patients, while other doctors might focus on scientific research that involves less patient contact. Your medical training will give you the opportunity to discover which appeals to you most and can involve studying abroad. Although the majority of doctors work within the NHS, opportunities exist in other settings, such as the armed forces, the Home Office, working as a police surgeon or as a prison doctor, and many others. In your future career, you will have good job security and further opportunities to work in another country. Medicine can take you wherever you want to go.

Once you become a doctor, you will need to register with the General Medical Council (GMC) and are strongly advised to acquire medical insurance. Most doctors also become members of the British Medical Association (BMA).

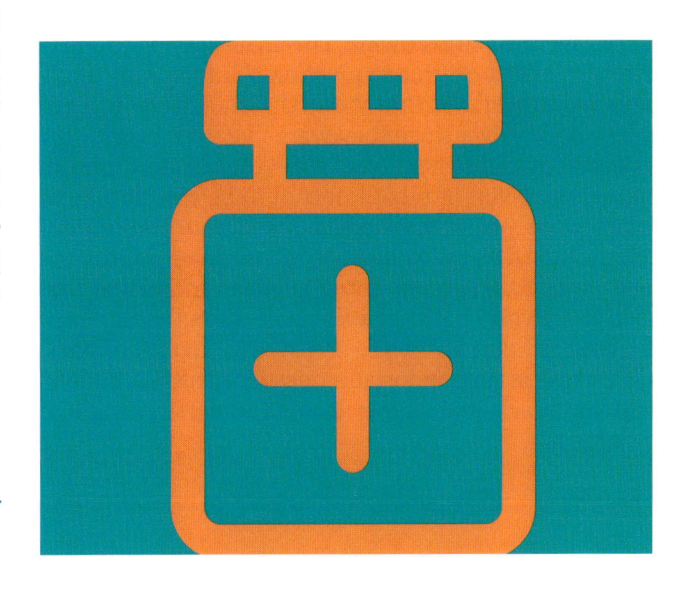

www.jobs.nhs.uk

GETTING INTO MEDICAL SCHOOL

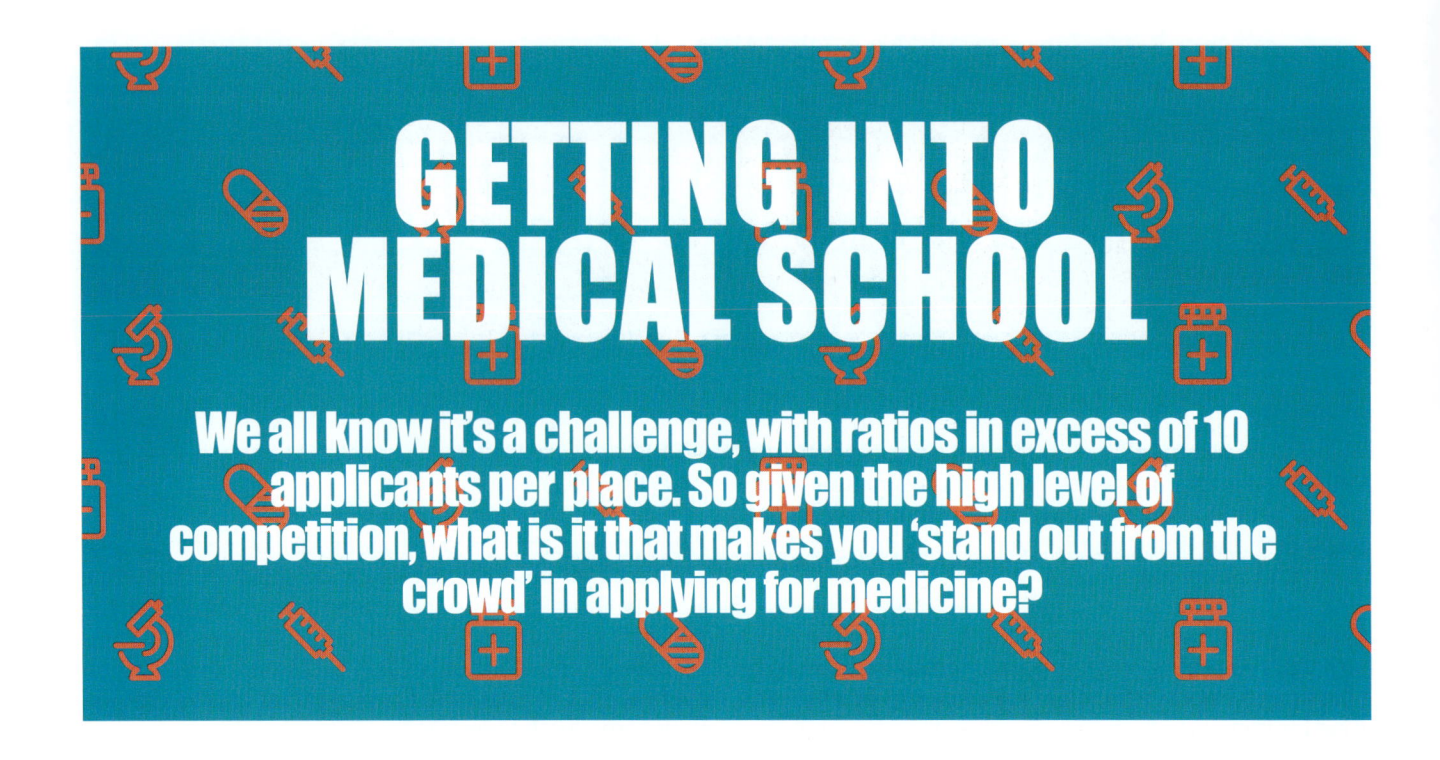

We all know it's a challenge, with ratios in excess of 10 applicants per place. So given the high level of competition, what is it that makes you 'stand out from the crowd' in applying for medicine?

The quick and pedantic answer is 'a poor-quality application'; with so many highly qualified, well-prepared and enthusiastic applicants, it's far easier to spot the poor-quality outlier from among the wealth of excellence. So rather than attempt the impossible in offering any sure-fire route to success, I'll instead offer broader guidance that helps you engage with the deeper thinking at play in selecting tomorrow's doctors.

MOTIVATION

All medical schools are looking for applicants with enthusiasm – individuals who are genuinely motivated by the idea of working in medicine. The challenge for you is to critically reflect on this motivation. All too often, applicants have told me in interviews that they have "wanted to be a doctor ever since they were five", so let's critically reflect on that statement – as a five-year-old, how well informed were you of what it meant to be a doctor? How aware were you of your abilities and your limitations? When I was five, I wanted to be an astronaut, but by the time I was 10, I'd grown out of it. As an individual, you need to actively challenge your motivation through constructive critique; always be prepared to step out of yourself and ask an uncomfortable question. This is what will help you reach that deeper level of understanding and engagement.

WORK EXPERIENCE

The challenge here is to get out of the 'tick-box' mentality, not to treat work experience as a test to complete, but as an opportunity to learn. You need a good understanding of what makes you tick; your strengths and, very importantly, your weaknesses (aka your opportunities for growth). A useful approach is to think of work experience (and voluntary experience, and life experience) as a chance to build evidence, both to help confirm your thoughts and to convince a medical school of your suitability. Identify the key skills that are needed to be a doctor – such as communication, empathy and integrity – and identify examples from your own life where you have demonstrated those skills. And genuinely do not be afraid to engage with your weaknesses – it is far healthier to have a mentality that recognises 'failure' as an opportunity to learn, rather than something to be ashamed of.

There are many different types of experience out there, ranging from shadowing a consultant in a hospital right through to working in your local shop. You might assume that the clinical experience is preferable, but not if you fail to demonstrate learning from it. Medical schools also recognise that access to clinical placements is not equitable (not everyone has an aunt or a neighbour who can help secure a place), so they consider the full breadth of potential experience, and consider your reflections on experience just as much, if not more so, than the actual experience itself. The key is to focus on opportunities to learn and opportunities to demonstrate the active application of key skills – take a look at www.tasteofmedicine.com for an in-depth exploration of the full range of potential experiences, recognising that all types of experience offer an opportunity to develop and to reflect.

CORE SKILLS vs SPECIFIC KNOWLEDGE

As a medical student, you will spend many years studying at university, taught by experts in their field who will help you develop the medical knowledge you need to be successful as a doctor. Concurrently, these experts will facilitate the development of your core skills (noting that is different to being 'taught'). That medical knowledge is not something expected of you before you start, but you are expected to be able to demonstrate and engage with the core underlying skills. It is important to recognise the differences between 'knowing facts' and 'knowing how to apply facts', and that is where demonstrating a propensity in core skills, such as empathy, resilience, insight and teamwork, will be of real value.

KEEPING PERSPECTIVE

Too easily the process of applying for medical school becomes a race, an all-encompassing focal point to your life. Yes, it is important, and yes, you need to devote time and attention to it, but to do so at the expense of other priorities can be damaging. It may be hard to read, but 'don't be in a rush to be a doctor'. As one of the very few genuine lifelong careers left in modern society, you can realistically expect to still be working as a doctor when you retire. Always keep in mind other routes, like clinical transfer from biomedical science, graduate entry, or joining medicine as a career change.

The other key perspective not to lose sight of is who you are – your friends, your family and your life. Focusing on academic work at the expense of your social life can hinder your application. You may find that, by spending your days in the library, you're able to secure excellent grades, but at what cost? Key skills of empathy, integrity, communication and insight can't be easily learnt from a book. It's engaging with life that helps you develop: meeting new people; experiencing new activities; and embracing what the world has to offer. So never underestimate the importance of maintaining a life-work balance, ensuring you fully engage with relaxing, recuperating and enjoying life.

CONCLUSIONS

DON'T BE IN A RUSH
If you want to be a doctor, then go for it, but don't be hard on yourself if you don't get in the first time. Keep in mind the alternatives, both in terms of related careers and other routes into medical training.

FOCUS ON THE CORE SKILLS
You are not expected to be an expert in all things medical, but you are expected to have the underlying skills and abilities necessary to develop as a medical student and a doctor. Focus on the core skills and link these to the experiences you've had.

KEEP PERSPECTIVE
Applying for medicine can dominate your life and become an urgent priority. But don't let the 'urgent' distract you from what is 'important' – a balance that allows you to enjoy life, develop as a human being, and achieve success in the widest sense of the word.

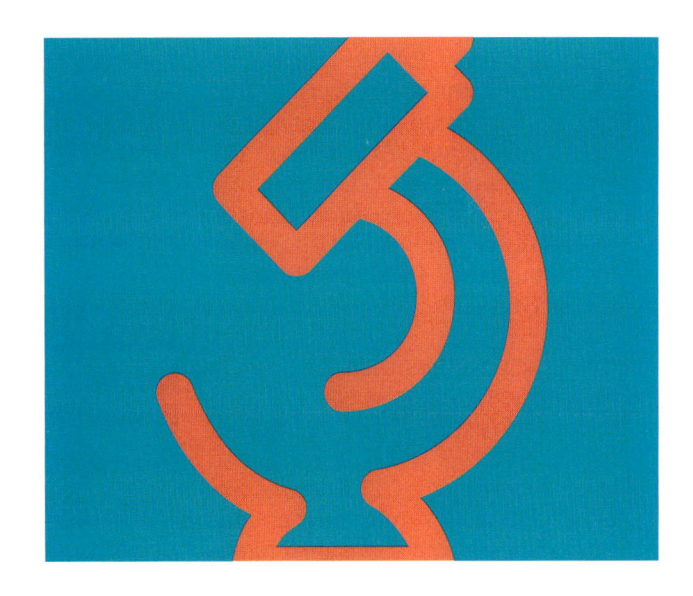

By Dr Kenton Lewis MBE

Dr Kenton Lewis MBE (www.kentonlewis.co.uk) is an independent education consultant and executive coach. He has guided and advised thousands of students, having worked at the University of Oxford, the University of Bristol and, for 10 years, running Student Recruitment at St George's, University of London.

ALTERNATIVE ROUTES INTO MEDICINE

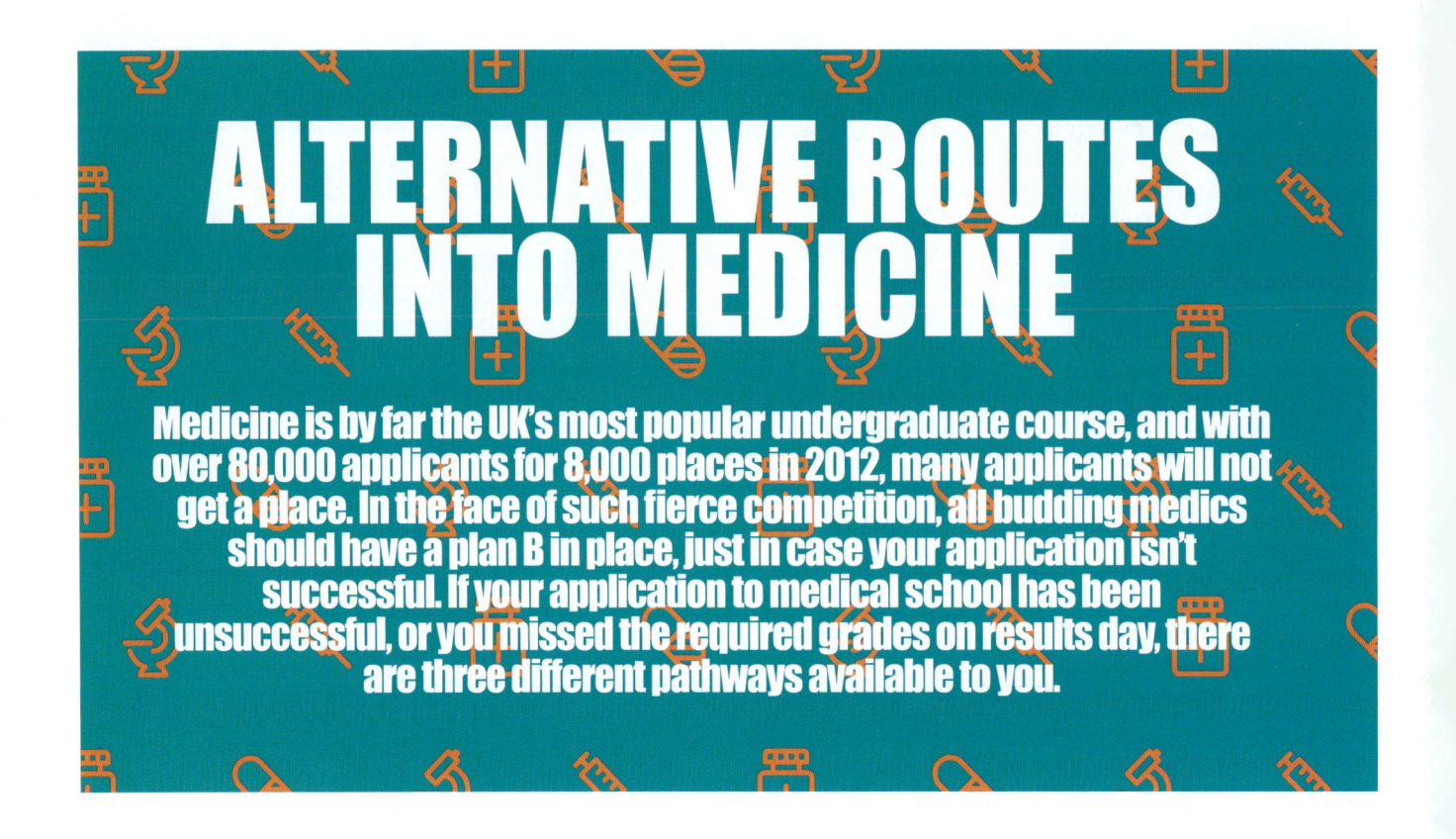

Medicine is by far the UK's most popular undergraduate course, and with over 80,000 applicants for 8,000 places in 2012, many applicants will not get a place. In the face of such fierce competition, all budding medics should have a plan B in place, just in case your application isn't successful. If your application to medical school has been unsuccessful, or you missed the required grades on results day, there are three different pathways available to you.

1. THE GRADUATE ENTRY PROGRAMME

The Graduate Entry Programme (GEP) is a four-year qualification that can be completed after graduating from university with a science degree. If you gain a 2:1 or higher in a subject such as biomedical sciences, biochemistry and natural sciences, then you would be eligible to apply for the GEP.

If you achieve less than 2:1 or your undergraduate degree was not in a science subject then you will need to take the Access to Medicine course prior to starting the GEP. These courses are primarily run by further education colleges, but there are a handful of universities that also offer the course.

It is important to bear in mind that some medical schools do accept students on their GEP courses without the Access to Medicine qualification, so it would be advisable to check the information on the UCAS website or the individual university websites.

2. OTHER RELATED COURSES

There are several other careers related to medicine for which you may be suitable, and which will provide a very rewarding career path. These include:

Clinical Psychologist
Healthcare Scientist
Dental Health
Nurse
Optometrist
Pharmacist
Radiographer
Physiotherapist
Sports and Exercise Scientist
Paramedic

This is not an exhaustive list, and there are many more careers worth investigating. Many of these professions require a very similar set of skills to that of a doctor and can be equally rewarding.

3. RETAKING & REAPPLYING

If you did not achieve the grades that you wanted, it is possible to take a year out to retake your exams and re-apply to medical schools. It is common for universities to accept retakes, but they may increase their standard offer so it is important to check this. If you did not secure an offer at a medical school but achieved outstanding results in your exams, you might be interested in taking a gap year and reapplying. The main advantage with this is that you can apply with your actual grades rather than predicted. When reapplying, we advise you to look back over your UCAS form and personal statement and look at ways to improve your application. The universities will want to know what you have done in your year out to make yourself a more attractive candidate. It would be very helpful if you could combine your year out with a relevant part-time job within the healthcare sector, as this would dramatically improve your personal statement and your chances of securing a place.

MY EXPERIENCE

Andrew Durnford
Neurosurgery Doctor at
University Hospital Southampton

"My day-to-day tasks vary from treating acutely unwell patients, including performing emergency operations, to seeing patients in clinic and managing conditions affecting the brain and spine, often with surgery. There are also opportunities to undertake medical research and potentially change the future treatment of patients. My role requires good relationships with many different colleagues in a hospital, including x-ray doctors to help make correct diagnoses and those involved in the rehabilitation of patients following surgery, such as physiotherapists.

As a trainee surgeon, I am paid a full salary. Although medical training can take many years, the continual learning and challenges represent one of the most enjoyable aspects of the job. I enjoy surgery, as it is practical and requires excellent problem solving, judgement and communication skills that enable you to help and care for people of all different ages and backgrounds. I went to a local comprehensive school and studied A-Levels and then studied at Oxford University and Birmingham University before becoming a junior doctor.

Becoming a doctor involves getting good grades at A-Level then studying medicine at university, typically for five years. You then start as a full-time junior doctor working for two years in a hospital before choosing to pursue a career often either as a GP or hospital doctor within many diverse branches of medicine, including surgery. Opportunities also exist to work abroad in both developed and developing countries, in the armed forces or in academic research at universities allied to NHS hospitals."

Amanda Williamson
Clinical Audit and Effectiveness Manager at a
District General Hospital

"I manage a team of 14 people who undertake a number of roles linked to governance. This means we take the local trust's annual audit plan for the hospital and ensure it is completed each year. We also help format clinical policies, procedures, and guidelines for clinicians and check them through an approval process. I review any guidance from external bodies (such as the National Institute for Health and Care Excellence or the National Confidential Enquires into Patient Outcome and Death) that is published and, if relevant to our trust, I send it out to clinicians to determine if the trust already complies with the recommendations or if we need to make any changes to ensure we meet them. The team also supports the NHS National Patient Surveys for our trust and I undertake a monthly analysis of patient feedback, escalating any concerns to senior nurses and identifying areas for improvement to patient experience while they're in the hospital. Every day is different!

You could definitely say I 'fell' into this role. I originally trained as a nurse and a midwife and worked in clinical practice for a number of years. I worked part time as a midwife for a few years and, during that time, I undertook a bachelors degree in law followed by a masters degree in family law and policy. Following this, I undertook a teaching role at a university for a number of years before returning to the NHS and clinical practice where I commenced my current role.

The best thing about my role is knowing that my job and my team helps to improve patient outcomes and patient experience in the hospital. I like being up to date with current clinical practice and national recommendations; I am always learning something new. The most challenging part of the role is trying to get some people to engage with us – we need excellent communication and diplomatic skills! Although this is quite a specialist role, you could approach it from a number of different ways. Some of my team have worked in clinics as nurses, some have undertaken degrees such as applied pyschology or English, and others have worked in administration. I think my top tip for getting into something similar would be to do a degree or course in something you enjoy and gain NHS experience working with people."

HOSPITALITY & CATERING

Hospitality and catering is all about making sure other people have a good time, so it can be a hugely rewarding and fun career. The main attribute you need is, of course, excellent people skills.

There are a huge range of career paths within this industry and, most often at the beginning, you will be asked to carry out a wide variety of duties, enabling you to discover what you enjoy before focusing on one role. If you excel in your field, you can be promoted and advance quickly up the career ladder. You will also need to be able to manage time very carefully, plan ahead meticulously, be a team player and be willing to work long hours from time to time. Helping other people enjoy themselves can be great fun for you too!

There are many different roles within this sector, and here are just a few to get you thinking:

Events Manager
Restaurants and Catering Manager
Hotel and Spa Manager
Catering Assistant
Conference Supervisor
Sous Chef
Hall Porter
Maître d'Hôtel
Bar Manager
Wedding Planner

We've picked a few interesting roles to explore in more detail...

EVENTS PLANNER
Maintaining a professional demeanour even when things go wrong and being able to communicate effectively to your team will stand you in good stead for a career managing events. From birthday parties to corporate dinners to large-scale public events to music festivals and even wedding planning, this is a career that will certainly keep you busy!

RESTAURANTS AND CATERING MANAGER
If you have a passion for food and drink (preparing AND eating, that is!) and think you can manage budgets and people well, then you may find this career suits you. Long hours are usually a requisite, so be prepared for hard work with potentially great rewards. From a small café to catering events, a school or office canteen or a five-star restaurant – the jobs within this area are widely varied.

HOTEL MANAGER
Have you ever been on a holiday or break that you really enjoyed? If you think about why you enjoyed it so much, and love the idea of making other guests experience a fantastic stay, then perhaps working in the hotel and spa sector could be right for you. You will usually be part of a huge operation, which can be very satisfying – the work that goes on behind the scenes is usually far bigger than a guest would ever get a glimpse of.

USEFUL RESOURCES

www.caterer.com
www.leisurejobs.com
www.jobsinhotels.co.uk

MY EXPERIENCE

Charlotte Dollin has worked in PR since graduating from Queen Mary's, University of London in 2010. She is currently the PR Manager for Virgin Limited Edition.

"The truth is that I fell into my career. Believe it or not, I actually applied to study travel and tourism while at college and was told that my grades were too high; with determination and persuasion, I was allowed to join the course and in the end, somewhat ironically, it is the only C I have ever received! From there, I was slightly put off pursuing that path any further and I set out instead applying to universities with the aim of becoming a teacher. I had used all of my six choices on teaching degrees and it was only when I met with the principal of my college, who advised me to pursue a subject I was passionate about and see where it took me, that I deviated from that plan. I'm eternally grateful for that advice, as I went on to study English literature which I absolutely loved and I would definitely be in a very different position today if it wasn't for those wise words.

While studying for my degree, like most students, I worked during the holidays and my first taste of the hospitality industry was at The Watermill Theatre in Berkshire in their restaurant and bar. Some of my happiest memories are from that job, but, at that stage, I struggled to see how I could turn it into a career and so I pursued my other interest at the time which was publishing.

As i had to read so many books, it is hardly surprising that the industry called out to me. As with most people who think of publishing as a career, I dreamt of being an Editor and began applying for work experience at the leading publishing houses. I was offered a work placement in the publicity team at Penguin and while it wasn't a department I had considered up until that point, it was an opportunity and so I took it. I'm so pleased I did as, based on that placement, I was hooked! I loved the buzz of the press office and meeting new people to spread the word about some fantastic books. After several work placements, I began my career at Penguin working with DK Travel as their Publicity and Marketing Assistant. From there, I moved to work for Random House as PR Assistant for Ebury before being promoted to Press Officer. We mainly looked after non-fiction titles and so I was able to work on a lot of cookery and lifestyle titles, as well as with a lot of brands. I can remember working on Sir Richard Branson's *Screw Business as Usual* and thinking that Virgin was where I wanted to be, so when a job came up to work for Virgin Limited Edition, I applied without any hesitation.

I joined the Virgin Limited Edition team as Press Officer for The Roof Gardens in Kensington. I can honestly say that, from day one, I felt like I had finally found my calling. The role combined everything I had learnt and enjoyed up until that point and I was able to be fully immersed in the hospitality industry. Not only was I able to promote a fantastic venue and profile some of the team who worked there, I was also able to work closely with our Restaurant Manager, who is a real champion for the hospitality industry; I would accompanied to visit schools and colleges across the country to highlight it as a career path.

My current role is PR Manager for Virgin Limited Edition, looking after nine luxury retreats around the world. No two days are the same and my role covers everything from drafting press releases and statements to hosting press trips, launching new ideas and properties to overseeing photoshoots and filming.

Looking at my journey, you perhaps wouldn't imagine an English literature graduate would end up working in hospitality, travel and leisure PR, but I firmly believe you have to pursue what you are passionate about and it is absolutely fine to not have a firm plan while you work out what that passion is. I loved my degree and I'm now in the fortunate position to love my job too. I think I realised at quite an early stage of my career that you could really go places, quite literally, and that was just another incentive to work hard. For me, hospitality is one of the most exciting industries to be a part of. It's an industry that is full of people with energy, enthusiasm and passion. It is also constantly evolving, so there's always an opportunity to be creative. I think it's safe to say that very few industries offer such variety, scope and… fun!"

MEDIA, TV & RADIO

If you have a love of films, TV and radio, newspapers, magazines, blogs and online content and are looking to put your creative and people skills to use, then have a think about joining this rapidly growing industry. Hard work, creativity and engaging with people from all walks of life will stand you in good stead in this sector.

As the media moves to a more digital world, there are many opportunities to use your digital skills too. There are 2.8 million jobs within the creative industry in the UK – meaning that 1 in 11 UK jobs are now in the creative economy, and 24% of them are freelance, meaning you don't work for a specific company but instead work on different projects for different employers. Jobs in media are fast-paced and exciting, usually involving the most up-to-date trends, technology and news.

There are many different roles within this sector, and here are just a few to get you thinking:

Advertising Account Manager
Editorial Assistant
Animation
Copywriter
TV Presenter
Broadcaster
Journalist
Publisher
Radio Scriptwriter
Special Effects Editor
PR Executive
Cameraman
Sound Engineer

We've picked a few interesting roles to explore in more detail…

EDITORIAL ASSISTANT
If you love to read, and are often finding yourself spotting mistakes and improving the writing of others (and yourself), then you may want to immerse yourself in the world of publishing. You will support the various stages a book, journal, magazine, website or online piece has to go through before it is ready for public view. You'll need excellent written and spoken English, as well as the ability to manage your time well, and be willing to work long hours from time to time.

PR MANAGER
A PR manager will be responsible for the external image, brand and reputation of an organisation. You can be a PR manager for a football team, celebrity, politician, business, product, book, TV show – pretty much anything! You will write press releases, which are essentially newsletters to the media (newspapers, magazines, TV and blogs) about a specific story that will have all the details you want the public to know. You will spend a lot of time building external relationships with the media, government or other influencers depending on your client.

ADVERTISING ACCOUNT MANAGER
The advertising account manager is the link between the client and the entire advertising agency team. Along with their team, the account manager acts as both the salesperson for the agency and as the client's representative within the agency. You will be the point of contact between the creatives and the client to oversee the advertisement for print, web, TV or radio from pitching to the client at the start to seeing your advert in the public domain.

USEFUL RESOURCES

www.thecreativeindustries.co.uk
www.theverge.com
www.technojobs.co.uk

MY EXPERIENCE

Rob Farris
Head of Production at Goldcrest Post Production

"I work at a market-leading supplier of picture and sound post-production services for film and TV in London.

My role is to oversee the client-facing side of our company, as well as act as producer for the films and TV series that complete their post-production with us. I've been fortunate enough to work on a huge range of shows, from *Skyfall* and *World War Z* to micro-budget short films.

I started in the industry – as most do – as a runner with little knowledge of the non-creative roles available. Head of Production wasn't the job that I had in mind through my studies but allows me to use the technical knowledge I learnt during a degree in audio visual media studies (at the University of Central Lancashire), as well as being client facing and therefore not stuck in a dark room all day!

I spend about 50% of my time at my desk, organising schedules with post-production supervisors, making sure we are charging for the work we are doing and drinking a lot of tea, and the rest of my time in various grading/edit suites reviewing VFX and talking with the directors and editors of the films to make sure everything is progressing as it should be.

No two days are the same when working in post-production – every film and TV show brings different challenges and the variety keeps things fresh and interesting. There are a whole range of roles in the industry; if you have a passion for film and TV, there is certainly one for you."

Daisy Morecroft
Studying Digital Television Production at Ravensbourne University

"Television has a huge impact on our lives: it makes you laugh, cry, and think. Deciding to study a degree in digital television production was an easy decision to make, because my aim in life is to inspire and educate the public through a creative platform.

At the age of 14, I was fortunate enough to secure work experience at the *Daily Mirror*, where I was involved in the advertising department (and a celebrity photo shoot!). Achieving this placement wasn't easy and involved a lot of persuasive emails explaining how passionate I was. However, once I had the *Daily Mirror* on my CV, other employers were happy to offer me work experience!

Since then, I have achieved a BTEC in creative media, an A-Level in media studies, and worked with a number of production companies and events as a runner/camera operator including Red Goat Films, Revolution and Soccer Six.

I am now a first year student at Ravensbourne University, where I am inspired every day, and also where I have learnt that there is more to TV than just presenting and directing! One piece of advice I would give to anyone wishing to enter and succeed in the creative industry, whether that be broadcast, online or paper journalism, is that it is 'who you know' in addition to 'what you know'. While studying, I am applying for a number of runner roles, but once I graduate, I plan to start as a Researcher and Production Assistant until I reach my dream job: 'Producer of Factual Entertainment' for a major channel!

From a young age, I always knew the traditional 9–5 office role was not for me, and achieving this degree will kick-start my career in the exciting, ever-changing, ever-growing industry of television."

FINANCE

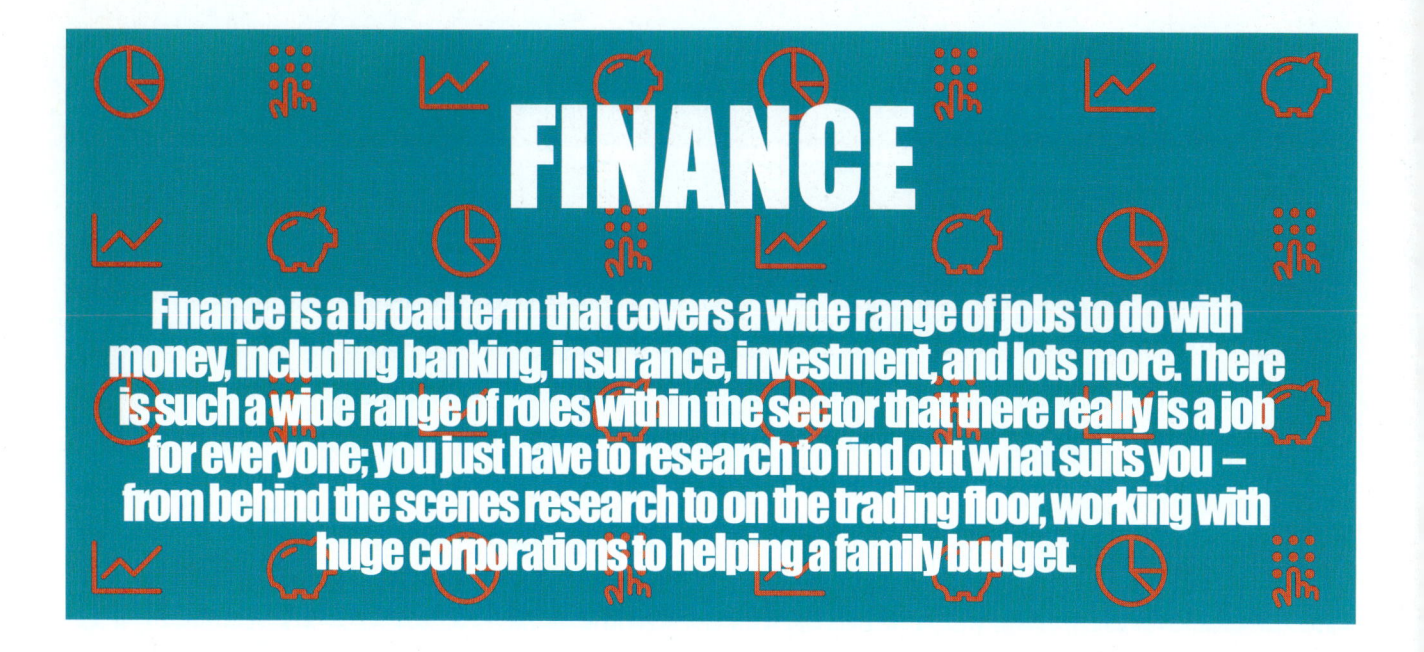

Finance is a broad term that covers a wide range of jobs to do with money, including banking, insurance, investment, and lots more. There is such a wide range of roles within the sector that there really is a job for everyone; you just have to research to find out what suits you – from behind the scenes research to on the trading floor, working with huge corporations to helping a family budget.

To succeed in this sector, you will need to be able to communicate well and be comfortable talking to people from across all levels. You'll need to be an effective negotiator and able to work well under pressure. Working in finance can mean working long hours in a fast-paced environment, so it particularly suits people who are highly motivated and determined. Contrary to popular belief, you do not need to be a mathematical genius to succeed!

There are many different roles within this sector, and here are just a few to get you thinking:

Accountant
Business Analyst
External Auditor
Financial Analyst
Tax, Finance Director
Mortgage Broker
Risk Manager
Actuary
Credit Analyst
Asset Manager
Hedge Fund Manager
Broker
Investment Manager

We've picked a few interesting roles to explore in more detail…

ACCOUNTANTS
Accountants generally work with the financial side of a business and interpret the figures and advise accordingly. There are many different kinds of accounting: tax, audit, government, bookkeeper and forensic (detecting fraud).

FINANCIAL SERVICES AND INSURANCE
If you like the idea of helping people plan their futures, then this area could be for you. By providing expert advice (gathered through research with doctors, lawyers, and fire officers to name but a few to assess risk), you can help families save money through insurance, mortgages and careful financial planning, and resolve claims against insurance companies.

BANKING
The biggest employers in the finance sector, these enable individuals and businesses to manage their money and access products such as loans, both in the UK and overseas. The term covers a huge range of jobs, from the high-street banks you probably walk past every day to the financial institutions that you hear about in the news.

INVESTMENT
Your job here would involve researching funds and making an educated guess on their likely performance. You would advise asset managers and, depending on the area you specialise in, you could be including trading and stockbroking, performance measurement, investment support, risk assessment and data management.

USEFUL RESOURCES

www.careers-in-finance.com
www.prospects.ac.uk
www.directions.org.uk

KPMG

Experience can be the greatest teacher

School and College Leaver Programmes

Give your career a flying start. Join KPMG straight from school or college and you'll receive training, qualifications, experience and rewards to help you thrive in the world of business. With opportunities across the UK, Live, Learn, Earn with KPMG.

kpmgcareers.co.uk/school-leavers

f KPMGRecruitment
○ kpmgtraineesuk

© 2016 KPMG LLP, a UK limited liability partnership and a member firm of the KPMG network of independent member firms affiliated with KPMG International Cooperative ("KPMG International"), a Swiss entity. All rights reserved. Printed in the United Kingdom. The KPMG name and logo are registered trademarks or trademarks of KPMG International.

At the National Audit Office, we offer something different – the chance to be part of work that has real impact on the nation. Our School Leaver scheme is amongst the best out there, providing you with an excellent path into accountancy and the public sector.

What do we do?

There are five main strands to our work; Financial Audit; Value-for-Money audit, Investigation and Insight, Parliamentary Relations and International Audit. Being a trainee at the NAO gives you access to these strands as well as valuable experience and a perspective that you would not get working anywhere else. Our unique clientele includes the Royal Household, Ministry of Defence, NHS and Nuclear Decommissioning Authority amongst many others.

Our people have a great reputation among our clients, Parliament, other international audit institutions and the wider accountancy profession. In addition to Accountants we employ Analysts, Statisticians, Economists and specialists in a variety of other disciplines to foster a fantastic learning environment.

Earn and Learn

Our school leaver scheme is a 5-year training programme which will see you right through to qualification as a Chartered Accountant (ACA) with the Institute of Chartered Accountants in England and Wales (ICAEW). Our pass rates are consistently at or above the national average.

Day to day you will be working in either our London or Newcastle office as part of our Six Clusters, each offering a range of exciting and challenging work. There are also opportunities to travel nationally to our different clients and stakeholders, a highlight for many of our current trainees.

In addition to our career opportunities, we offer a list of benefits including:

A starting salary of £23,610 (London) or £18,122 (Newcastle), which will increase year-on-year and be subject to increases for success in exams to take it around £36,00 (London) and £30,000 (Newcastle), 25 weeks College and study leave, interest free season ticket loan, an on-site gym and activity centre at our London office and post-qualification earning potential of £50,000 plus.

Training with the NAO School Leaver scheme will open a world of career opportunities.

Please visit our website today to find out more about the programme and how to apply. At the NAO, we're committed to helping you build your career, so take yours further in public sector audit.

National Audit Office

Career. Influence. Impact.
Build yours in public sector audit while training as a Chartered Accountant

The NAO scrutinises public spending for Parliament to help the nation spend wisely and improve public services. You can support that work by joining our School Leaver scheme in London or Newcastle.

You will receive first-class tuition over the five-year programme to qualify as a Chartered Accountant whilst learning the latest auditing techniques and working with a unique set of public sector clients.

Find out more about how you can open up a world of career opportunities whilst doing work which has a real impact on the nation.

nao.org.uk/school-leavers

What are you working for?

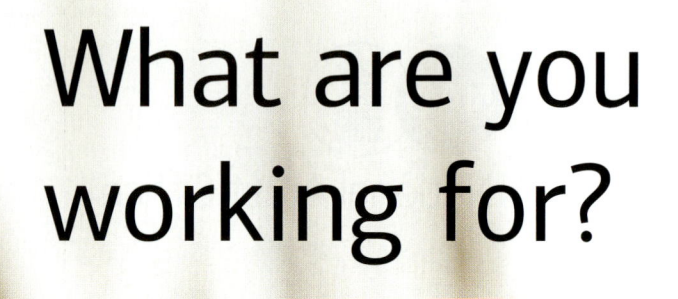

Join us for an insight day where you'll learn more about the variety of career opportunities available within an investment bank. It's never too early to think about your future.

Chester events
20 February – Futures, Year 13
4 & 5 April – Insight Day, Year 1 Uni
31 May – Futures Insight, Year 12

London events
16 February – Futures Insight, Year 12
13 April – Female Futures, Year 13
13 July – Futures, Year 13

Get started. Apply now at:
campus.bankofamerica.com

©2016 Bank of America Corporation.

Bank of America
Merrill Lynch

Is a head start sometimes the best start?

At EY, school leavers can go as far as graduates, with just as many career options.

Choose what's right for you.
ukcareers.ey.com/schools

EY
Building a better working world

The better the question. The better the answer.
The better the world works.

97

of the world's 100
global leading brands employ
ICAEW Chartered Accountants

Find out more and start your career
journey at **icaew.com/purepotential**

ICAEW

Source: ICAEW member data at January 2016, Interbrand Best Global Brands 2015.

MY EXPERIENCE

Shyam
National Audit Office School Leaver

Why the NAO?

At the NAO, the firm prides itself on its culture, as the focus is around one person and that's you. This means you get vital experience from the start to establish your auditing career.

The second reason why I chose NAO over other firms is that, simply put, no one else audits the government, so the experience on offer was unrivalled. Where else would I be able to to say that I am continuously protecting and saving the taxpayer's money?

My day-to-day life at the NAO...

I am based in the Department for Transport, where I have been assigned to work on Network Rail, Highways Agency and the Vehicle Certification Agency.

Although I'm at the most junior grade, I'm not given mundane tasks such as photocopying. I am allocated my own account areas to audit and, as I've developed, been given more responsibilities when interacting with clients. I feel valued at the NAO.

The NAO has lots of opportunities on offer. I get to travel across the UK as part of my regular work, and I even get the chance to go oversees. Wherever government money goes, you get to go too!

Attending college...

College is a key part of learning and development. The best thing I like about college is you learn the theory in class and put it into practice when working for clients. No one asks or expects you to work while you are at college or revising for an exam, neither do you attend college during our main busy period. All this helps reduce the stress of exams and promotes a good work-life balance.

You go to college with the rest of your intake, which makes the experience less daunting and the teachers don't expect you to know much about accounting either. The teachers I've had to date have all been qualified accountants with years of experience, so it's good learning from people who were once in your situation.

School leaver scheme vs going to university

I knew I wanted to work in accounting when I was studying my A-Levels. That meant I had a choice of going to uni first, then studying all over again to become a chartered accountant, or I could choose something better. Instead I got to start off day one with a prestigious employer and with a good salary. Instead of six years of study and at least £27,000 of debt, I got five years of experience with none of the drawbacks. It was a no-brainer.

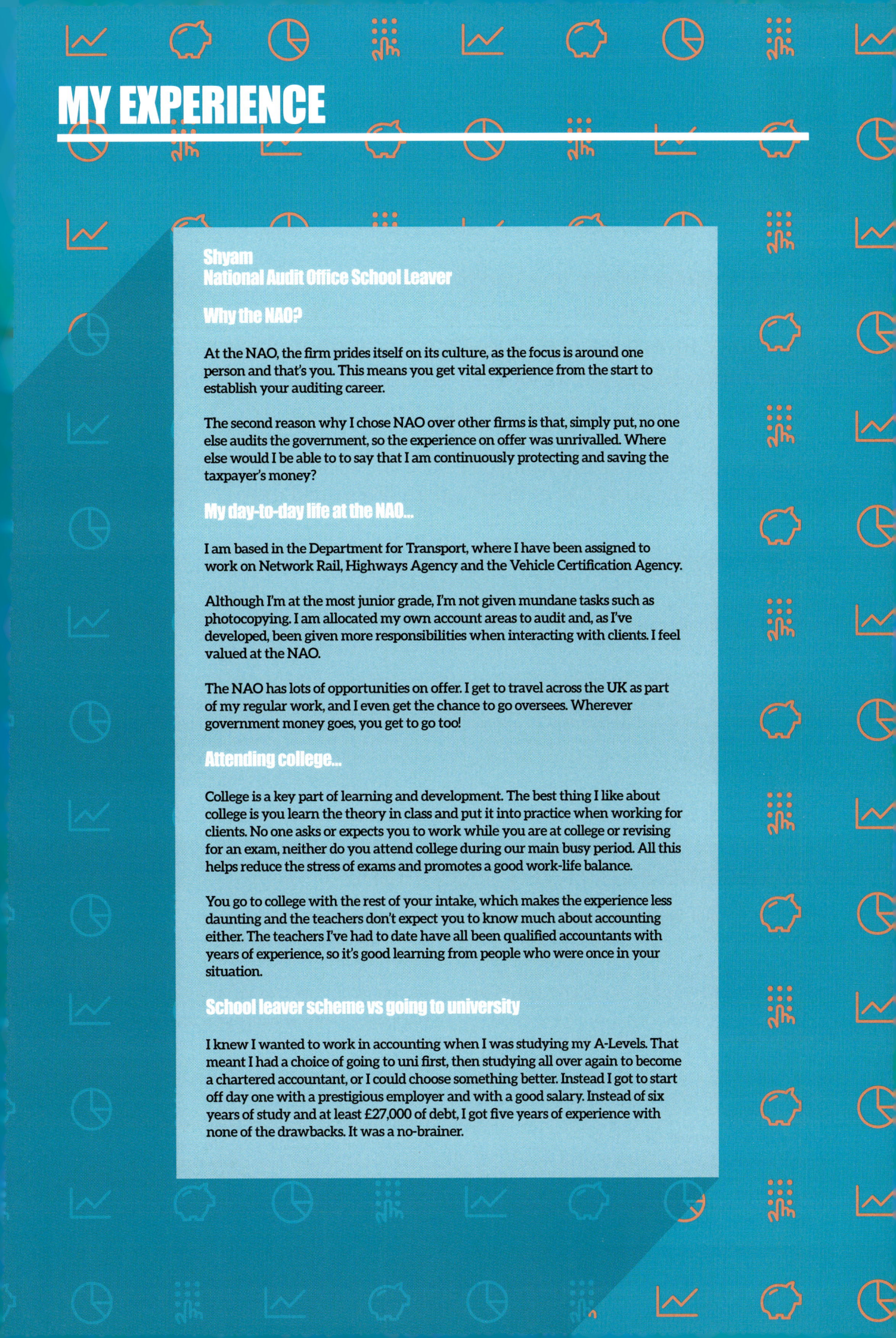

Imagine a career where you can investigate fraudulent activity and act as an expert witness in court? Or a career that gives you the opportunity to make a real difference, through making sure a charity has the funds to deliver its work? Perhaps you want to be in charge of a global business, or start up your own company?

As an ICAEW Chartered Accountant you'll have an exciting and fulfilling career, which will open the door to all of these opportunities – and more.

What do chartered accountants do?

Chartered accountants are people who tackle the most important challenges in business, using their skills and experience to help companies improve their performance, solve their financial problems and drive their future plans.

The role of chartered accountants goes much beyond the numbers. It requires analysis and interpretation. For example, calculating the worth of a company's physical goods may be straightforward, but how do you measure the value of a brand?

Chartered accountants are often involved in big, strategic decisions. Companies turn to them when they want advice on how risky a business proposal is, where they can improve efficiency and more. That's why so many move into Chief Executive Officer (CEO) and senior leadership roles.

Why become a chartered accountant?

You'll do meaningful, important work
Chartered accountants build trust because they give confidence that financial figures are true. Without this trust, there would be no investment or lending. Businesses would cease to operate, factories would grind to a halt and public services would go undelivered.

You'll have a prestigious qualification
Being 'chartered' means you're recognised as being at the top of the profession. It shows the world you have both the technical skills and the practical experience needed to tackle complex challenges.

You'll be financially well rewarded
Chartered accountants earn more. For those who qualify with ICAEW and work in business, the average salary globally is £90.2k.

You'll enjoy more opportunities
Go into chartered accountancy and you won't find a shortage of job opportunities. The accounting and professional services sector employs more students on Higher Apprenticeship and graduate programmes than any other.

You'll significantly enhance your long-term prospects
Chartered accountancy is widely recognised as a strong foundation for business leadership. In fact, almost one in four CEOs in the top 100 companies in the UK is a qualified chartered accountant.

You'll be able to take your skills anywhere
As a chartered accountant, your skills will always be in demand – and not just in organisations with a financial focus. You could help to run a sports team, an airline, a charity, a film company or an international relief effort even.

BUSINESS WITH CONFIDENCE

How to become an ICAEW Chartered Accountant

ICAEW is a world leading professional membership organisation that promotes, develops and supports over 147,000 chartered accountants worldwide. Through us, accountants can complete a globally-recognised professional qualification called the ACA and become ICAEW Chartered Accountants.

If you're about to leave school, there's more than one route to becoming an ICAEW Chartered Accountant. You can go straight to work or you can go to university first.

Whichever route you choose, you'll train for the globally recognised ACA qualification while working for an ICAEW authorised employer. Training to become an ICAEW Chartered Accountant is rigorous and challenging – but that's why our chartered accountants are always in demand.

Find your route

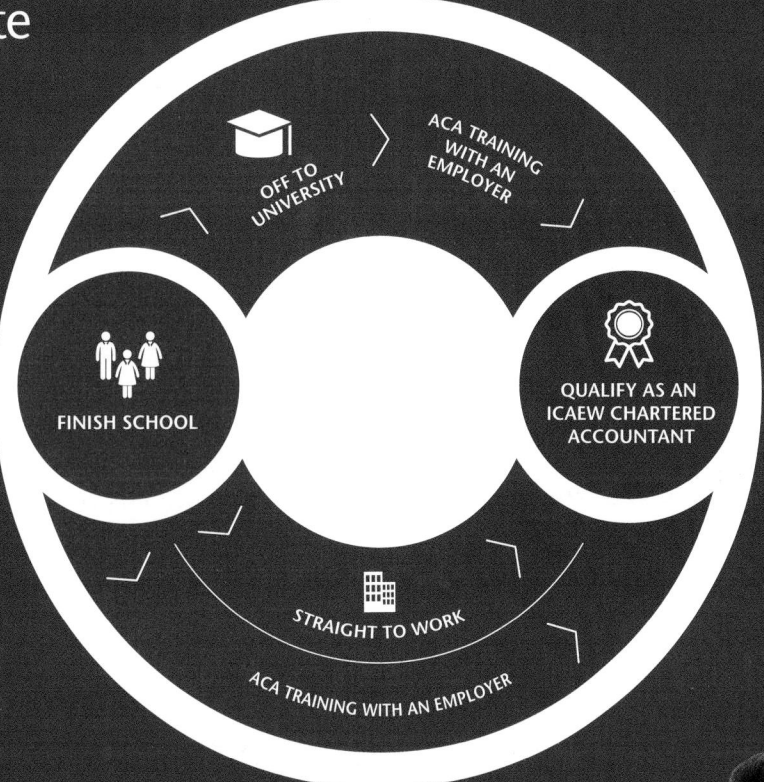

- FINISH SCHOOL
- OFF TO UNIVERSITY
- ACA TRAINING WITH AN EMPLOYER
- STRAIGHT TO WORK
- ACA TRAINING WITH AN EMPLOYER
- QUALIFY AS AN ICAEW CHARTERED ACCOUNTANT

> I'm currently studying the ACA through the EY school leaver programme. From beginning to end, the whole process should take five years, but it will be worth it. I've met a lot of people here who joined as school leavers and who are now in senior positions.

Laura Matthews, ACA Student, Assistant Tax Advisor at EY, UK

For more information on becoming an ICAEW Chartered Accountant, visit icaew.com/purepotential

ENTREPRENEURS

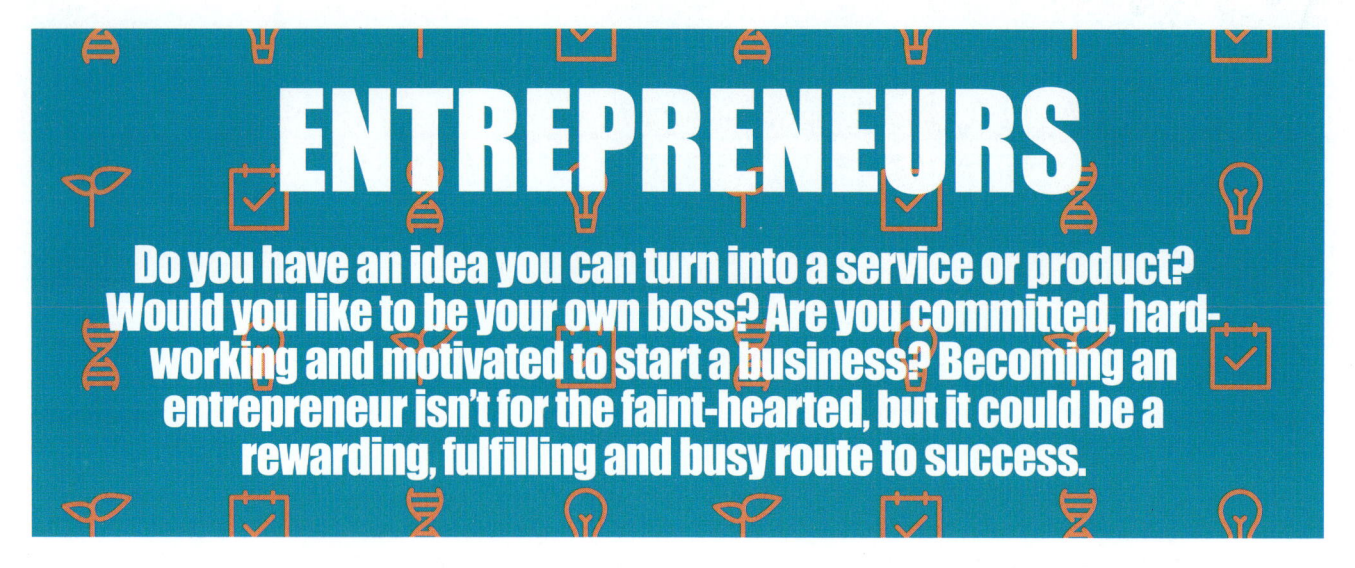

Do you have an idea you can turn into a service or product? Would you like to be your own boss? Are you committed, hard-working and motivated to start a business? Becoming an entrepreneur isn't for the faint-hearted, but it could be a rewarding, fulfilling and busy route to success.

You could start a business or social enterprise in any area that you can think of: it could be selling a service or product or you could be a successful middle man – think Uber (world's largest taxi company that owns no taxis), Netflix (world's largest movie house that owns no cinemas) and Facebook (most popular media owner that creates no content). There isn't a specific qualification you need to gain or a direct route through training to become an entrepreneur; it all depends on having the right skills, ideas, tenacity and determination. You might have developed some of these skills through your education, others might be natural to you and part of your character already. Either way, they will all be useful if you are considering starting a business of your own.

There are many skills and attributes you'll need to start your own business and here are just a few to get you thinking:

Creativity
Resilience
Risk-taking
Selling
Self-reflection
Leadership
Self-reliance
Forward planning
Motivation
Research and analysis
Planning and development
Fundraising
Budgeting
Trendspotting

USEFUL RESOURCES

www.entrepreneur.com

We've picked a few of these attributes to explore in more detail…

CREATIVITY
You'll need some ideas to get your business off the ground and you will need to get used to adapting to the changing situation around you with new innovative ideas to solve problems you may be faced with.

RISK-TAKING
You need to be bold, brave and confident and not shy away from taking risks. Take risk management very seriously but sometimes you may need to be prepared to take a leap of faith.

LEADERSHIP
You need to be able to convince people that your business is worth investing in and that you have the ability and commitment to lead the business.

FORWARD PLANNING
A clear vision for the future of your business is important to ensure your business stays relevant as things around you change.

MOTIVATION
With no set hours or a manager to keep track of your time you might find yourself working long hours so will need to stay motivated and focused on the end goal.

RESEARCH AND ANALYSIS
Identify potential customers, talk to them and find out if your idea is meeting a real need. Research your competitors and find out why they are a success, and how you could do even better.

PLANNING AND DEVELOPMENT
Test your product or service with real customers, make changes, and test it again. Keep doing this and tweaking your product until you're sure there is a demand for it.

FUNDRAISING
Explore different sources of business finance, from bank loans to government-backed schemes to private investors.

MY EXPERIENCE

Lauren Robinson
Founder of Engaging Communications

"I didn't always have a grand plan for setting up on my own, but I have always focused on what I enjoy, what my strengths are, and seeking opportunities to learn new skills.

After graduating from De Montfort University (Leicester) with a BA (Hons) Politics & Media, I joined a graduate programme at a public affairs company where I worked as an account handler. I soon realised that the parts of my job I most enjoyed were the marketing elements (the newsletters, the events, the collateral and meetings with key stakeholders) so I completed my Chartered Institute of Marketing Professional Diploma as a stepping stone. I changed industry and worked my way up to director of communications for a business process outsourcing business. Keen to widen my network and understand how other companies approach employee engagement, I sought out an opportunity to be seconded to Engage for Success. This is a movement dedicated to raising the profile of employee engagement and shining a light on good practise and was invaluable. I met so many great people and it gave me the confidence to set up my own business. I was keen to have a portfolio career: a more flexible approach to work while working with a wide variety of clients.

So in 2014, Engaging Communications (UK) was launched, a business to business (B2B) marketing and communications consultancy specialising in internal communications and employee engagement. The approach is simple, small companies and start-ups often cannot afford a dedicated marketing or internal communications team. Instead, they need these services on an ad hoc basis, so Engaging Communications acts as a virtual marketing team. It might be a stand-alone event, a change communication programme (for a company acquisition or restructure) or a rebrand. A company may need a marketing strategy developed, or a social media strategy to raise its online presence. They may want to focus on an employee engagement strategy or require marketing coaching to develop the team and provide advice. This variety and constant learning is what excites me."

Vinit Patel
Co-Founder of Excel With Business and an investor in start-ups

"I believe any young person can start and run their own business. No formal skills or experience are required. But you must be prepared to work hard relentlessly, and experiment. And your business needn't be an entirely brand new product or service that will take the world by storm; many great, successful businesses are small, local and simple.

With that mindset, I helped start an online skills training business (www.excelwithbusiness.com) as I was leaving university six years ago. We have since launched another business line, and I have personally invested in four other start-up businesses. All of these experiences are truly fascinating, as I get to work with a very diverse group of people tackling problems big and small.

When I was younger, I had no idea I'd end up where I am but I did know that I was prepared to work hard, challenge myself, be a nice guy as much as possible (important!) and never give up, especially when things get tough. I also got involved with as many business-related projects as I could, including:

- Young Enterprise. Excellent way to learn about starting a business. Ask your school about starting one with your peers.

- Target 2.0. Usually for students studying economics A-Level. If you don't study economics but are interested, ask if you can join their sessions.

- ICAEW BASE. Ask your school's business studies department to enter a team from your school.

- University (if you go) societies for business and entrepreneurship are brilliant and you meet lots of like-minded people.

- Start up loans are a great way to actually apply for funding to kick-start your own business idea (www.startuploans.co.uk).

Finally, if any of this interests you and you'd like some direct advice, I'm always happy to help. Please email me on vinit@filtered.com."

THE THIRD SECTOR

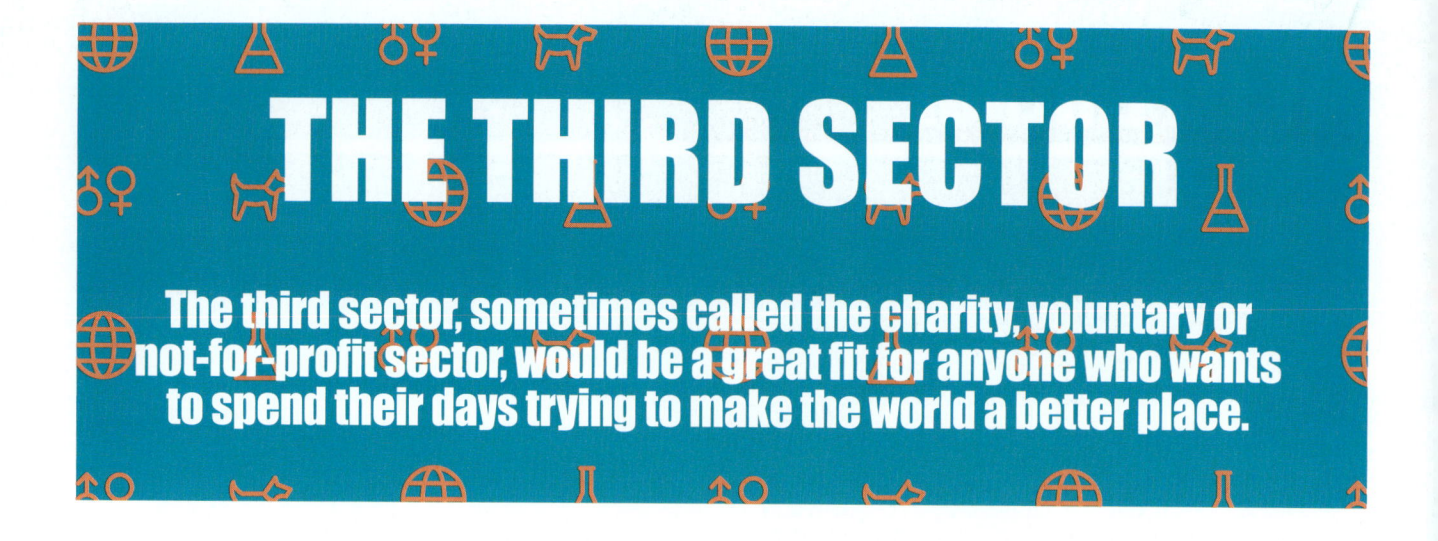

The third sector, sometimes called the charity, voluntary or not-for-profit sector, would be a great fit for anyone who wants to spend their days trying to make the world a better place.

The third sector is all about contributing to your community, helping other people and focusing on improving the future. Many people find working in the third sector to be a hugely rewarding experience. There are all sorts of third sector organisations out there, whether you want to work internationally or closer to home, with animals or children or adults, or focus on religion, human rights, sports or housing. In a smaller organisation, you're likely to need to be able to demonstrate a broad range of skills and a willingness to 'muck in' across all aspects of the organisation. This can be a great opportunity to really build your experience, which can then be applied to non-charity companies. In contrast, larger charities often look for people with specific skills or experience such as accountancy, project management or campaigning.

There are many different roles within this sector, and here are just a few to get you thinking:

Fundraiser
Corporate Account Manager
Policy and Research
Individual Giving Manager
Governance
Finance Director
Management
Team Administrator
Marketing Executive
Trust Fundraiser

USEFUL RESOURCES

www.purepotential.org
www.diana-award.org.uk
www.charityjob.co.uk
www.thirdsector.co.uk
www.vsointernational.org

We've picked a few interesting roles to explore in more detail...

FUNDRAISING
Fundraising is a key area for many charities and a growing area of graduate recruitment. It very much does what it says on the tin – you'll be raising money for the charity that you're working for in order to enable them to continue to function properly. Fundraising is all about building relationships and being innovative in thinking of new ways to increase contributions from people.

POLICY AND RESEARCH
Many non-governmental organisations (NGOs) and think tanks produce their own research exploring the ideas and issues that relate to their aims and focus areas. This research will normally culminate with some suggestions for policy changes.

CAMPAIGNING AND LOBBYING
Campaigners and lobbyists work on behalf of charities to try and change external policies and popular opinion for the better. They raise awareness of the charities' causes and work to influence and persuade the relevant people to effect change.

GOVERNANCE
Governance is key in making sure that a charitable organisation moves in the right direction, achieves its objectives and complies with all legal requirements. It's a big responsibility and governance is a great place to gain a broad knowledge of the whole organisation as you'll be working closely with all teams.

MANAGEMENT
Charities are made up of all sorts of management roles that you would find in other companies - from finance and IT to HR and project management. This is a great chance to put your specific skills to use in an area where you can make a difference.

MY EXPERIENCE

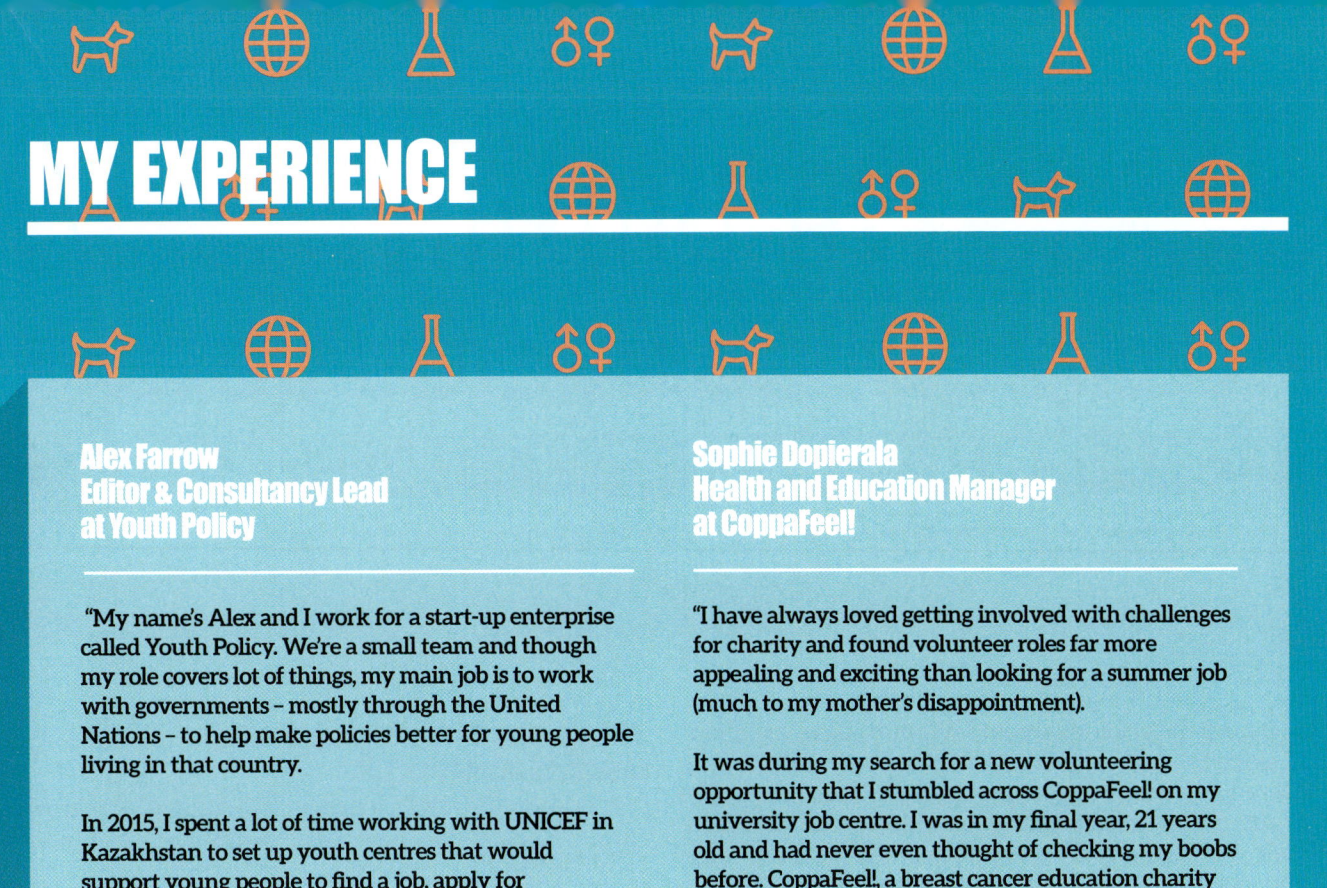

Alex Farrow
Editor & Consultancy Lead
at Youth Policy

"My name's Alex and I work for a start-up enterprise called Youth Policy. We're a small team and though my role covers lot of things, my main job is to work with governments – mostly through the United Nations – to help make policies better for young people living in that country.

In 2015, I spent a lot of time working with UNICEF in Kazakhstan to set up youth centres that would support young people to find a job, apply for university, get a health check-up or advice on a problem troubling them. It's about getting the government to provide all the things a young person needs to grow up, be happy, healthy, and know what to do with their future.

When I was at school, I had no idea that this kind of job existed. I always knew that I wanted to do something more than just earn money: I wanted to contribute in some way to society and make the world a better place. This wasn't just to 'do good' but to do something meaningful with my 50 years of work.

My training as an actor helps me deliver training and meet new people, and my masters from Birkbeck College (which I did part time while working full time) has given me the skills and critical thinking that's vital for my job.

We're not a charity – we're a social enterprise – and that can be tough work. When you're trying to create something of your own, not just join a company that's already up and running, it can mean a lot of late hours, demanding deadlines and never enough people around to help.

But doing a job that contributes to society, that creates jobs, and building our own organisation is what I love. Working for another company or organisation just isn't for me – I want the challenge!

I travel a lot for my job – maybe two weeks of every month – and that's both an adventure and a demand. But it is my favourite part of the job: getting to experience so many interesting places, people and cultures is pretty cool – especially as they aren't normally countries you would often go to on holiday."

Sophie Dopierala
Health and Education Manager
at CoppaFeel!

"I have always loved getting involved with challenges for charity and found volunteer roles far more appealing and exciting than looking for a summer job (much to my mother's disappointment).

It was during my search for a new volunteering opportunity that I stumbled across CoppaFeel! on my university job centre. I was in my final year, 21 years old and had never even thought of checking my boobs before. CoppaFeel!, a breast cancer education charity aimed at spreading the importance of being breast aware to younger audiences, struck a chord and I haven't looked back since. After volunteering for them in every role possible, I got the job as their first health and education manager. The title seems quite broad and that is for a good reason. Alongside my main responsibilities of running our school education programme and overseeing our #RETHINKCANCER campaign, I have found myself arranging photo shoots, writing scripts, doing media requests and running a fundraising campaign. A small charity allows you to try your hand at many different things and really develop your skills across the spectrum. No day is the same and I often find myself out and about in the community with volunteers. If you love working with people and being faced with new challenges, this is certainly the sector for you.

The third sector does have it's downsides and aside from the obvious (no big banker bonus each year), it can often mean working extra hours, being under-resourced and having to create your own structure. However, the enthusiasm, passion and dedication to making the world a better place really does shine through in this sector and you can certainly look forward to working alongside inspirational people and returning home knowing your job matters – feeling that is ultimately way better (in my opinion anyway) than a bonus that would soon be spent!"

TECHNOLOGY

One of the best things about this industry is that you will find yourself at the cutting-edge of the latest ideas that can help the world be a better place: healthier (see Big Health), more convenient (see Apple Pay), more global (see Facebook and Skype) and more fun (see Angry Birds!).

Although it is obviously important to have excellent IT skills to work in this sector, other soft skills are required for many roles, such as an ability to solve problems, be creative and be able to communicate well. You will work within a team to develop ideas and make them a reality. You'll be pleased to hear that many big companies like Google and Facebook are renowned for their innovative efforts to create a happy workplace culture. For example, at the Google office, there is a room full of sweets that all employees and visitors can help themselves to!

There are many different roles within this sector, and here are just a few to get you thinking:

Software Engineer
IT Manager
Games Developer
Software Programmer
App Developer
Website Manager
Systems Analyst
Information Security Analyst
Technical Support
Network Engineer
Business Analyst
Product Manager
Networks and Systems Manager
Web Designer

We've picked a few interesting roles to explore in more detail...

IT MANAGER
You'll need excellent organisational skills for this role, because you'll be in charge of every aspect of a project, including timings, budget, and being the point of contact between your team and the client.

SOFTWARE PROGRAMMER
If you love coding, and you want to learn more about creating websites and apps, and languages such as Python and C++ make sense to you, then there are a huge number of roles at a wide range of companies that need your skills. Attention to detail is essential here, as one tiny error in a complex code can mean the making or breaking of a website.

INFORMATION SECURITY ANALYST
We have all read the news about hackers exposing company secrets, stealing bank details and causing major websites to malfunction – but how do we stop them? Defence against cyber attacks is a huge and growing industry that helps companies protect their data through prevention and keeping track of threats. To do this role you'll need to analyse evidence and make educated guesses on the hackers' next move as well as build relationships with the media, government or other influencers, depending on your client.

USEFUL RESOURCE

www.thetechpartnership.com
www.techcrunch.com

MY EXPERIENCE

Matilde
Data Scientist at Excel with Business

"I work as a data scientist at a company called Excel with Business. We create personalised online training in essential business skills. Using algorithms, we train people in what they don't know and leave out the stuff they do know.

My role is to help design the algorithm that selects the best possible syllabus for each individual learner. How? Using machine learning algorithms to look at the data we have already and calculate the most probable set of subjects for this new student, after comparing their profile with the historic data. And those predictions get better each time, as we update our databases whenever someone uses our courses. The job at Excel with Business appealed to me because I get to deal with data and use my programming skills to develop and improve the algorithm that selects the optimal course.

Researching new techniques and dealing with data are the favourite parts of my job! I am no stranger to research and learning new topics, as I did a PhD in Particle Physics from Queen Mary University of London. The subject of my PhD was to analyse data coming from one experiment called ATLAS, from the CERN laboratory in Switzerland. ATLAS is a particle accelerator that is as high as seven buildings and is designed to study the fundamental forces and particles that constitute our universe. My focus was on one of these particles, called the top quark. I studied its properties and proved that it was detected with ATLAS, if the conditions were optimal.

This study implied braving through terabytes of data to discover the signal I was looking for. Not an easy task and it involved a lot of computer programming, statistics and, of course, physics knowledge!

Who would know that, by choosing a degree in Physics, I would end up as a data scientist! I'd never have guessed it, but I definitely like it!"

Andrew
Technical Consultant at Softcat

"As a Microsoft Technical Consultant within Softcat's Professional Services department, the majority of my time is spent working directly with Softcat's customers to design and build identity and email solutions with a focus on Microsoft's server technologies.

I've been interested in technology, and specifically computing, from an early age when I first started learning how to use my family's first home computer, a Sinclair ZX Spectrum 48K in the 1980s! I'd played video games at home, but being able to build your own programmes is really what fired my imagination about what computing and technology could do so I pursued the sciences at school and A-Levels at college. I studied Computer Systems Engineering (MEng) at the University of Sussex in Brighton as this would give me a solid grounding in both electronics and software engineering.

After graduation I started work as a systems engineer researching synthetic environments for training at the Defence Evaluation Research Agency (DERA), once part of the Ministry of Defence. After a few years I decided that a research position wasn't really for me, I wanted to be in role where I could build the solutions as well as design them so I moved to an IT managed services company in London. Here, I continued to build upon the skills that I rely upon today as a consultant, to understand a requirement and how to design and troubleshoot a solution to a problem.

Working as a consultant means that I deal with a range of customers from small businesses to large multi-nationals and as a result I get to work with different people and projects on a regular basis. This is great for me because the problems I encounter will be different from customer to customer so it keeps my skills current and most of all interested and engaged with what I love to do. Because of the project based nature of the job, I don't necessarily work a regular 9-5, but considering the amount of satisfaction I derive from a job well done, I can take this in my stride."

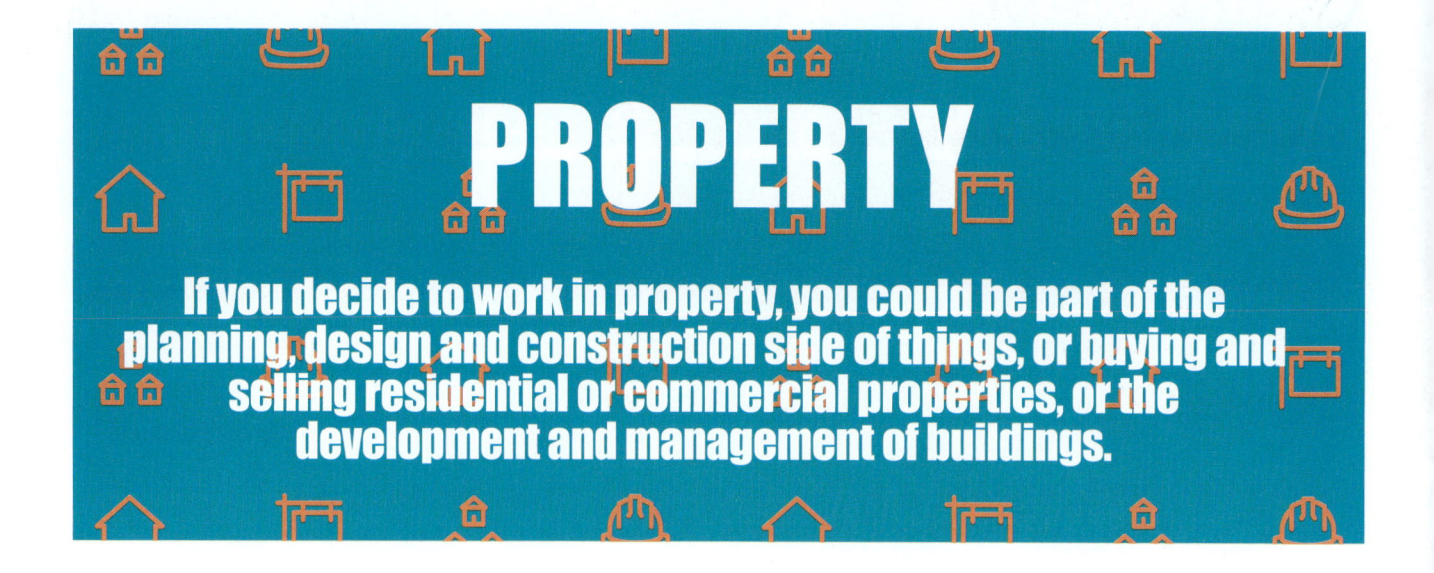

PROPERTY

If you decide to work in property, you could be part of the planning, design and construction side of things, or buying and selling residential or commercial properties, or the development and management of buildings.

The property sector can be particularly enjoyable because you are dealing with real buildings that can bring to life the work you are doing – which is great for job satisfaction. There are a huge variety of careers, regionally and in the cities, dealing with the buying and selling of homes (think Kirstie and Phil on 'Location, Location, Location') to the planning of a new block or flats, or designing and building a brand-new state-of-the-art gleaming office tower, redoing a crumbling old country estate or national treasure, to the management of an entire shopping mall like the Bullring or Westfield - there is something for everyone, so it's worth looking into.

There are many different roles within this sector, and here are just a few to get you thinking:

Town Planner
Chartered Surveyor
Project Manager
Developer
Investor
Engineer
Construction Worker
Architect
Interior Designer
Commercial Property Manager
Portfolio Manager
Landlord
Estate Agent

We've picked a few interesting roles to explore on more detail...

COMMERCIAL PROPERTY MANAGER
To manage a commercial property requires a wide range of activities including ensuring rent is collected on time, negotiating the terms of leases and contracts to get the best deal for the owner of the property, and ensuring the property is well maintained, secure and complies to regulations. The property could be anything that isn't residential – a restaurant, retail park or even a car park!

TOWN PLANNER
This is an important role that has a significant impact on the appearance and purpose of towns and cities across the country. Their roles is to ensure that the development of a building or piece of land is done in compliance with certain rules and preserves the local environment. Graduates from any degree subject can get into town planning, although specific degrees in planning are available.

CHARTERED SURVEYOR
Surveyors design, build, manage, value and protect everything from skyscrapers to shopping centres, industrial sites to houses, woods to big rural estates – in fact, everything you see around you. There are three main areas in which surveyors work, and these are land, construction and infrastructure, and property. You could be involved in everything from the purchase and sale of properties, to their development, management and valuation, and to helping to manage and change landscapes to fit in with the environment. A career in surveying is definitely not your standard 9-5 desk job so, if you'd like to work in a sociable industry with opportunities to get out and about and to see the tangible outcomes of your work, this could be the career for you.

USEFUL RESOURCES

www.apropertycareer.co.uk
www.naea.co.uk
www.rtpi.org.uk

RREF
Reading Real Estate Foundation
Registered charity no. 1092627

Have you ever wondered how properties are developed, who is responsible for them and how much they are worth?

You may know something about pursuing a career in law or even accounting but working in property is not so well known – even though there are countless career opportunities. Want to know what they are?

Pathways to Property

Pathways to Property is a free programme led by Reading Real Estate Foundation at the University of Reading for sixth form students. Supported by British Land and some of the biggest players in the real estate sector and by the Sutton Trust, the programme will help you find out where a career in property could lead.

Opportunities include:
- A free residential Summer School at the University of Reading each July
- Industry led talks in schools throughout the year
- A mentoring programme
- Work experience placements in real estate firms

Pathways to Property introduces careers in property by connecting you with those already working in the sector. Industry volunteers from some of property's leading firms work with students across the programme to share their expertise and talk about their routes into the profession.

For further information and to get involved visit
www.reading.ac.uk/pathways-to-property
or email pathways2property@rref.reading.ac.uk

'The talks from the graduates were very inspiring. I would definitely recommend the summer school to anyone.'

Anita, Summer School participant

'The experience improved my understanding of the various ways to pursue a career in property and it gave me an insight into higher education courses in property and real estate.'

Toni, Summer School participant

Henley Business School
UNIVERSITY OF READING

ENGINEERING

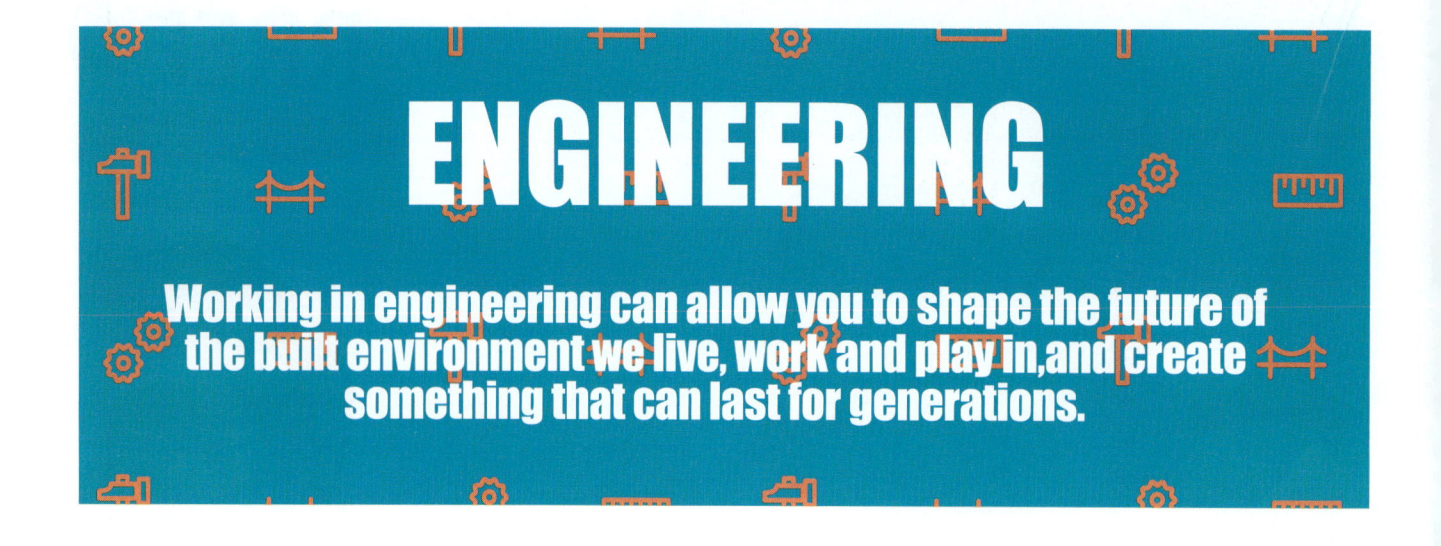

Working in engineering can allow you to shape the future of the built environment we live, work and play in, and create something that can last for generations.

You get to see designs turned into reality and can work to help overcome some of the biggest problems faced in society today – whether it be preparing for a natural disaster or implementing infrastructure to aid development in countries around the world. Engineering and construction is relied upon by every single person, every day. If you're interested in the design and structure of buildings, the way things work, have a lot of creative ideas, like solving problems, and want a practical and varied career then this could be the ideal industry for you.

There are many jobs within this sector, and here are just a few to get you thinking:

- Industrial Engineer
- Civil and Structural Engineer
- Electrical Engineer
- Computer Engineer
- Architect or Architectural Assistant
- Aerospace Engineer
- Manufacturing Engineer
- Mechanical Engineer
- Agriculture & Biosystems Engineer
- Nuclear Engineer

USEFUL RESOURCES

www.discovere.org
www.educatingengineers.com
www.theiet.org/

We've picked a few interesting roles to explore in more detail...

INDUSTRIAL ENGINEER
If you are highly organised and like things to be efficient, you could consider career as an industrial engineer. They ensure that systems run optimally in range of settings that create a product or provide a service. This job involves meticulous logistical planning, managing staff, machinery, tools and technology as well as eliminating waste, including wasting time!

CIVIL AND STRUCTURAL ENGINEERING
As a civil engineer you would plan, design and manage a variety of construction projects. You could work on everything from bridges and tall buildings to transport links and sports stadia. These tend to be very long term projects, sometimes taking a decade to complete! You'll need to test them to ensure they can withstand all weather conditions, as well as natural and other disasters such as earthquakes, bombs or accidents.

AEROSPACE ENGINEER
Imagine what it might be like to work on a real space craft! You may also work on more planet earth-based projects such as aeroplanes, military jets, high speed trains or even a submarine! This career is varied and fascinating and requires working with the latest technologies.

MANUFACTURING ENGINEER
Working on the manufacturing process of anything from oil we put in our cars, the food we eat, the drinks we consume or the medicine we take to make ourselves better could be the career for you if you have close attention to detail and use the technical skills you learn along the way to invent or improve upon processes, and solve some of the problems the world faces.

MY EXPERIENCE

James Horn
Apprentice Engineer
at Virgin Trains

"I've always had a slight interest in engineering. I've spent my life around old cars and since around the age of seven, I've helped my dad repair and restore cars. My high school encouraged people to look into engineering due to the large amount of engineering opportunities in the local area around Edinburgh. In my sixth year of school, my teacher informed me of the engineering apprenticeship scheme run by the local college. Applicants fill out a form, sit an aptitude test and have an interview – this information is then sent to several different companies who decide if they want to give you an interview. The interview wasn't too bad but I was surprised when I got the job because I didn't think my interview was that great due to nerves!

In the three years I've been with the company, I've done everything from changing light bulbs to replacing full engines. The opportunities within the company to take part in different tasks are amazing. I've also taken part in modification and improvement projects. Personally, I prefer to work on mechanical jobs but you do feel good when you solve an electrical fault.

The apprenticeship has given me lots of different opportunities to learn new skills. I've also had the chance to travel around the country and work with other companies. The social aspect is good too - the apprentices regularly plan trips, events and nights out together. The only thing I'm not a fan of is the 30-mile drive to work. The start and finish times put me right in the worst traffic!

After my apprenticeship finishes, I plan to stay with the company as long as possible. The job and wages are too good to throw away. The experience and qualifications I've gained also mean I could easily move on to a new career in Canada or the US. I would definitely recommend the railway as a career. It's very unpredictable, so rarely gets boring. Plus, it really is a job for life. I'm now 21 with a promising career, good friends, a steady above-average income and no student debt. All thanks to the railway!"

Jessica Dabrowski
Chartered Building Surveyor at
Lambert Smith Hampton

"I have always had an interest in property and the idea of undertaking a self-build project one day. At school I spent my Year 12 work experience with the building control department at my local council. Each day was spent visiting different building sites and discussing with the contractor how they were meeting the building regulations. I also spent a week with a residential building surveyor at a local estate agent, and a week in a commercial property practice in Bristol. This gave me a real insight into the work that building surveyors do.

I undertook a full-time BSc (Hons) in Building Surveying at the University of Reading, graduating in 2012. I undertook three separate summer placements in my second year of university and was offered a job on graduation with one of the firms.

I have recently passed the Assessment of Professional Competence set by the Royal Institution of Chartered Surveyors (RICS). This is a globally recognised qualification and the benchmark that all surveyors aspire to achieve.

I now work in a commercial property practice, inspecting commercial, retail and industrial properties. My day-to-day activities include inspection and advising clients of the expected cost and time frame to repair the property, meeting contractors to discuss and procure refurbishment works, and taking written and photographic records of the condition of properties prior to a tenant taking a lease.

The best part of my job is that I get out of the office regularly, visiting different properties and speaking to a variety of people including clients, contractors and tenants.

The worst part of my job is that I have to climb a lot of ladders and I'm scared of heights!"

RETAIL

The retail industry employs almost 3 million people in the UK and generates over £250 billion a year in sales. It's a fast-paced industry that must keep up with customer demand and even predict future trends.

Retail covers everything you can think of that you buy; from fast-moving consumer goods (FMCG) such as soft drinks, toiletries, over-the-counter drugs and processed foods, to clothing, furniture, cars and luxury goods. Working in retail doesn't just mean working on a shop floor, there are many exciting areas you can get involved in, from the source of the product to the consumer.

If you love shopping (both online and in-store), and you have excellent communication skills, like to use your initiative, and are prepared to work hard, then whatever products you love, you could find yourself working for a company that sells them. The retail sector workforce is on the rise, with the biggest growth in online shopping (think ASOS, Ocado and Amazon), so IT skills can be extremely useful.

There are many jobs within this sector, and here are just a few to get you thinking:

Food Production Technologist
Visual Merchandiser
Fashion Buyer
Textile Technologist
Quality Assurance
Production Manager
Ordering and Logistics Manager Purchasing Manager
Textile Designer
Visual Merchandiser
Supply Manager

USEFUL RESOURCES

www.arts.ac.uk/fashion
www.retailchoice.com
www.textilehouse.co.uk

We've picked a few interesting roles to explore in more detail...

VISUAL MERCHANDISER
Visual merchandisers will come up with a visual concept that will promote brands and increase sales. Their role could include dressing a shop window, developing an in-store feature, or designing photo shoots and catalogues. Most visual merchandisers are employed by retail stores, but could also be self-employed and offer consultancy to brands or smaller shops, or be employed by a national brand where they travel around to different stockists. You don't need to be a graduate to enter this profession, but some FE colleges have foundation degrees that specialise in this area if you are interested in learning more about the role. Many visual merchandisers work their way up from the shop floor.

LOGISTICS MANAGER
Logistics is the process from the point that someone makes an order online through manufacture to storage and distribution. There are many pressures and constraints to consider, particularly at peak times such as Christmas, so it requires very effective management. The main aim is to get A to B in the most cost-effective, fast and environmentally friendly way possible. Many major retailers have graduate schemes to enter logistics and this area of work is only set to need more employees as online sales increase.

TEXTILE TECHNOLOGIST
Textile technologists design, develop and produce fibres, yarns and fabrics. They work in a range of areas including research and development, engineering, production and quality control. If you're interested in fabrics and have lots of creative ideas to develop new uses for textiles, this job could suit you well.

FASHION BUYER
Buyers usually work closely with designers or brands, and ensure that suitable items are purchased for their stores. For example, the fashion buyer at a boutique will know the local clientele and buy clothing and accessories they believe will sell. Buyers attend trade fairs, wholesale showrooms and fashion shows to observe trends, so it can be a very exciting and sociable career.

MY EXPERIENCE

Alice Austin, Harrods School Leaver Programme Alumni

Why the Harrods Retail Academy?

"It was everything I was looking for. Not only is Harrods one of the most amazing department stores, but the idea of three different six-month rotations also appealed to me, as I love to continuously learn and progress."

How would you sum up the programme?

"It is the perfect way for passionate and dynamic individuals to kick-start their career in retail management."

What opportunities has it brought you?

"Working with the best brands in the world, serving prestigious clients and successfully delivering three retail projects."

Most memorable moment?

"It would have to be taking a trip to the distribution centre at Thatcham and also the Harrods at Heathrow Terminals. It was really interesting to see the 'behind the scenes' aspect of the business and also to see how we lay out the Heathrow Terminals to suit our international customers' shopping habits."

What did you find challenging?

"Balancing training commitments with shop floor experience. Attending courses, preparing presentations, calling clients, visual merchandising and getting to know your brand is a lot to accomplish! Now I carry a notepad and pen everywhere I go."

Best thing about working at Harrods?

"Every day is different; there's never a dull moment. I learnt new skills and systems and made friends for life."

Riki Brockman Apprentice Cutter at Gieves and Hawkes

"We have been making bespoke suits the same way on Savile Row for over 200 years. Famous for its history and its royal, celebrity and civilian clients, the street is synonymous with quality, luxury, and world-class service. It's hardly a wonder then, that this is an amazing place to work. Recently, there has been a real resurgence of employment on the Row. Since 2004, over 50 new apprentices have been introduced to the various tailoring houses on Mayfair's infamous golden mile.

I currently work at Gieves & Hawkes, No1. Savile Row, as an apprentice cutter. The role of the cutter is varied. It's our job to consult with each individual customer about cloth choice (there are over 15,000 to choose from) and style details. We take measurements and body configurations and make an individual paper pattern that reflects their unique body shape, chalk around the pattern, chop it out of the cloth and give it to the tailors to sew, fit the suit onto the customer (making notes of any alterations), rip it down flat and completely re-cut it! This can happen three or four times for a new customer. Evidently, there is a lot to learn, which is why it takes in excess of five years to become a fully fledged bespoke cutter. Although this may seem like a long time, it's a small price to pay for the knowledge that, when it comes to this specific skill, will literally make you one of the best in the world.

Unfortunately, there is no guiding light on how to become a tailor or cutter. You don't need a degree or five A-Levels, but everybody has to do their time as an apprentice. One of my colleagues studied as an architect, and trained at a military tailors in the city. Another studied engineering and started selling ready-to-wear suits for extra pocket money at uni. I obtained a first-class degree in drama and film studies, and then went back to college to undertake a bespoke tailoring course, before being offered my apprenticeship at Gieves. There are many different routes in, but most houses on the Row will want to see some evidence of tailoring or sewing, which means doing a course or finding some practical experience.

The process of making a bespoke suit is both a technical discipline and a creative discipline. Despite what they show in the movies, not one person alone creates the entire garment. Up to six people can be involved in any one suit, so there are lots of potential career options. Each role is specialised to ensure consistency and brilliance throughout every part of the process. Cutters, coat makers, waistcoat makers, trouser makers, finishers (who make beautiful button holes by hand) and pressers all work together towards the same goal: to make the finest hand-made suits in the world."

START YOUR STORY

Do you want to work for a global business with lots of famous brands and innovative ideas?
Working in our forward-thinking business, you'll gain invaluable experience and be given real responsibility from the start!

"MY APPRENTICESHIP HAS JUMP-STARTED MY CAREER. I'M GAINING UNPARALLELED EXPERIENCE, A WEALTH OF SKILLS AND KNOWLEDGE AND FORMING REAL CONNECTIONS WITH INSPIRING PEOPLE WHO ARE TRULY PASSIONATE TO HELP ME DEVELOP."

Samantha Whitbread, Business Administration

MY EXPERIENCE

Charlotte Mitchell
Food Operations Apprenticeship at Nestlé

"Before joining Nestlé, I was studying for A-Levels at sixth form and decided that I wanted work experience that would lead me to a career. The scheme was recommended to me through a friend who already worked at Nestlé in York. I chose the food operations apprenticeship because of diversity of the job. As part of the scheme I spend four six-month placements in departments such as KitKat and Polo. This means that I have the opportunity to understand four completely different types of machinery and fully understand the importance of each department to the business. From this, I am gaining hands-on production experience, as I am running multimillion-pound machines that are producing tonnes of product each shift. Therefore, I am responsible for the machines I run.

Through the apprenticeship, I have become a functioning member of my shift by attending meetings and representing my area. The scheme allows me time to study towards my Level 3 in Food Industry Skills by collecting work-based evidence for my portfolio.

On a day-to-day basis, I complete work around safety, quality and hygiene, which means there is a lot of variation and I am able to spot problems quickly. I have developed my problem-solving and teamwork skills around the challenges I faced. Working shifts on a rotation also means I enjoy some great time off – four and five days off at a time, which is ideal for hobbies such as going to the gym.

At the end of my apprenticeship I hope to become a process operator in the factory in one of the areas I have worked in and hope to eventually become a shift manager."

LAW

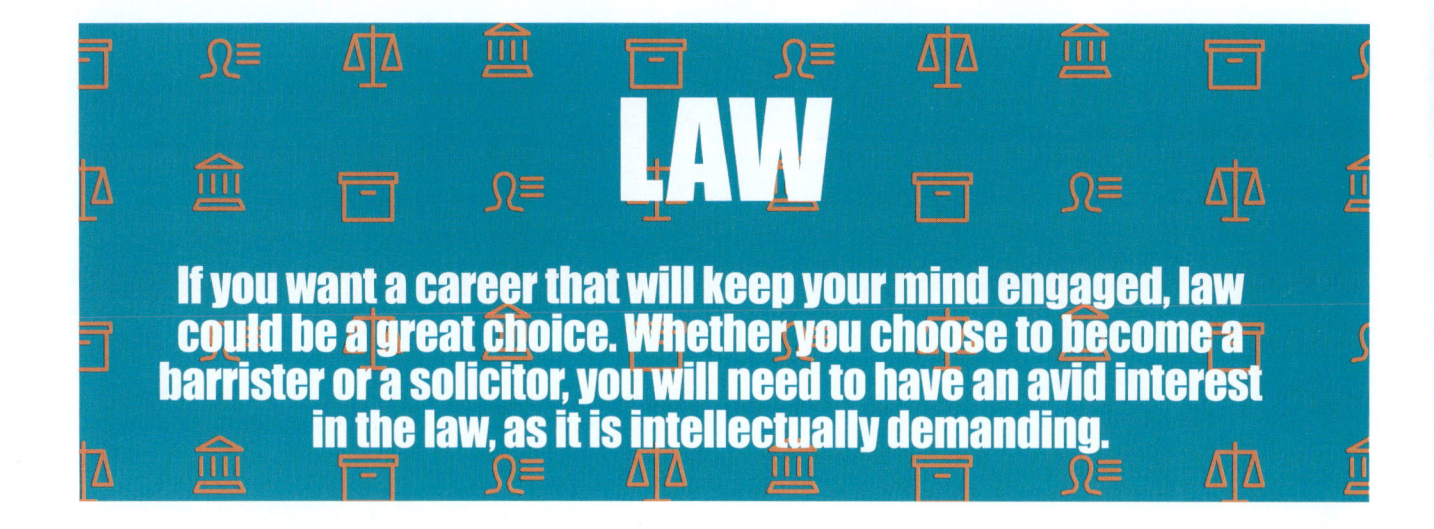

If you want a career that will keep your mind engaged, law could be a great choice. Whether you choose to become a barrister or a solicitor, you will need to have an avid interest in the law, as it is intellectually demanding.

Every aspect of our society is governed by law and, accordingly, there are all kinds of lawyers. Whatever your interests, there will be an area of law governing it and legal professionals practising it.

If you feel passionately about human rights or international politics, a career in public or European law may await you. If you find yourself attracted to business and commerce, you might find a perfect home in one of the big City firms. If you find yourself waiting with bated breath for the new edition of *Heat* to fall through your letterbox, defamation and media law could be the area for you. The rewards of a career in law are as varied as the different areas of practice. Corporate law in a large firm will bring with it a secure and hefty salary. Criminal law may provide the satisfaction of preserving an innocent person's liberty or ensuring that the guilty are brought to account.

Many lawyers would say that the main attraction of working in the law is the intellectual challenge it presents.

The law is evolving all the time. Textbooks are changed and revised constantly, as new concepts come to light and new rights are recognised. This means that lawyers in all fields are always innovating and adapting to new circumstances.

You DO NOT need to study law at university to become a lawyer. Thinking that studying law is a must is the most common misconception that students have about a legal career. Whether you want to work as a legal executive, city lawyer, in family law, at an international firm, as an in-house lawyer or as a barrister for a chamber, there are a number of routes in, and studying law as an undergraduate student at university is not the only one. In fact, some law firms prefer students who have broader interests and have studied something other than law.

There are three main routes into law, outlined below.

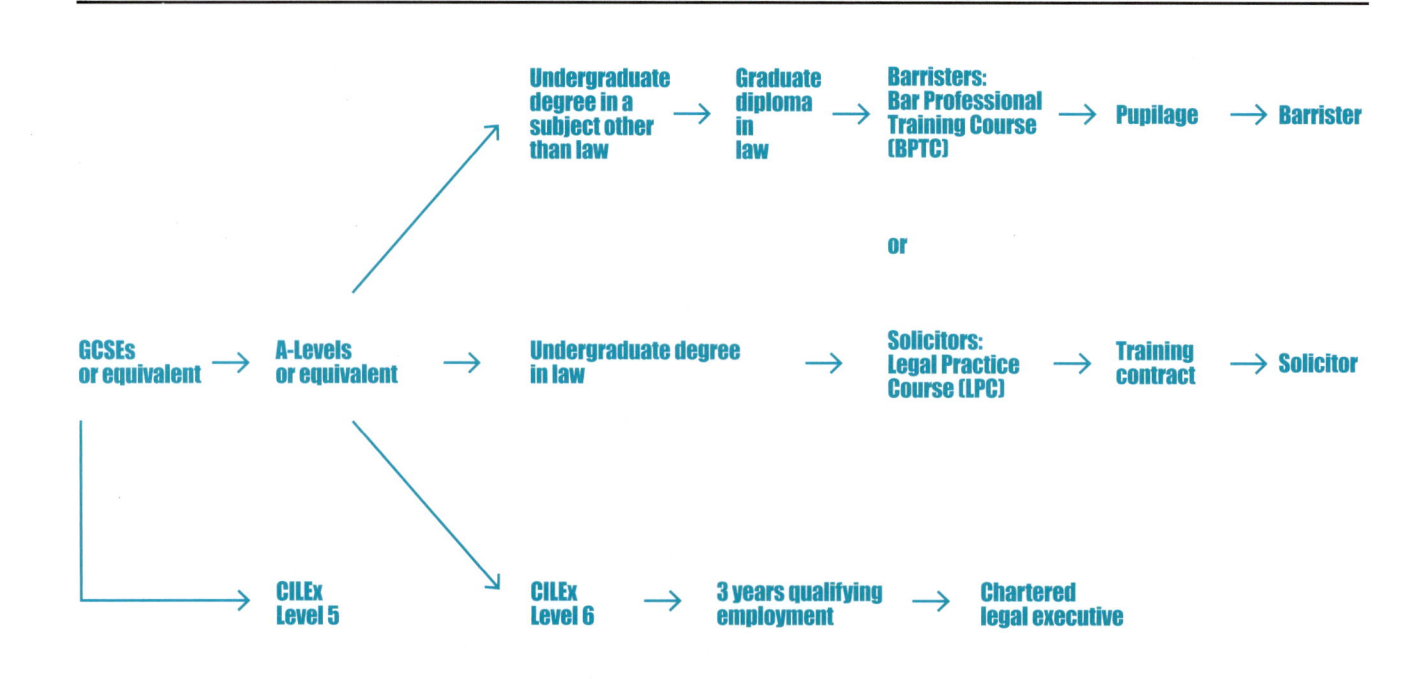

Route 1: GCSEs or equivalent → A-Levels or equivalent → Undergraduate degree in a subject other than law → Graduate diploma in law → Barristers: Bar Professional Training Course (BPTC) → Pupilage → Barrister

or

Route 2: GCSEs or equivalent → A-Levels or equivalent → Undergraduate degree in law → Solicitors: Legal Practice Course (LPC) → Training contract → Solicitor

Route 3: GCSEs or equivalent → CILEx Level 5 → CILEx Level 6 → 3 years qualifying employment → Chartered legal executive

There are many jobs within this sector, and here are just a few to get you thinking:

Solicitor
In-house Lawyer
Barrister
Legal Executive
Judge
Paralegal
Researcher for the Law Commission
Court Usher
Conveyancer
Legal Secretary

USEFUL RESOURCES

www.l2b.thelawyer.com
www.cilex.org.uk
www.lawsociety.org.uk
www.barcouncil.org.uk www.theiop.org

COURT USHER
A court usher is a position in a law court. You will need to escort participants to the courtroom, check that witnesses, defendants and lawyers are all present, direct the taking of oaths, correctly label evidence and handle it carefully where required, ensure the secure transaction of legal documents within the courtroom and decide the order of cases. You'll need to have strong people skills to deal with every member of the courtroom.

LEGAL SECRETARY
Legal secretaries are an essential part of all legal practices, and this career oath can be an excellent way to embark on a legal career without committing to further study. If you enjoy the work that you do, you can upskill as you go along, gaining law qualifications while you work.

CONVEYANCER
A licensed conveyancer is someone who deals specifically with property transactions, so you would only need to gain the knowledge and qualifications for this specific area of law, i.e. the buying and selling of domestic and commercial properties. This qualification can be gained without going to university, so you avoid racking up debt.

PARALEGAL
A paralegal is a person qualified through education and training to perform substantive legal work that requires knowledge of the law and procedures but who is not a qualified solicitor or barrister, although their work does overlap. They usually specialise in just one specific area of law and become an expert in it.

Paralegal job roles vary depending on where you work and the experience and qualifications you have – you could work for a huge firm being part of a large team, or at a high-street solicitor assisting on smaller contracts. Work can range from administrative and legal secretarial tasks to undertaking research and providing legal information to clients. You will need to have excellent communication skills to deal with clients from a wide range of backgrounds, and manage your time well to meet deadlines.

It is common for a budding solicitor to work as a paralegal for a year or two while they apply for training contracts.

SOLICITOR
To succeed as a solicitor, you need to be determined and willing to work hard. It will take at least three years to train if you are a law graduate, at least four years if you are a non-law graduate and at least six years if you are not a graduate. It is intellectually challenging, and there are a wide range of areas you can specialise in, including family law, criminal law, banking and finance law and corporate law.

JUDGE
Judges are the public officers who decide cases in a law court, and you will probably have seen them portrayed in film and television. They preside over court proceedings, sometimes as part of a panel. Judges are only appointed by the Judicial Appointments Commission after practising law for a number of years; you cannot train to be a judge straight from school or university.

MY EXPERIENCE

Nilufar Anwar
In-house Solicitor at
EDF Energy
(Litigation and Commercial)

"I attended UCL and studied physiology and pharmacology, as I loved science. After graduation, I was torn between applying to study medicine or go into law and so I did work experience in both fields and had lots of conversations with doctors and lawyers about their jobs – what they liked, disliked, what I should take into consideration when making my decision, and a honest overview of what a career in each field entailed. I quickly decided I wanted to do law as I loved problem solving, debating, and generally preferred working in an office environment compared to working in hospitals. I underwent the GDL and LPC at BBP University and put in good effort to secure a training contract at Hogan Lovells LLP. I then moved to King & Spalding LLP, working on incredibly interesting cases concerning fraud and commercial litigation. I wanted to have a deeper understanding of how legal advice was implemented in business and how it changed from advice to a reality. This drove my move to EDF Energy, where I advise colleagues from all over the business, from directors to people who run the power stations to people who deal with customer complaints on the telephone. As a solicitor advocate, it is my job to help ensure that the company is fulfilling its legal, contractual and regulatory obligations, that it has limited exposure to risk, and that its customers and employees are working in a safe environment. I act as a troubleshooter, so when a team within the business has a legal hurdle to overcome they contact my team to explain the issue and then we work together to formulate a solution. Last week, I visited a power station to understand how certain remedial work was being carried out and I worked with health and safety professionals in the company to ensure it was being done in a safe way according to the zero-harm safety policy. I love my job and I work with great people who are passionate about what they do. Plus, I get to check out nuclear power stations – what more could one desire in their job?!"

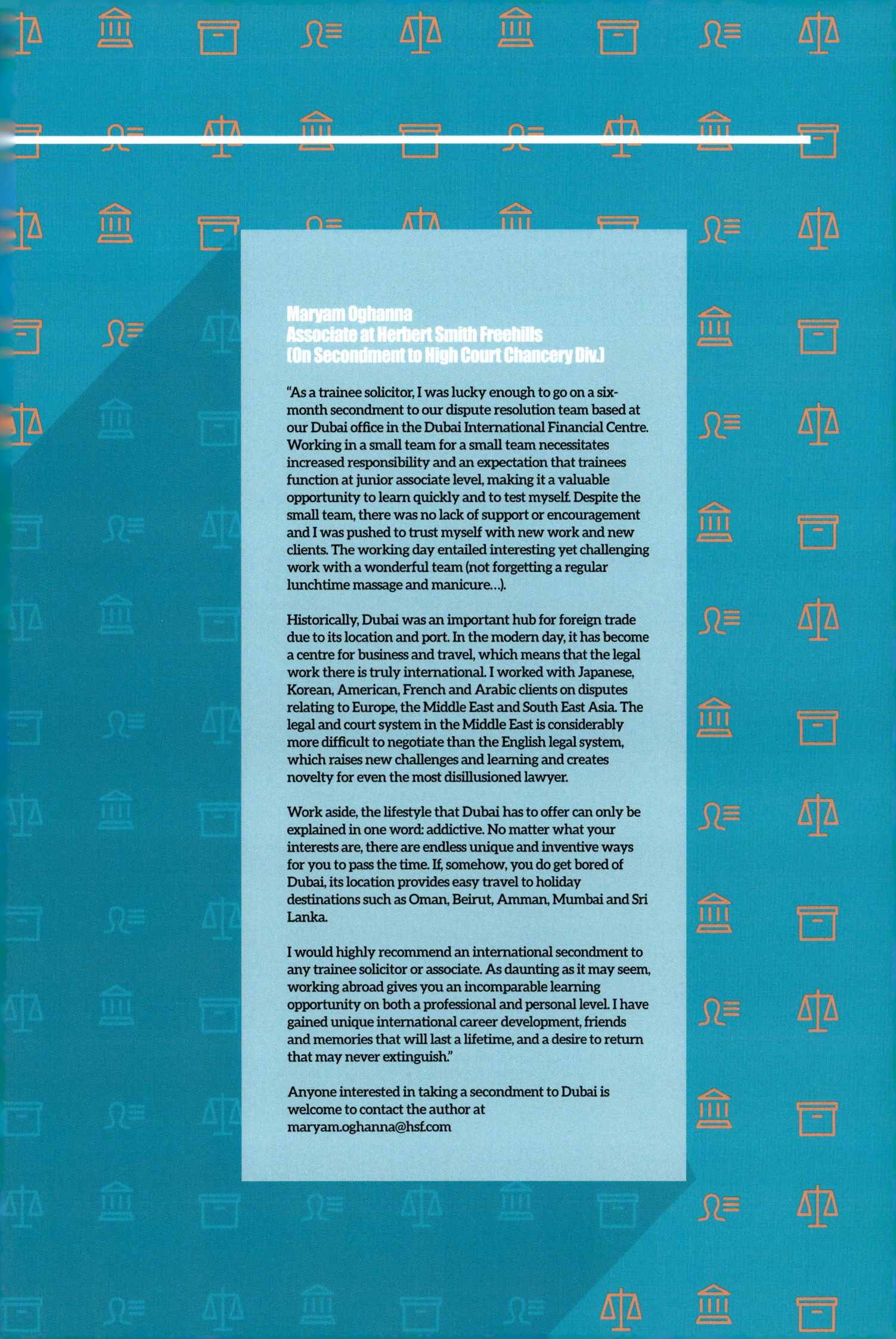

Maryam Oghanna
Associate at Herbert Smith Freehills
(On Secondment to High Court Chancery Div.)

"As a trainee solicitor, I was lucky enough to go on a six-month secondment to our dispute resolution team based at our Dubai office in the Dubai International Financial Centre. Working in a small team for a small team necessitates increased responsibility and an expectation that trainees function at junior associate level, making it a valuable opportunity to learn quickly and to test myself. Despite the small team, there was no lack of support or encouragement and I was pushed to trust myself with new work and new clients. The working day entailed interesting yet challenging work with a wonderful team (not forgetting a regular lunchtime massage and manicure…).

Historically, Dubai was an important hub for foreign trade due to its location and port. In the modern day, it has become a centre for business and travel, which means that the legal work there is truly international. I worked with Japanese, Korean, American, French and Arabic clients on disputes relating to Europe, the Middle East and South East Asia. The legal and court system in the Middle East is considerably more difficult to negotiate than the English legal system, which raises new challenges and learning and creates novelty for even the most disillusioned lawyer.

Work aside, the lifestyle that Dubai has to offer can only be explained in one word: addictive. No matter what your interests are, there are endless unique and inventive ways for you to pass the time. If, somehow, you do get bored of Dubai, its location provides easy travel to holiday destinations such as Oman, Beirut, Amman, Mumbai and Sri Lanka.

I would highly recommend an international secondment to any trainee solicitor or associate. As daunting as it may seem, working abroad gives you an incomparable learning opportunity on both a professional and personal level. I have gained unique international career development, friends and memories that will last a lifetime, and a desire to return that may never extinguish."

Anyone interested in taking a secondment to Dubai is welcome to contact the author at maryam.oghanna@hsf.com

MY EXPERIENCE

Abbi Lavill
CILEx Legal Apprentice
Gowling WLG LLP

"I didn't want the rising tuition fees or to land myself in debt and the student lifestyle never once seemed like something I'd enjoy."

Despite not being sure what I wanted to do when I left school, one thing I was sure about was that I didn't want to go to university – I was completely adamant that it wasn't for me. Instead, I wanted something that meant I could get a head-start on everyone else in the world of work, earn a salary and ultimately use those three years to get my foot in the door of a firm and start carving out a career for myself. I started looking at apprenticeships as an alternative after one of my friends told me about CILEx. I applied for two legal apprenticeships and after several aptitude tests, a phone interview, and a formal interview and securing the required grades, I was offered a position at Gowling WLG where I've now been working since September 2015.

My day can consist of anything from drafting and reviewing documents and speaking to clients/other solicitors on to attending all party meetings and site visits. The work is incredibly varied so you can't help but find it interesting and it's so satisfying to see the things that you're studying come alive in what you're doing day-to-day – it really helps to motivate you to keep learning and makes the work you put in seem all the more worthwhile.

Go with your gut! If university isn't something you're interested in then don't convince yourself that it's right for you purely because it's considered 'the next step'. Remember that there are other options out there for you, and so far the CILEx route has been perfect in helping me to achieve my goals."

Playing The Game

aspiringsolicitors
access | opportunity | assistance

Key hints and tips about becoming a solicitor, by Chris White, founder of Aspiring Solicitors

So, you have decided to become a solicitor. That is great news as it is a fantastic career to pursue and one I can thoroughly recommend. Unfortunately, deciding to become a solicitor is the easy part...

Having secured the best grades possible throughout your academic career (including your first year at university) and having completed legal/non-legal work experience to enhance your CV, you arrive at the daunting prospect of starting your vacation scheme/ training contract application to your dream firm. If you get the application right, you know that it could shape your future. If you succeed in securing a training contract it could be worth between £35,000 to £100,000 to you over three years, depending on the training contract provider you apply to and your stage of academic study. Still, getting the application right is only part of the game. You still have to succeed at interview and assessment centres. This article sets out the key stages of the training contract application process and provides you with useful tips on how to improve your chances of success.

THE FIRST HALF
COMPLETING THE APPLICATION

Most aspiring solicitors apply for training contracts with "private practice" law firms, i.e. those whose sole purpose is to provide legal advice to clients in return for fees. Application processes for vacation schemes and training contracts can either be fixed (via a set application form with various questions) or non-fixed (by submitting a CV and covering letter). Most City and national firms require these applications to be submitted online via a fixed application. These applications should take hours to complete because they require research, both online and in person (i.e. by meeting people from the firm at Open Days, Workshops etc) to complete questions such as "why do you think you will be a good City lawyer and what qualities could you bring to our firm" and "describe a situation where you demonstrated your initiative". Most answers to these questions have word limits between 200-500 words, so they are like mini essays.

THE SECOND HALF
THE INTERVIEW & ASSESSMENT CENTRE

When you receive the golden news that you are being invited to an interview and/or assessment centre at your dream firm, you begin to realise that the most challenging part is still to come- the interview. By securing an interview, you should feel confident that you are good enough for the firm on paper – you just have to prove it in person!

The interview/assessment centre tests everything else, including your personality, interest in the firm and whether you will fit into the firm and its culture. Most law firms will require you to attend at least two interviews throughout the process (each lasting approximately 45 minutes to one hour) during which you will be interviewed by different representatives of the firm e.g. representatives from the graduate recruitment team, associates/senior associates of the firm and/or partners. Each interviewer will probe the different competencies and skills you possess e.g. your personality/communication skills or your knowledge of the law. However, certain qualities are required in every interview e.g. you will need to (i) know your CV/application back to front and inside out (ii) demonstrate why you want to train at that firm specifically and (iii) persuade the interviewer that you would be a great addition to the team.

More and more law firms use assessment exercises as part of the recruitment process. They are designed to test various skills and abilities, over and above those which could be evidenced in an interview. Assessments recruiters use include:

Group exercises. Here you will be in a small group (usually 4-6 people). You will likely be given a fact pattern with different points for each member to consider and negotiate in a set period of time. The key skills being assessed here are communication skills, teamwork, logical reasoning and working under pressure.

Presentation exercises. This will require you to consider a particular task and to present it to the other applicants and assessors. This will normally last between 5-10 minutes. Again, communication skills are being tested here as well as your confidence to speak to an audience and composure.

In tray exercise. This requires you to prioritise several tasks or issues from a list/particular matter, giving logical explanation of your choices. Your choices will then be challenged by the assessor and you need to further justify your reasons.

Written tests. This can cover a range of different tasks. These tests can take between 30 to 90 minutes. They test your ability to assimilate large amounts of written information quickly and write a report analysing the information.

THE FULL-TIME WHISTLE
GETTING THE JOB

Being offered a training contract is an amazing feeling and one that will change your life. For access, opportunity and assistance for aspiring solicitors visit www.aspiringsolicitors.co.uk

---

Facebook/LinkedIn/Instagram/YouTube "Aspiring Solicitors"
Twitter "@access2law"

BAKER & McKENZIE

Graduate careers
– in Law –

Training Contract | **Vacation Scheme** | **International Vacation Scheme** | **First Year Programme** | **Open Days**

At Baker & McKenzie, we pride ourselves on being a global law firm with a personal touch, and a friendly approach that will make your career really go places.

We're looking for the best and brightest talent to turn into the well-rounded commercial lawyers that make our Firm stand out from the crowd.

bakermckenzie.com/londongraduates

Journeys can begin anywhere. Yours begins at Baker & McKenzie.

Baker & McKenzie International is a Swiss Verein with member law firms around the world. In accordance with the common terminology used in professional service organizations, reference to a "partner" means a person who is a partner, or equivalent, in such a law firm. Similarly, reference to an "office" means an office of any such law firm.

BRIGHT SPARKS

Giving young talent the chance to shine

Work experience with an international law firm for talented year 12 students

If you're thinking of a career in Law, Marketing, HR, Finance or IT, this is the perfect place to start. A chance to develop your personal and professional skills, brush up on your CV and interview techniques, get some real-world experience and find where your strengths and interests lie.

For full details and an application form email
graduate.recruitment@shlegal.com

PRIME
FAIR ACCESS TO QUALITY
WORK EXPERIENCE

STEPHENSON HARWOOD

THE HONOURABLE SOCIETY OF THE INNER TEMPLE: HOW TO BECOME A BARRISTER

Barristers provide specialist legal advice and represent their clients in courts and tribunals. The work is intellectually challenging in an intense and demanding professional environment. It is also a very rewarding career. Barristers' work varies considerably depending on the area of law they practise in and their seniority.

TYPICALLY, BARRISTERS DO SOME OR ALL OF THE FOLLOWING:

- Advise clients on the law and the strength of their legal case
- Hold 'conferences' with clients to discuss taking their case forward and giving them legal advice
- Represent clients in court. This can include presenting the case, cross-examining witnesses, summing up all relevant material and giving reasons why the court should support the case
- Negotiate settlements with the other side

Most barristers are self-employed and work in chambers, although approximately 20% are 'employed barristers' and work for an employer, an industry, commerce or central or local government. The role of an employed barrister can vary greatly depending on the employer. The majority will work in specialist legal departments advising only the organisation they work for.

Self-employed barristers work in offices called chambers that they may share with other barristers. On completion of their training, barristers apply for a permanent position called tenancy in a set of chambers.

Students are expected to demonstrate the following skills in order to both qualify as a barrister and succeed in the competitive professional and business world:

- Academic ability (at least a 2.1 at degree level)
- Outstanding written and oral communication skills
- An ability to absorb and analyse complex information, often very quickly
- Numeracy skills
- Interpersonal skills
- Good judgement
- Self-motivation
- Commitment to continuing professional development
- Total integrity

SCHOLARSHIPS

The Inns of Court award more than £5million annually in scholarships to students undertaking the BPTC.

HOW TO GAIN RELEVANT WORK EXPERIENCE

Before committing yourself to a career at the Bar, it is wise to get an insight into what a barrister does. The best way to do this is by undertaking work experience in the form of a 'mini pupillage'. These usually last a week in which you might be reading papers, discussing cases, shadowing a barrister and attending court. Mini pupillages can help to decide whether life as a barrister would suit you while also exposing you to areas of law you may want to practise in at a later date. Relevant legal experience is also helpful, but undertaking at least three mini pupillages by the time you apply for pupillage is seen as a must. To apply, you can contact chambers directly or search www.legalhub.co.uk, which is the Bar directory for all the chambers in England and Wales. While you are in sixth form, you may also want to look into whether you are eligible to apply for the Bar Council's 'Bar Placement Week' and, during university, you should research the Inner Temple's Pegasus Access and Support Scheme. Both of these schemes offer students from less advantaged backgrounds the opportunity to undertake relevant work experience at the Bar.

For more in-depth information, read the Inner Temple's 'Guide to becoming a Barrister', available on their website: www.innertemple.org.uk

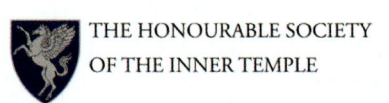

THE HONOURABLE SOCIETY OF THE INNER TEMPLE

MY EXPERIENCE

Baroness Helena Kennedy, QC, Doughty Street Chambers

"I grew up in Glasgow in a working-class family, the first to go on to higher education. Neither of my older sisters had stayed on at school because family circumstances had made it impossible at the time. It was really through the encouragement of teachers that I decided to try for law and ended up coming to the Bar. I had no connections, no real understanding of how it all worked and found out it completely mystifying. However, I was unwilling to admit defeat and determined to succeed – even when I was told by sets of chambers that they did not take women – which they could do in those days!

At first, I felt like a fish out of water because I had not gone to public school, was not male and I had an accent – which was very unusual then. However, I soon realised that my difference became my strength. My background gave me insight into the lives of many of the people for whom I acted and I had a ready empathy with the hard experiences of life that often brought people before the courts. In fact, having an accent distinguished me from others and made me memorable, which is always a good thing at the Bar. They used to say 'Let's get that Scots girl' especially when Scotland supporters were arrested after cup finals having consumed too much alcohol or young Scotswomen had ended up on the game.

I have loved my life in the law. I think it is vital that people from hugely different backgrounds come into the profession because the law should have input from every quarter of our society. The knowledge that comes from diversity enriches law and makes it more likely that law translates into justice."

BE A PART OF EVERYTHING

HERBERT SMITH FREEHILLS

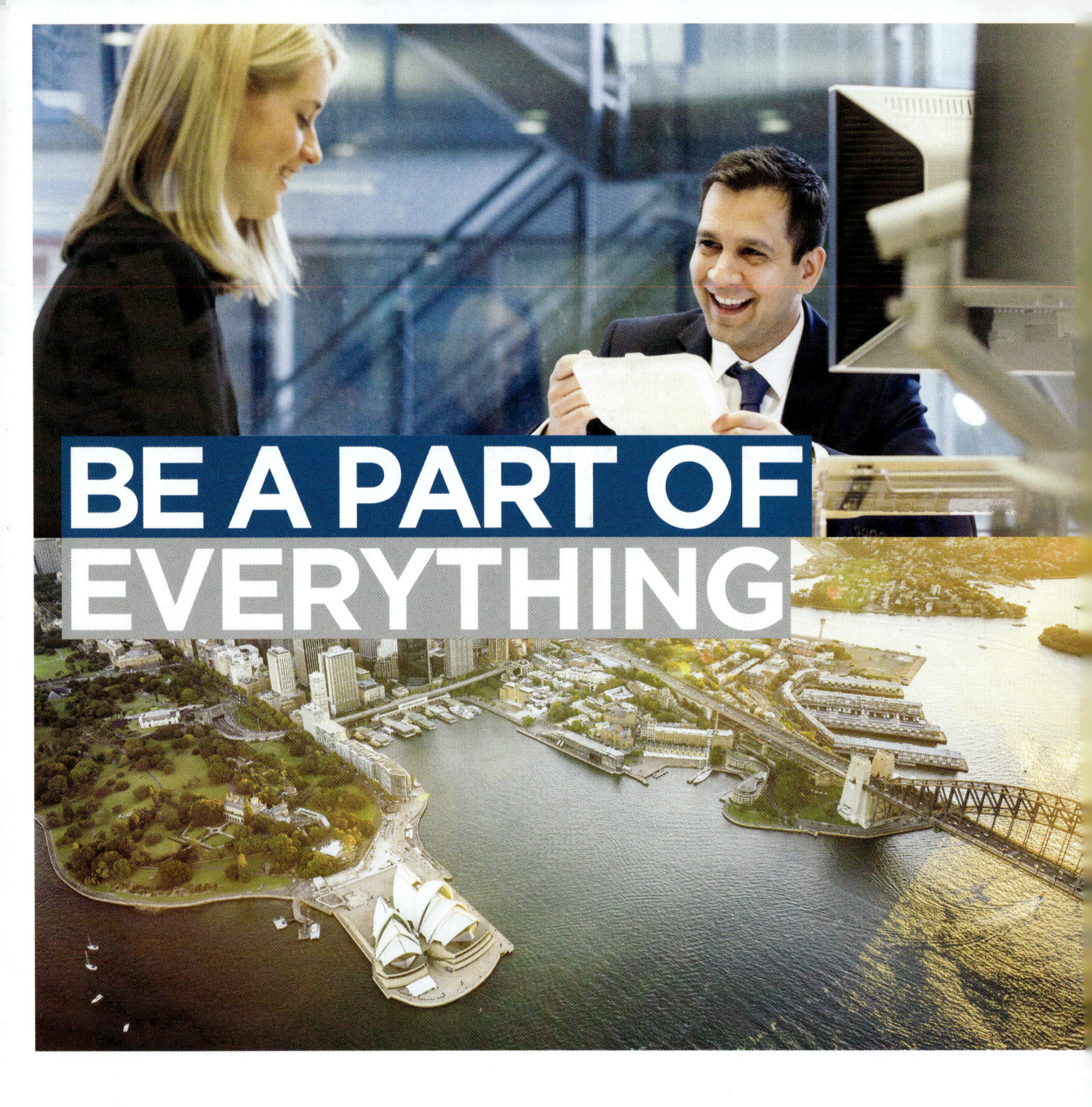

INTERNATIONAL GRADUATE CAREERS IN LAW

Advising clients on front-page matters in London. Reading about your work in the newspaper the next day. We work with some of the biggest international organisations on some of their most ambitious projects. So be prepared to see the impact your hard work makes in the real world.

When you join Herbert Smith Freehills you get so much more than a job. You'll have the chance to gain the skills and experience you'll need to become a brilliant lawyer. As a full service global firm, our work is incredibly varied and there is no limit to where your career could take you. From first-year workshops to vacation schemes and training contracts, we have a wide variety of opportunities for you.

Don't just experience everything, be a part of it.

careers.herbertsmithfreehills.com/uk/grads

SEARCH HSF GRADUATES FOR MORE

26 OFFICES GLOBALLY • 22 INTERNATIONAL SECONDMENTS • £44k IN FIRST YEAR